P9-BAT-465

Taunton's

BUILD LIKE A PRO®
Expert Advice from Start to Finish

WORKING with TILE

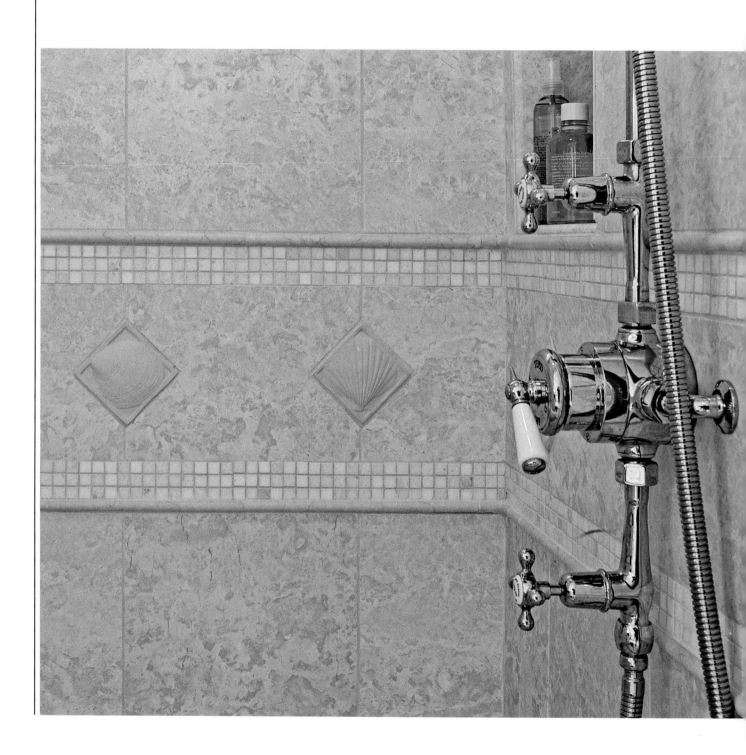

Expert Advice from Start to Finish

WORKING with TILE

TOM AND LANE MEEHAN

The Taunton Press

Text © 2005 by Tom Meehan and Lane Meehan

Photographs © 2005 by Tom Meehan and Lane Meehan, unless otherwise noted on p. 199.

Illustrations © 2005 by The Taunton Press, Inc.

All rights reserved

The Taunton Press
Inspiration for hands-on living®

The Taunton Press, Inc., 63 South Main Street, P.O. Box 5506, Newtown, CT 06470-5506

e-mail: tp@taunton.com

EDITORS: Jeff Day and Scott Gibson

COVER AND INTERIOR DESIGN: Lori Wendin

LAYOUT: Susan Fazekas

ILLUSTRATOR: Chuck Lockhart

PHOTOGRAPHER: Rob Karosis, Lane and Tom Meehan and crew

Taunton's Build Like a Pro® is a trademark of The Taunton Press, Inc.,
registered in the U.S. Patent and Trademark Office.

Library of Congress Cataloging-in-Publication Data

Meehan, Tom.

  Working with tile : great results from start to finish /

Tom and Lane Meehan ; photographs by Tom and Lane Meehan, unless otherwise noted.

      p. cm. -- (Taunton's build like a pro)

  ISBN 1-56158-677-3

  1. Tile laying. I. Meehan, Lane. II. Title. III. Series.

  TH8531.M44 2005

  698--dc22

                          2004030436

Printed in the United States of America

10 9 8 7 6 5 4 3 2

The following manufacturers/names appearing in *Working with Tile* are trademarks: 3M®, Bonsal®,
Chloraloy®, Corian®, DeWalt®, Ditra®, Felker®, Hardibacker®, Kerdi®, Laticrete®, Mapei®,
MK®, Nobleseal®, Nuheat®, Schluter Systems®, Sharpie®, Stabila™, Suntouch®, Superior Tile
Cutter®, Target®, Velcro®, Wonder-Board®

Construction is inherently dangerous. Using hand or power tools improperly or ignoring safety practices can lead to permanent injury or even death. Don't try to perform operations you learn about here (or elsewhere), unless you're certain they are safe for you. If something about an operation doesn't feel right, don't do it. Look for another way. We want you to enjoy the remodeling process, so please keep safety foremost in your mind whenever you're working on your project.

For our kids

Acknowledgments

The process of creating this book has been a learning and growing experience for our whole family. In the beginning, our four boys, Christopher, Tyler, Connor, and Ryan, would refer to our writing as "homework." In many ways it has been. Thank you, boys, for being interested, concerned, curious, and understanding of this undertaking. Thanks also to their big sister Lindsay for her excitement and support.

Writing this book has definitely been a project of larger magnitude than writing articles for *Fine Homebuilding* magazine. We would like to thank Roe Osborn for introducing us to the other side of The Taunton Press. Without encouragement from Roe, Kevin Ireton, and Chuck Bickford, I'm not sure we would have finished. We do look forward to returning to being *Fine Homebuilding* authors again.

At the point that we thought this was just too big of an endeavor for us to accomplish without losing our family, friends, and minds, Jeff Day made us believe that we could do anything, and with him we did. The process of creating something like this involves many people and we are thankful to all who worked to make this book happen. The group at Taunton worked effortlessly to teach us how to take what we know and organize it on paper and share it with everyone else. We'd like to thank Tim Snyder for both his hard work and his confidence. Thank you Scott Gibson for helping us put the final touches on the book.

We would also like to thank Dave Holbrook of the *Journal of Light Construction* for being a good friend and neighbor, and for helping us learn the art of researching. Thanks to all of our employees at Cape Cod Tileworks: Linda Dunne, Marion Newell, Marcus Verteramo, Jan Richmond, Robin Decoteau, and the installation crew of James Mahony, Kyle Bowman, and Dave Powers, all of whom have encouraged us and kept our business afloat while we have taken on this endeavor. To our friends, who must be tired at this point of hearing that we can't get together or make it to karate class because we are working on the book, we say thanks. We couldn't have done it alone.

Thanks to my dad, Don Meehan, an old master tilesetter who taught me skills rarely developed by contemporary tilesetters. Not only did he give me the knowlwedge of old-world methods, but he also incouraged me to explore and incorporate the modern day methods that have made me what I am today.   —LM & TM

I'd like to make special acknowledgment of my co-author, business partner, best friend, and wife, Lane Meehan. Without her, this book would not have been possible—or as beautiful. All sections on tile design are exclusively her doing. Also, while I took care of the installation work, Lane was more often than not behind the camera or working on the manuscript long into the night. Lane is a talented design professional with whom I count myself lucky to share my business, this book, and my life. Thank you, Lane.   —TM

Contents

Introduction 2
How to Use This Book 4

■ CHAPTER ONE

Getting Started 6

Living in Style 8
Look to the Future 8
Translating Ideas into Tile 10
Materials Are Better, More Versatile 12

■ CHAPTER TWO

Tiling a Floor 22

Maintain a Familiar Style 24
Tiling a Floor 24
Installing an Uncoupling Layer 26
Layout Is Next 30
Installing Tile Is the Fun Part 32
Finishing Up 36

■ CHAPTER THREE

Tile Wainscott 40

Wainscoting Is a Practical Choice 42
Layout Is Key 45
Checking for Obstructions 46
Now Check the Horizontal 47
Installing the Tile 49

■ CHAPTER FOUR

Tiling a Fireplace 56

Design for the Whole Room 58
Planning a Hearth and Mantel 58
Tiling over the Firebox 61
Building a Mantel 64

■ CHAPTER FIVE

Tiling a Backsplash 72

Color, Patterns, and Accents 74
Installing a Tumbled Marble Backsplash 76
Sealing and Grouting 81

■ CHAPTER SIX

Tiling a Countertop 86

Keeping It Clean 88
Getting Started 90
Cut the Tiles First 92
Adding Edge Trim and Grout 93

■ CHAPTER SEVEN

Tiling a Tub Surround   96

Before You Start 98
Use a Story Pole for Layout 99
Planning the Installation 102
Now for the Installation 104
Finishing Up Corners and Edges 105
Finishing Up 107

■ CHAPTER EIGHT

Tiling Showers   110

Reviving a Bathroom with Tile 112
Out with the Old 113
Installing a Pan and Backer Board 116
Story Sticks Guide Layout 118
Cutting Tiles to Fit 121
Installing a Glass-Block Shower Wall 122

■ CHAPTER NINE

Installing a Shower Pan   128

Getting It Right 130
Start with the Subfloor 130
Installing the Waterproof Membrane 135
Attaching the Drain and Liner 137
Installing Backer Board and Tile 140
Building a Curbless Shower 143

■ CHAPTER TEN

Tiling with Stone   148

Choosing the Stone and the Look 150
Choosing Thinset and Trowels 152
Cutting and Installing Stone Tile 153
Stone Should Be Sealed 158

■ CHAPTER ELEVEN

Glass Tile   162

Glass Tile Installation Is Different 164
Glass Tile in a Tub Surround 166
Getting the Thinset Right 167
Have Patience with Cutting and Grouting 169

■ CHAPTER TWELVE

Tile Repairs   174

Planning a Repair 176
Replacing Tile around a Shower Valve 177
Replacing a Large Area of Tub Surround 182
Replacing Floor Tile 184

Resources 186
Appendix A   A World of Tile 190
Appendix B   Tools and Materials 194
Appendix C   Trowels for Tiling 195
Appendix D   Preventing Cracked Tile and Grout 196
Credits 199
Index 200

Introduction

WHEN TOM WORKED with his father 30 years ago, installers went to the customer's home and helped pick the tile. They would show up with 10 or 12 sample boards and walk out an hour later with all the choices made.

Not that it was easy: There were 40 or so possible colors for bathroom tile alone. The lower 4 ft. of the wall was usually tiled, forming a wainscot. There was a trim tile, called a cove base, where the wainscot met the floor, and another trim tile, called a cap or a tile chair rail, that could be used at the top. Customers could pick a matching, contrasting, or complementary color. Most bathrooms also got a full set of ceramic fixtures—towel bar, soap dish, toothbrush, and toilet paper holder.

Those relatively simple days are gone. We have a wider variety of tile shapes and sizes today than we did back then. Probably the most popular is 6-in. by 6-in. tile, which gives walls a clean look and a minimum number of grout lines. Rhomboids, or diamond shapes, have been making a strong impact in the past few years. They're most popular on backsplashes, but they add a wonderful texture to any wall. New decorative borders and trim pieces make it easy to interrupt the wainscot part way up, and once you do, you can turn the tiles diagonally to create different visual textures.

Ceramic fixtures are on the decline. Today's toothbrushes just don't fit into the holders once common over the sink. Standard toilet paper holders don't accommodate the larger rolls of toilet paper sold today. Old-fashioned tub soap dishes with the handle across the top are a thing of the past, too. They've been replaced by grab bars. Given the tendency of soap dishes to pop out of the wall when you grab them, it's probably just as well. The shampoos, conditioners, body washes, and other beauty products we use today would overwhelm an old-fashioned shower stall. Now, we cut shampoo niches into the wall, sizing them to meet the customer's needs and tiling them to match the shower.

Floor tiles are becoming larger, too. In the past, a floor tile commonly would have been 8-in. or 10-in. square. Now we tend to use tiles 12-in. by 12-in. or even larger. They reduce the number of grout lines, making the room look bigger and less busy. On the other hand, we are also seeing a great deal of small stone mosaic patterns. Mosaic patterns can make a big impression in a small powder room.

In the old days, a high percentage of foyers would have been red, gray, or green slate in one of a number of random block patterns. Today, the possibilities are endless. You can create a formal marble entry or a more rustic entry using tumbled marble. Borders and patterns can be combined to imitate rugs, making wonderful welcome mats, especially inside sliding or French doors. We have even filled entryways with what look like ponds of water made with fish- and shell-shaped tiles surrounded by tumbled stone.

What's new in the kitchen

When Tom was doing kitchens with his father, the floors were usually either quarry tile, 8-in.-sq. Italian tile, or Mexican terra-cotta tile. Today, the combination of tile technology and our fast-paced lives has changed how we design kitchen floors. The most popular kitchen floors are now ceramic or porcelain 12-in. squares made to look like stone.

The varied texture hides a multitude of sins, such as juice spills, sand, dirt and pet hair. The matte finish keeps footing reliable even when the surface is wet. Porcelain and ceramic tiles come in many patterns and variations. The trend is to make tile that looks like tumbled marble or limestone, and it's amazing how real the tiles look. Both porcelain and ceramic tiles are reasonably priced and very durable—a great way to update a kitchen without breaking the budget.

Slate also has become increasingly popular for kitchens. Unlike the flat slate of the '70s, available in three colors, slates today come in a wide variety of colors and textures. Surfaces today are more forgiving than the flat, chalkboard finish that showed scratches and was very difficult to maintain. Many slate tiles have a beautiful cleft texture that helps prevent slipping but still lets you move your kitchen chairs across the floor. Slate is usually slightly more expensive than ceramic tile but is a nice compromise if you want all the wonderful colors and textures of real stone without paying for a more expensive stone such as tumbled marble or limestone.

Tile still a smart choice

People we meet at our tile store on Cape Cod or through Tom's tile-setting business often assume we have fantastic tile in our own home. And the fact is that we do. But we also have four active boys in the house, and tile makes a lot of sense for us from a practical as well as an aesthetic point of view. Like many other parents, we'd like to keep our house spotlessly clean and well organized, but the reality is that if we're not working, we probably are racing to a karate class or a baseball game or some other activity. Tile is not only durable and good looking, but it also hides our housekeeping shortcomings as no other material could do.

A lot has changed since Tom began working with his father a generation ago. It's not just that there many more colors, sizes, and types of tile to choose from. There also are better and more varied materials used to install tile—everything from grout and thinset cement to special floor membranes and sealers. All of it helps ensure that the beauty and practicality of tile remains as compelling as it's ever been.

How to Use This Book

I F YOU'RE READING THIS, you're a doer who is not afraid to take on a challenging project. We've designed this book and this series to help you do that project smoothly and cost effectively.

Many doers jump in and do, reading the directions only if something goes wrong. It's much smarter (and cheaper) to start by knowing what to do and planning the process step by step. This book is here to help you. Read it. Familiarize yourself with the process you're about to undertake. You'll be glad you did.

Planning Is the Key to Success

This book contains information on designing your project, choosing the best options for the results you want to achieve, and planning the timing and execution. We know you're anxious to get started on your project. Take the time now to read and think about what you're about to do. You'll refine your ideas and choose the best materials.

There's advice here on where to look for inspiration and how to make plans. Don't be afraid to attempt drawing your own plans. There's no better way to get exactly what you want than by designing it yourself.

Finding the Information You Need

We've designed this book to make it easy to find what you need to know. The main part of the book details the essential parts of each process. If it's fairly straightforward, it's simply described. If there are key steps, they are addressed one by one, usually accompanied by drawings or photos to help you see what you will be doing. We've also added some other elements to help you understand the process better, find quicker or smarter ways to accomplish the task, or do it differently to suit your project.

Alternatives and a closer look

The sidebars and features included with the main text are there to explain aspects in more depth and to clarify why you're doing something. Some describe a completely different way to handle the same situation. We explain when you may want to use that method or choose that option, as well as detail its advantages. The sidebars are sometimes accompanied by photos or drawings to help you see what the author is describing.

There's a pro at your elbow

The authors of this book, and every author in this series, have had years of experience doing this kind of project. We've put the benefits of their knowledge into quick tips that always appear in the left margin. Q&As are brief answers to some common tiling questions. While not essential to doing the job, they are meant to help you get professional results.

Every project has its surprises. Since the authors have encountered many of them already, they can give you a little preview of what they may be and how to address them in the "What Can Go Wrong" sidebars. And experience has also taught the authors some tricks that you can only learn from being a pro. Some of these are tips, some are tools or accessories you can make yourself, and some are materials or tools you may not have thought to use.

Building Like a Pro

To make a living, a pro needs to work smart, quickly, and economically. That's the strategy presented in this book. We've provided options to help you make the best choices in design, materials, and methods. That way, you can adjust your project to suit your skill level and budget. Good choices and good planning are the keys to success.

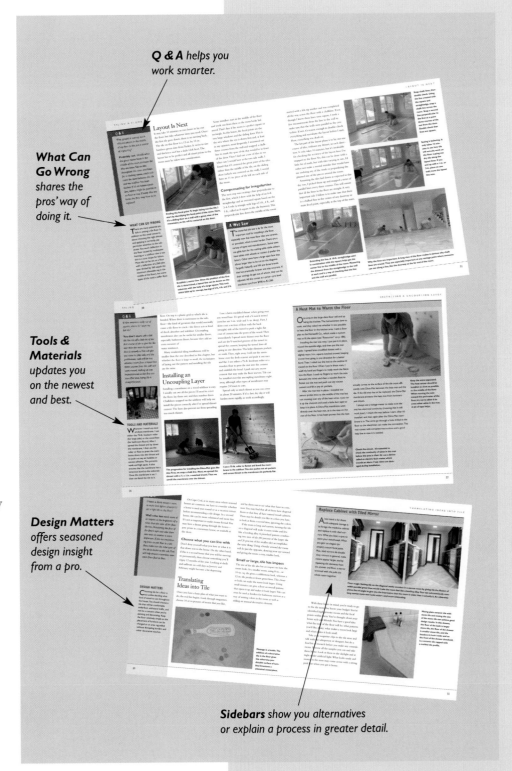

Q & A *helps you work smarter.*

What Can Go Wrong *shares the pros' way of doing it.*

Tools & Materials *updates you on the newest and best.*

Design Matters *offers seasoned design insight from a pro.*

Sidebars *show you alternatives or explain a process in greater detail.*

Getting

CHAPTER ONE

Started

1 Living in Style, p. 8

Faced with a new design project, most people are overwhelmed. Breaking the project into manageable sections will make it easier, and a good first step is to set a budget. Don't be embarrassed to let your designer or the salesperson at the tile store know what you're willing to spend. It won't help anyone if you fall in love with something you can't afford. And there's no reason you can't get the look you want even with self-imposed spending limits.

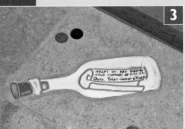

2 Look to the Future, p. 8

Next, decide which areas are a priority. Want to dress up the first floor powder room that all your guests will see? You can afford to splurge here because a little money goes a long way in a small room. The kitchen backsplash is another small but highly visible area where small expenditures yield big results. But watch your expenses in large areas where costs can really pile up.

3 Translating Ideas into Tile, p. 10

Once you've chosen the rooms in which you want to use tile, focus on what's important in each of them. If you are tackling a bathroom, for example, think about the first thing you see when you walk in. If it's a tub, make it your focus and go all out in tiling it. If the shower is hidden behind a door, on the other hand, maybe you should invest money in the floor. Everyone sees the floor, and a little money can go a long way here, too.

4 Materials Are Better, More Versatile, p. 12

Q & A

I've been told that the best place to start a floor is in the middle of the room and then you work your way out. Is this so?

In a perfect world, yes. If the room is square or rectangular in shape, that approach often works. But most floors have jogs or hallways. Try looking at a room as people will live in it. The eye is draw to windows or an entrance. Always think of the area that is seen first and most frequently. Use full or larger pieces there. Make sure you don't end up with small pieces of tile in any areas that have visible importance.

DESIGN MATTERS

Adding one simple, unexpected tile to the floor can make an otherwise inexpensive tile look like a million bucks.

Living in Style

The style of your house is another factor. There are plenty of appealing tiles to choose from but not all of them will look appropriate in all houses. We live in a 230-year-old house on Cape Cod. We see thousands of beautiful tiles in our shop, and most of them would look great—in someone else's house. Many just aren't suitable for the architectural style of our house.

Lifestyle plays a role, too. For example, we have four active boys, a dog, and a cat. We also work crazy hours and enjoy entertaining. So for us, high-relief handmade Mexican tiles are out of the question. We don't want our tile to emphasize every bit of dust or animal hair, and it has to stand up to heavy foot traffic. As a result, we've gone with stone and ceramic tile, both of which are durable and forgiving.

If you are designing a tile installation for only one room, think about how you've used color in the rest of the house and the atmosphere you'd like to create. If your house is contemporary, then continue that same clean, simple look from room to room. Change the color, if you like, but not your style.

Remember the flow

If you are designing tile for a whole house, take each room one at a time. Look at the blueprints repeatedly, and take mental walks from one room to the next. Think of the floors as if they flow from one room to the next—wood followed by carpet and then tile, for example—and design them so they blend. For instance, if the kitchen opens into a great room, chose a kitchen tile of the same tone as the great room, even if the floor there is carpet. The point is not to have any jarring contrasts in color from one floor surface to

Special decorative tiles can be used as accents to highlight sections of walls or floors.

the next. Matching tones creates a visual flow and makes the room look larger and more open. When two tiled floors run into each other, use the same tile on both, but consider changing the size in one area or adding a decorative border to make it a little special.

Look to the Future

If you know you're going to be reselling your home in a few years, go ahead and buy that wonderful tile you've got your eye on, but keep the colors basic. You can still be imaginative. Just turning a tile on the diagonal or creating a pinwheel pattern on the floor gives the tile a great texture without introducing a color that a prospective buyer may hate. In the same vein, think about who uses the room. If you are tiling your children's bathroom, remember that they grow up. Make sure that the bathroom scheme isn't too juvenile.

REPLACE CABINET WITH TILED MIRROR

A hot trend for those with adequate storage is to forego the medicine cabinet and replace it with tiled mirrors. What you lose: a spot to store your mouthwash. What you gain: an elegant (or simple) custom focal point. Plus, tiled mirrors do double duty; mirrors in general, make rooms appear larger, and by repeating tile elements from the shower and floor, a mirror trimmed with tile pulls the whole room together.

Custom mirror frames. The nice thing about making your own mirror frames is that not only can you choose the colors you like but you can make the finish opening to your exact specifications.

The use of handmade, handpainted tile makes these mirrors a focal point of the room.

I have a dark room *I want to make look lighter; shouldn't I use a light tile on the floor?*

Wall color has *much more of an impact on the brightness of a room than the color of the floor tile has. Maintaining the flow of the floor's style and color from one room to another is more important. If you are transitioning from an oak floor to a tile floor, make sure the color tone of the tile is similar to the oak. That will help ensure a seamless transition from floor to floor.*

DESIGN MATTERS

Choosing tile for a floor is not unlike deciding what kind of wood to use throughout the house. You should choose a tile that will be comfortable underfoot, withstand traffic, and not be a concern when you're painting and decorating. Keep the floor relatively simple so the placement of furniture can be changed or an area rug added without disrupting borders and other decorative touches.

On Cape Cod, as in many areas where seasonal homes are common, we have to consider whether a home is used year-round or as a vacation retreat before recommending a tile design. In a second home, tile can be more whimsical and more fun. It's not as important to make rooms formal. You may have a theme going through the house— paw prints in a mountain house, or seashells at the shore.

Choose what you can live with

Don't deny yourself what you love or what it is that draws you to the home. On the other hand, if this is a second home that you will be moving to permanently, then choose something you'll enjoy 12 months of the year. Looking at shells and sailboats on cold days in January and February might become a bit depressing.

Translating Ideas into Tile

Once you have a basic plan of what you want to do, the real fun begins. Look through magazines, choose 10 or so pictures of rooms that you like,

and lay them out to see what they have in common. You may find that all of them have diagonal floors or that they all have natural wood cabinets. There may be details you like in colors you hate, so look at them a second time, ignoring the colors.

If the room is long and narrow, turning the tile on a diagonal will make it seem wider and less like a bowling alley. A pinwheel pattern combining two sizes of tile (80 percent of the larger tile and 20 percent of the smaller tile) accomplishes the same thing. Using a border around the room will do just the opposite, drawing your eye inward and giving the room a cozy, smaller look.

Small or large, tile has impact

The size of the tile also has an impact on how the room looks. In a smaller room, using 8-in.- or 10-in.-sq. tile gives a cobblestone look, whereas a 12-in. tile produces fewer grout lines. This cleaner look can make the room look larger. Using small mosaics can give a floor an overall pattern that opens it up and makes it look larger. Tile can even be used as borders for bathroom mirrors as a way of uniting colors in the room as well as adding an unusual decorative element.

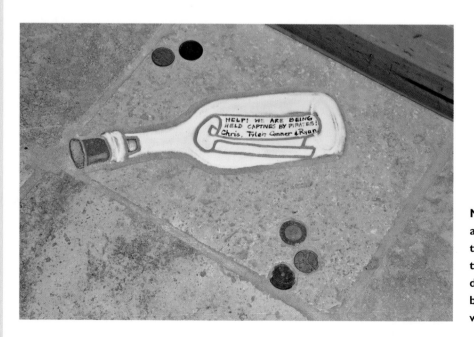

Message in a bottle. The addition of a decorative tile in the floor gives this otherwise predictable surface of tumbled limestone a whimsical centerpiece.

Can You See the Difference?

Floor magic: Setting tile on the diagonal works wonders in a narrow room by giving tile the illusion of width; parallel grout lines would make the room feel like a bowling alley. Your eye subconsciously completes the triangle to give you the impression that the room is wider than it actually is. An otherwise long narrow room now looks wider—and more interesting.

With these basics in mind, you're ready to go to the tile store. You know your budget. You've identified high-priority rooms and the focal points within them. You've thought about your house style and lifestyle. You have a good idea what the tone of the floor will be; what patterns you'd like, if any; what makes a room look large and what makes it look small.

Take your magazine clips to the tile store and talk with the salesperson or designer, but do a final bit of research before you make any commitments. Borrow all the samples you can and take them home. Look at them in the daylight and at night under artificial light. What looks sandy and neutral in the store may come across with a strong pink hue when you get it home.

Mixing plain ceramic tile with stone tile and mixing the size of the stone tile can achieve good design results. In this shower, the floor of the bath is larger stone tile, the floor of the shower is smaller stone tile, and tile baseboard, both inside and on the front of the shower threshold, is a ceramic tile capped with a molded tile profile.

Q & A

We are thinking *of using a softer surface like linoleum or wood on the kitchen floor because we're afraid if we drop something like a tea cup on tile, the cup will break. Isn't tile too hard?*

I hear this question *all the time. Yes, if you drop something breakable, it will break. If you drop a glass on any floor, unless it is carpeted with a thick pad under it, it will break. The difference is that if you drop your hammer on a tile floor, you won't have dings or cuts permanently imbedded. And, a chipped floor tile (if it gets chipped at all) is a do-it-yourself fix. Linoleum and wood don't have that going for them.*

DESIGN MATTERS

When choosing grout, remember you want to focus on the tile, not the grout. If you are using a stone or stone look-alike, remember mortar comes in two main colors—gray and white. Keep that idea and it will give the tile a more natural look.

Tile material and design possibilities are endless. With specialty tiles in metal, glass, stone, and slate, you are no longer limited by the run-of-the-mill porcelain variety. So if your project and budget allow, be creative in your tile choices.

Now find a good tile store

Then, at last, it's time to pick tile. Work with the tile store to get a balanced look. That is, you don't want people to come into a room and say, "Oh, what a great backsplash." You want them to say, "I love what you did with this room." A good tile store has a good designer who will help you balance the needs you've identified with your budget. It's a free service. Take advantage of it.

What you'll find is an enormous variety of tile, everything from natural stone to handmade ceramics in many colors, textures, and price ranges. Whether you're looking to tile a single shower or use tiled surfaces extensively, there should be plenty to choose from. For details, see "A World of Tile" on p. 190.

Materials Are Better, More Versatile

Forty years ago, tile was set only over a wire and mortar base (called a "mud job") or over water-resistant gypsum drywall. Special membranes, cement board, and latex-modified thinsets had yet to be introduced. Grouts were simply colored cement without additives, and sealers were basic silicon (and not very effective). It took a lot more skill to do a good job then. Working with installation materials today is easier than it was, and more productive.

Cement backer boards

Cement board was invented in the mid–1970s to replace gypsum drywall in tile installations. This alone saved the tile industry from the onslaught of fiberglass tub and shower units. It was almost too late because drywall jobs were breaking down. Grout was turning black from mold and mildew that thrived inside the tile substrate. Modern backer board changed that. There are three types (for more detailed information, see "Tools and Materials" on p. 194).

Thinset cement

Thinset is the adhesive in which tile is bedded. Many companies make a variety of types for different applications (for more, see p. 194). Most manufacturers offer a few different grades. Don't buy the cheapest product if the project warrants special attention. Each grade has certain proportion of chemicals or polymers that make the cement work with different types of tile. For instance, glass tile should be installed with thinset that has flexible, adhesive qualities. Using another type will lead to failure. With any type of installation, it's worth your while to do your homework and choose the right type.

In general, thinsets should be mixed slowly, allowed to set for a couple of minutes (to "slake"), and then quickly mixed again. If the thinset starts to harden during the job, throw it out and make a new batch. Do not add more water to revive old thinset.

Mastics are used when you're tiling over drywall and sometimes cement backer board in tub surrounds, but not in shower stalls where the water spray is more concentrated. We use mastic on wainscot walls and backsplashes. Use only all-purpose nonstaining or non-yellowing mastic. When installing very light-colored stone tile on a backsplash, switch to white thinset.

Grout

A good grout job is almost as important as the tile installation itself. It is the final step that either makes or breaks the job. Portland cement grouts of years ago have been replaced by grouts containing latex additives. These products are more flexible and more water-resistant. Latex additives

Thinset cement is used almost 100% of the time in floor installation. When I install tile in a shower stall or tub area (wet areas) I also use thinset cement instead of mastic. I use different types of spreading trowels with different size notches depending on the type and size of the tile: The larger the tile, the larger the notches in the trowel.

Whether it is floor grout (with a ⅛-in. or more joint) or wall grout (⅛-in. or less), grout is spread with a rubberized grout float trowel. The grout is spread over the complete surface of the tile and then allowed to set for 15 minutes or so before it is washed off and toweled dry or to a shine.

also make colors more consistent. In addition, there are epoxy grouts (for more, see p. 194).

It's very important not to add too much water when you're mixing grout. This thins out the latex, weakens the grout, and also makes the color inconsistent.

At least two companies, Laticrete® and Mapei®, offer antimicrobial products that inhibit the growth of stain-causing bacteria, mold, and mildew in grout. Most good-quality grouts that have been properly sealed will provide a lot of this protection, but in some extremely damp areas, these products may be a good idea.

Q & A

We are tiling *a room that does not have its own heat source. If we put an electric heating system under the tile floor, will that adequately heat the room?*

No, most electric heat *systems today are comfort heat systems. These systems feel great under your feet and will help take a bit of the chill out of the room, but they will not provide an even, comfortable temperature throughout the room.*

DESIGN MATTERS

Whether they are built into the floors of a new house or added during a renovation, electric heating elements beneath the tile in selected areas are an affordable luxury. Most heating elements are designed to run on ordinary household current and are available in several types. They can be connected to automatic timers so they provide added warmth only when it's really needed—early morning and evening hours, for example.

An electrical heat mat under tile flooring provides a comfort heat system. The tile is installed over the heat mat using thinset cement. The thermostat is linked to a sensor probe located in the middle of the mat.

Membranes and heat mats

Like cement board, membranes have been saviors of the tile industry. There are a variety of types for different applications, but in general they are useful for either waterproofing or protecting tile from changes in the substrate below. The three main types are stress-crack–isolation membranes, waterproofing membranes, and uncoupling membranes (see p. 194).

Electric heat mats that go under the tile are not designed for heating an entire room, but they make the floor more comfortable underfoot. Most operate on 120-volt household current. In one type, wires are sandwiched between two layers of fabric that is put down with latex-modified thinset and pressed flat into the floor. Tile is then installed over the mat. It is the easiest system we know of, and it's reliable.

Another system, made by a few companies, is a roll of webbed wires. The wires are rolled out on the floor to make sure they all will fit in place before thinset cement is spread. Some of the web-bing is cut back (be careful not to cut the wires) in order for the roll to go up the room one way and then double back the other way. Rolls come in different widths (12 in. or 24 in.). It takes a little more effort to install this type, which uses thermostat probes. Always read and follow the manufacturer's instructions carefully.

A third type is a line of wires that is looped back and forth on the floor and then screwed or stapled in place. Thinset is troweled over the wires and tile is then set in place.

Great care must be taken with all these mats, and all should be checked with a voltage meter for continuity along the way.

Sealers

A sealer is the best investment available to protect many types of stone tile, and there are a number of good products on the market. Sealers also are important for sealing grout—nothing is worse than grout that has become stained or just plain looks dirty. If a good sealer is used, the grout will still get dirty but you will be able to clean it up without too much trouble. If it is not sealed, it may stain and will never look as good as it did when it was new.

Sealers today are impregnator sealers, which go into the pores of the grout or stone and seal from the inside out. These sealers allow the surface to breathe, unlike topcoat sealers of the past, which trapped moisture and could produce a cloudy haze or worse on the surface of the tile.

Sealers are either water based or solvent or oil based. We rely on what old-timers used to say, "If it doesn't stink, it doesn't work." Oil- or solvent-based sealers are very strong and get the job done. We've found that overall, the performance of water-based sealers is limited. The best sealers will protect stone from hot grease and other damaging products like ketchup and wine. However, if you spill red wine on your granite countertop, clean it up before you go to bed. We have not found any sealer that will prevent a red wine stain on stone after it sits for 12 hours.

An impregnator sealer allows the stone tile to look dry. It does not darken the tile or give it a shine. If you want a shine or you want to bring out some color in the stone, use an enhancer or a finish.

It's important to use the correct cleaning and care products. There are a variety of products out there. Always read the label and never feel funny about calling the manufacturer's toll-free hotline for help.

Tools for installing tile

Not too long ago, $1,500 would buy you all the tools you needed to get into the tile business—an electric wet saw, a snap cutter, nippers, trowels, and a few other hand tools. I can still do many jobs with just those basic tools, but a variety of new tools have made jobs that were seemingly impossible almost routine. New tile-cutting machines and layout tools have opened many doors, and even something as simple as the trowel has changed dramatically for the better.

Levels and lasers

Levels are among the most important tools in my truck. I don't look for a bargain brand because quality really counts (I prefer levels made by Stabila). I have a number of sizes: 16 in. for backsplashes, 32 in. and 58 in. for tub surrounds, and 6-ft. and 8-ft. levels for large installations or detailed door jambs.

Lasers offer great advantages. Being able to shoot accurate lines around a room for a tile wainscot or for leveling or squaring off a floor saves a tremendous amount of time and keeps labor costs down. Lines that I shoot with a laser are marked with a pencil and recorded all around a room. If I'm laying out a floor and find the

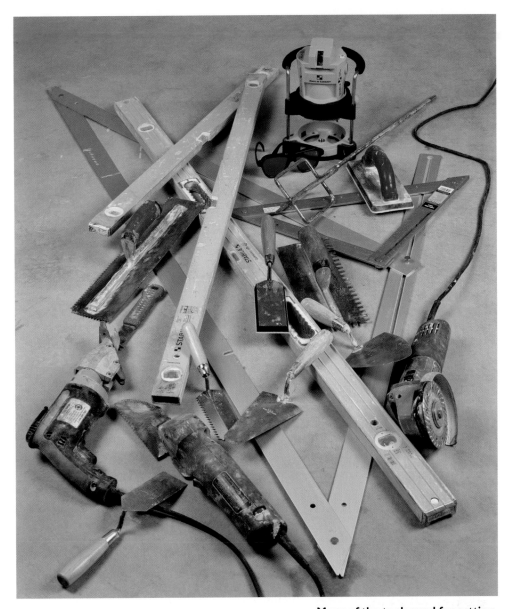

room is out of square, I just shift the laser slightly and don't have to re-snap any chalklines. The laser also can also be used for finding highs and lows in an existing floor. Once you have one, you'll wonder how you ever got along without it.

Trowels for spreading cement and grout

Good-quality steel trowels make a big difference in performance, and they tend to last longer than cheap ones. I stick with name brands. When I've bought bargain trowels in the past, the handles often broke under pressure, and the thinset

Many of the tools used for setting tile are still relatively simple and affordable. A variety of new tools, including lasers and more sophisticated tile saws, have made complicated installations easier and less time-consuming.

Q & A

I have done *some tiling over the years. I now would like to go a step further and get a number of tools that will help me step up to the next level and tackle the more complicated jobs. Where would I look for good tools?*

Any good ceramic tile *store that sells to contractors would be a good source. Another is the National Tile Contractors Association (NTCA) trade publication, which is called the TileLetter. The very best tile-setting tool companies advertise in it. Go to www.tileletter.com.*

DESIGN MATTERS

Modern tiling tools allow installers to create more varied designs in tile than ever. New tile cutting tools can create intricate designs by cutting heretofore impossible curves in tile. This technology allows us to cut decorative tile into a field of tile in minutes. Modern lasers shoot a continuous level line around a room for laying out border tile. We can also cut a bullnose profile into the edge of porcelain field tile when bullnose trim pieces are unavailable.

cement does not apply as smoothly after a short period of use.

There are different trowels for different jobs, including steel and wood floating trowels for spreading cement, notched trowels for spreading thinset or mastic, and rubber grouting trowels (for a complete explanation, see "Trowels for Tiling" on p. 195).

Using a trowel correctly takes practice. The National Tile Contractors Association has produced a great video called *Trowel and Error* that explains working techniques.

Water saws and snap cutters

Many companies make electric tile-cutting saws. Most of them have a 10-in., 6-in., or 7-in. diamond blade cooled by water. They work by friction, not with cutting teeth, and are much safer than woodcutting sawblades. In 30 years of tiling, I have never known anyone to get cut by a tile saw. But that does not mean it can't happen.

Most of these saws have a rolling table that's pushed toward the sawblade. I feel that these are the strongest, most accurate, and easiest to use. Saws come in different sizes. The smaller ones are great for backsplashes and small floors, but they are limited in the size of tile they are able to cut (especially on the diagonal). Larger machines have bigger motors so they can cut through larger and harder tile. Some of the cutting tables can accommodate an 18-in. tile on the diagonal.

The Gemini Revolution saw can make radius cuts that no other saw can (except for a water jet). In my opinion, the new and improved version is the cutting saw of the decade. Because the blade doesn't vibrate or chatter, it allows the most delicate cuts to be made. Its 10-in. rim blade is table mounted, so that radius cuts are made by pivoting the tile, but it also has a slide table that can be used for straight cuts. Its only drawback is that on the radius cuts the blade has a 10-in. working area, so it takes a little creative maneuvering to make some larger cuts.

Score-and-snap cutters are less expensive than electric saws and work well with ceramic tile. To use one, you score a line in the face of the tile,

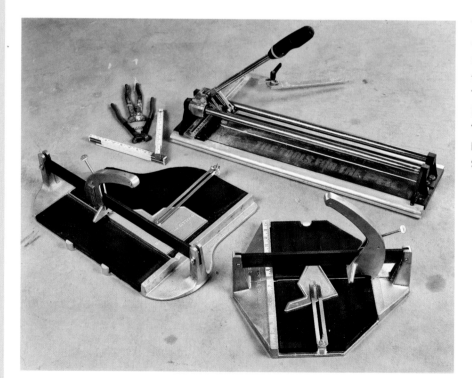

These are popular snap cutters and tile nippers made for quick, dry cutting of different size tiles. The top cutter is from **North American Tile Tool Company** and the bottom two are made by **Superior Tile Cutter, Inc.**

then push down on the tile to snap it along the line—much like cutting a piece of glass. Now that most floor tile is made of porcelain, these cutters are not as popular because the surface sometimes cuts inconsistently. The Superior Tile Cutter® was the one that I grew up with and I still like it today. There are other score-and-snap cutters with a double glide bar that are very popular, and many installers swear by them. They seem to work very well on larger tiles.

Nippers and hole cutters

Tile nippers are really companion tools to the snap cutter. When I tiled bathrooms with my father 30-plus years ago, we cut all the wall tile with a snap cutter and tile nippers. L-cuts and U-cuts (called a "pair of pants") were scored with a snap cutter and finished with nippers. Back in those days, a real tile man did not use a tile saw for bathroom walls. Boy, have things changed.

Hole cutters are mounted in a drill, and the diamond or carbide core cuts very nicely (with the exception of porcelain, which is difficult no matter what you use). I frequently cut a hole from the back side with the water saw (for more, see "Punching a Hole in Stone" on p. 159).

Layout tools

A measuring tape and chalkline are two essential tools. A chalkline is not needed every day, but it is invaluable on any large floor and on many other projects. A measuring tape is used all day long— it's just as important as a level.

The collapsible 3/4/5 A-square is the best tool for doing quick layouts on large or small floors (it gets its name from the fact that a triangle with legs of 3 ft., 4 ft., and 5 ft. forms a right angle at one corner). With an A-square, I can use either lines or straightedges and quickly check and adjust my layout lines so they are square. It is great for dropping into place to start the next section of

The 3-4-5 A-Square (Hanson Tool Co.) is the best layout tool to come on the market in years. It allows me to lay out a floor quickly and with confidence that everything is dead-on accurate. This three-sided tool folds up into one piece for easy storage.

tile. These squares come in different sizes and also with a 45-degree angle, which is great for doing a floor on the diagonal.

Edge-forming tools

Putting a bullnose edge on marble, limestone, and porcelain tile can be done in several ways. I have used diamond profile wheels on a tile saw, although results can be inconsistent if the machine is not brand-new and perfectly set up. More often, I cut an ⅛-in. chamfer on the edge of a limestone or marble tile with a tile saw and then use a polishing grinder with different grits of sandpaper to form the edge. With harder granite and porcelain tile, I use 4-in. diamond pads with a water feed instead.

I also have a water-fed router-profiling machine with a small automatic conveyer table. It was expensive ($2,700), but I had three large limestone jobs in a row, and the machine paid for itself in the first month. It makes a consistently perfect bullnose edge.

Q & A

How do I make *a bullnose or rounded edge on a stone tile?*

There are a few *different ways to make a bullnose. If I am using a uneven slate tile, I round it with a sander after I ease the edge with the tile saw. If I am doing a lot of limestone or marble pieces, then I do it with a bullnose edging machine, which you can rent. These machines make consistently perfect bullnose profiles every time. If I am using marble, I have to follow up by hand with diamond-coated polishing pads to bring the edge to a finished shine. Many marble shops will do that for you as well.*

DESIGN MATTERS

If you can wait until the kitchen is all put away before designing your backsplash, you'll be able to see the negative space created by toasters and coffee pots and create a good balance. Installing a backsplash is not a disruptive job, but the backsplash is a very visible area.

Other specialty tools

An undercut jam saw is used to cut door casing so floor tile can be slipped underneath. That presents a very clean look, and it's much easier and better looking then cutting tile to fit around the casing.

Another miracle tool is the right-angle grinder with an aggressive diamond-abraded blade. This is used to cut out any tile in place that needs modification. With practice, this tool can be used with pinpoint accuracy. A vacuum and a helping hand to hold the nozzle close to the grinder to catch all the dust is a big help when you're working inside.

The most widely used tool for cutting cement board is the carbide-tipped scorer, which costs about $10 or less. It works like a utility knife with drywall, although it takes a little more effort. Special shears are good for cutting Hardibacker®, a type of tile substrate. These shears are absolutely amazing. They offer pinpoint accuracy in cutting with the greatest of ease, and they create no dust. A grinder or a circular saw with a diamond blade also cuts cement board, but these tools create a lot of dust and should only be used outside (and with a dust mask).

Safety tools

Good safety glasses can be bought almost anywhere, and they should be with you at all times. When you're using dangerous chemicals or working with tools that have tile chips flying everywhere, safety glasses will be your best friend. When using chemicals such as cleaners and sealers, it may be even better to wear goggles, which prevent splashes from the side. Wear a dust mask when grinding or sanding.

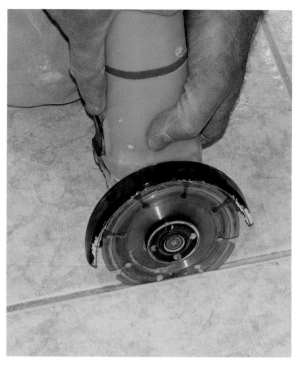

The right-angle grinder is great for demolition or pinpoint cutting. It is used to remove tiles and for cutting out detailed corners.

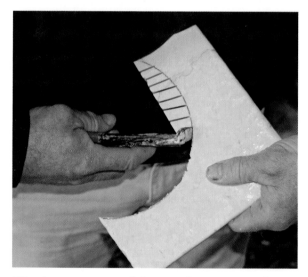

Tile nippers are one of the most important tools an installer has. They perform the delicate job of nipping away to make a cut fit around a pipe or corner of a window. They are like a light pair of pliers and with a downward motion when squeezed, they will break off little pieces of tile until the cut is complete. It takes time to master this tool.

Safety glasses or goggles offer protection against flying tile chips and chemical sealers or cleaners. Earmuffs or foam plugs protect hearing when working with tile saws, grinders, and other power equipment

Ear protection is also needed with continuous use of loud tile saws and grinders. There are a couple of different types, including soft foam plugs and earmuffs. When I'm cutting for an extended length of time, I use a set with a built-in radio.

Tile educational courses and seminars are also important tools. You can have the best set of tools in the world, but if you don't know what to do with them, you may become the master of disaster. The Ceramic Tile Education Foundation and the National Tile Contractors Association offer the best courses I know of.

New Tools of the Trade

New to the market is the DeWalt 10-in. compound miter wet saw. This is the saw that tile installers have been waiting for. It does just about everything and makes perfect miter cuts on any kind of raised-trim pieces. Not only does it cut miters but it makes the heavy duty straight cuts, too. It weighs only 69 pounds and has such good spray guards that you can almost eliminate drop cloths while running it. It is noisier than the other machines and takes up more space with its spray guards. Also, it should be cleaned more thoroughly at the end of the day.

If I had to do a full day of cutting porcelain tile, I would use my old standard tile saw, which is belt-driven and considered a bulldog among tile saws. But after using the DeWalt miter saw, I could not work with my old saw when doing detailed miter work, which has become almost an everyday task in the industry.

DESIGN OPTIONS

Tile offers a world of design possibilities. It's easy to feel overwhelmed at the start of a project, especially if you're planning to use tile extensively. Staying true to the design of your house and attacking one section at a time will help keep the job in perspective.

Take advantage of advice and design services that a tile store has to offer. An expert's suggestions on colors and textures and where to best use different types of tile can be invaluable. The author (right) works with a client selecting tile.

Classic black and white tile will never date your home and they're easy to coordinate with changing colors.

The stone and hand-painted tile in this log home's bathroom gives the room an earthy, rustic feel.

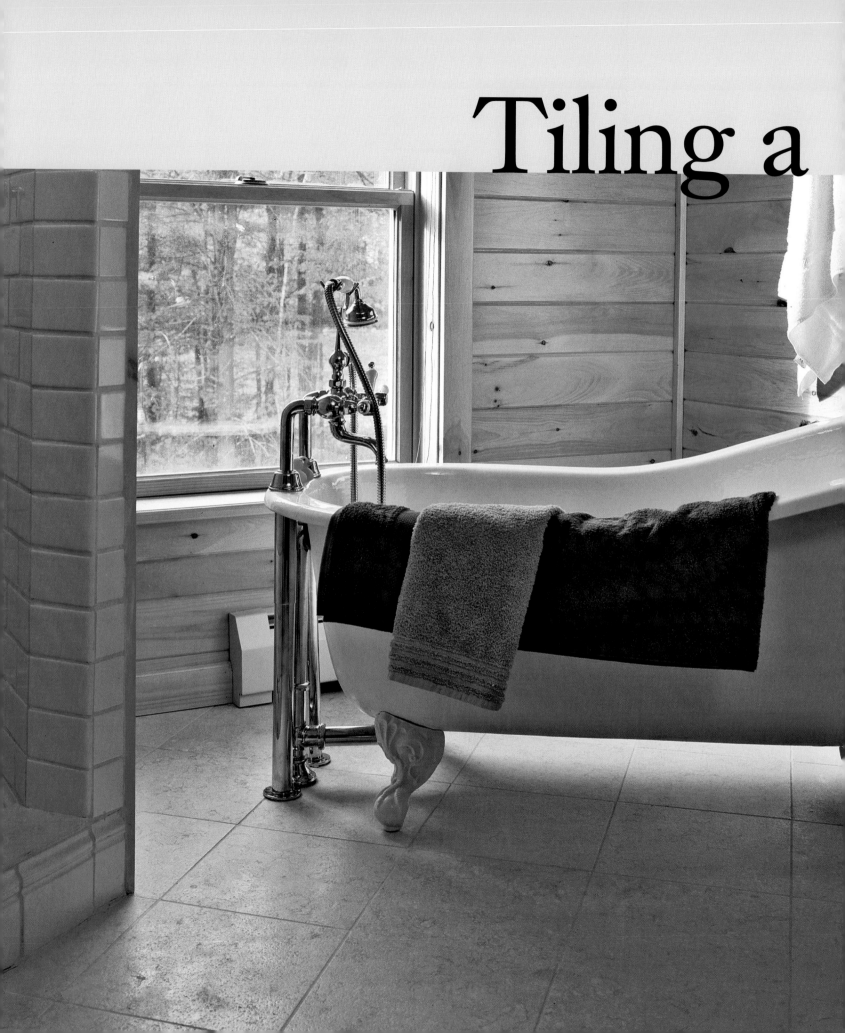

CHAPTER TWO

Floor

1 Maintain a Familiar Style, p. 24

2 Tiling a Floor, p. 24

3 Installing an Uncoupling Layer, p. 26

4 Layout Is Next, p. 30

5 Installing Tile Is the Fun Part, p. 32

When I ask people at our store how I can help, they often reply that they're just looking for floor tile. It's never really that simple. What kind of floor, for example, and is it in a small bathroom or a large sunroom? In fact, the size of the room and how you use the room are both important considerations.

The size and shape of the room will help dictate the size and layout of the tile. In a foyer or entryway, for example, consider decorative patterns if you don't plan to use a rug. You may want to consider bordering the room and then tiling the center on the diagonal, or you could clip the corners of the tile, or introduce a medallion into the center of the room. If you are considering a rug, its size and shape will affect the pattern of tile you choose, and you should keep the layout simple. If you create a dramatic design, you will not only lose the look under the rug but the outside edge that is visible can begin to look cut up and busy. Tile should complement the rug or the furniture in the room without becoming the main focus.

Q & A

I have a *small bathroom. What size tile should I use to make it look larger?*

Either a 12x12 *or a small mosaic will do. A 12x12 will give the room a clean, open look with fewer grout joints for the eye to catch. Or, use a small mosaic to create a wallpaper-like pattern, which will also open the room up.*

DESIGN MATTERS

Always keep the size of the room you're tiling in mind when planning the room. If you're tiling a large floor, plan the room as if the floor were made of oak. For instance, you'd never refuse to have oak floors because they might clash with your sofa; floors should be neutral enough that they go with everything. The same design principle should be applied when deciding which tile to use. If you're tiling a small powder room, you can (and should) add colors or patterns without limiting yourself. But for larger spaces, keep it neutral.

Maintain a Familiar Style

In choosing floor tile, stay true to the style of the house. Tile evokes a feeling. When tile has rustic, chiseled edges, for example, it may go better in a bungalow than in a contemporary house. Natural stone tends to have more variation than ceramic tile, although this isn't always the case.

Keep the flow, too. If you bring tile from the back entrance down the hall and right into the kitchen and powder room, keep tile the same color so there is a nice transition. You can still use the same tile to define different rooms—creating a smaller rug pattern in the powder room, for instance, or clipping the corners of tile in the kitchen and adding a contrasting dot every 4 ft. This maintains the flow but eliminates thresholds

The authors embellished their own tile floor with polished stones and seashells from a Cape Cod beach, but you don't need to be a professional installer or designer to incorporate a personal touch in your tile job.

and prevents the floor from looking like a patchwork quilt.

In bathrooms, remember the slip factor. Whether I am considering my children's bathroom as they splash in the tub and then jump out onto the floor or just myself getting out of the shower, I want something that will be both visually appealing and safe. There are some wonderful stone look-alikes that are neutral in color, with a matte texture that helps prevent slips.

Natural stone is also a terrific choice for just those same reasons. With natural stone you never have to get fancy, either. Every piece of stone is unique and therefore creates its own pattern; you don't have to fuss it up and make it something it isn't.

Always ask to see several pieces of the tile that you'll be installing. Once it's been installed, there is nothing that can be done if it's not the look you wanted, except to rip it out or learn to live with it. Keep the amount of variation in mind as well when you are deciding on a pattern. The way a pattern looks when drawn out with a pencil and what it looks like in reality are somewhat different. Also, when you are looking at a rendition of the layout, it's in black and white. Color changes everything.

Tiling a Floor

Why is it that some tile floors in Europe are perfectly intact after 1,000 years, while others fail in less than one-tenth of that time? Laying a large tile floor can be one of the most challenging of all tile installations. Cracks can telegraph upward from floor framing. Use the wrong cement, or even the wrong trowel, and tiles may break or work loose. I frequently get telephone calls from people who report loose grout in the middle of the floor, and when I inspect one of these problem floors I can tell by rapping on a tile with my knuckles that it has worked loose.

There actually is an answer to this puzzle. It's not the tile that goes bad but the substrate on which it sits. It seems that many years ago, European tile craftsmen developed a method of uncoupling the tile from its substrate. The layering process went something like this: A bottom layer of mortar formed the base, followed by ¼ in. of sand, another layer of mortar, and finally the tile. The sand absorbed any movement in the substrate and allowed the top level to float, unaffected by expansion, contraction, and settling.

This same approach, although with modern materials, is the secret to installing trouble-free tile floors today. The uncoupling membrane I'm using on this floor is called Ditra®-Mat, made by Schluter Systems® (see Resources on p. 186). On one side is a fleece backing bonded to the subfloor.

Classic glass. Glass tile can have a classic as well as a stark, contemporary look, as is the case with this bathroom floor.

Get Rid of the Bounce

Adding a membrane to a floor is a great way of ensuring a long-lasting installation, but if the floor is not structurally sound it's not going to do a lot of good. For most tile applications, the standard L/360 formula (the span divided by 360 equals the maximum allowable deflection, or sag, at the center of the floor) provides a firm enough foundation for tile. At least that's the old standard. There are now recommendations within the industry for new guidelines on the spacing of edge and end joints in plywood subfloor and underlayment, designed to minimize the risk of too much deflection. See "Preventing Cracked Tile and Grout" on p. 196.

Instead of using plywood or cement board as the underlayment over the subfloor, I used this uncoupling membrane (made by Schluter Systems), which will help prevent movement in the subfloor from affecting the tile.

An exception to the current L/360 rule is for setting natural stone, which may be more susceptible to breakage than ceramic tile. Some types of stone, although not all, are softer than today's very hard porcelain tile. Another layer of plywood should be added, bringing the total thickness of the subfloor and underlayment to 1⅛ in. The Marble Institute of America recommends cutting the maximum deflection in half, to L/720 (both the Marble Institute and the Tile Council of America maintain telephone hotlines for advice on this and other subjects). When I start a job, I check the floor to see if there is any bounce and, if possible, look at the floor framing from the basement. The bottom line is this: If the floor is not structurally sound, do not install the tile floor, no matter what anyone says.

Q & A

If the room *is really out of square, where do I start my full tile?*

You don't start *with a full tile. You cut off a little bit of the first course of tile to give the illusion than the room is squarer than it actually is. This will give you room to play with, and the problematic walls will be less obvious. I start from a layout line three courses from the wall and work inward, making up any inconsistencies in this first section. After that, laying tile is straightforward.*

TOOLS AND MATERIALS

Whenever I install any kind of sheet membrane, I use either the 75-lb. linoleum roller (for large jobs) or the wood float (for bathroom floors). After I spread the thinset and lay down the membrane, I then use the roller or float to press the membrane down into the thinset and to push out any air bubbles or excess adhesive. This prevents voids and high spots. It also ensures that the membrane has a tenacious bond to the substrate. Once the membrane is set, I then can bond the tile to it.

On top is a plastic grid to which tile is bonded. When there is movement in the subfloor—the kind of gyrations that would normally cause a tile floor to crack—the fleece acts as kind of shock absorber and stabilizer. Uncoupling membranes also can be useful for smaller floors, especially bathroom floors, because they add an extra measure of water resistance.

Many residential tiling installations will be smaller than the one described in this chapter, but whether the floor is large or small, the techniques of laying out the pattern and installing the tile are the same.

Installing an Uncoupling Layer

Installing a membrane on a wood subfloor is easy. I usually cut out all the pieces I'll need to cover the floor, lay them out, and then number them. Chalklines snapped on the subfloor will help me install the pieces correctly after I've spread thinset cement. The lines also prevent me from spreading too much thinset.

I use a latex-modified thinset when going over any wood base. It's spread with a V-notch trowel (notches are ¼-in. wide and ³⁄₁₆-in. deep). First, I skim-coat a section of floor with the back (straight) side of the trowel to push a tight, flat coat of cement into the pores of the wood. Then immediately I spread more thinset over the floor and use the V-notched grooves of the trowel to spread the cement, keeping the trowel lines all going in one direction. This helps eliminate pockets or voids. Then, right away, I roll out the membrane over the fresh cement and push it out nice and flat. I use either a 75-lb. linoleum roller or a wooden float to press the mat into the cement and establish the bond. I push out any excess cement that may make the floor uneven. Tile can be installed over this uncoupling membrane right away, although other types of membranes may require 24 hours to cure.

Spread only as much thinset as you can cover in about 20 minutes. If it's a hot, dry day it will harden more rapidly, so work accordingly.

The progression for installing the Ditra-Mat goes like this: First, we snap a chalk line. Next, we spread the thinset with a ³⁄₁₆ in. x ½ in. v-notched trowel. Then we unroll the membrane over the thinset.

I use a 75-lb. roller to flatten and bond the membrane to the subfloor. This also pushes out air pockets and excess thinset so the membrane sits perfectly flat.

A Heat Mat to Warm the Floor

One area in this large slate floor will end up being the kitchen. The homeowners love to cook, and they asked me whether it was possible to heat the floor in the kitchen area. I sent a floor plan to the Nuheat® Co., which made a custom mat to fit the space (see "Resources" on p. 186).

Installing the mat was easy. I just put it in place, traced the outside edge, and then put the mat aside. I spread latex-modified thinset with a slightly worn ¼-in. square-notched trowel, keeping trowel lines going in one direction for a better bond. Then I rolled out the mat to the outline I'd traced on the floor. When I put in these mats, I used my hand and fingers to really work the fabric into the floor. I used my fingers to work the area between the wires and then a wooden float to flatten out the mat and push out any excess cement and fill in any air pockets.

After the mat was in place, I installed the sensor probe close to the middle of the mat but not crossing over any of the heat wires. I just ran it up the channels and used a little duct tape to keep it in place. A Ditra-Mat membrane went directly over the heat mat, as is the case on the rest of the floor. It has been proven that the heat actually comes to

the surface of the tile more efficiently with Ditra-Mat between the heat mat and the tile. If the tile ever has to be replaced, the Ditra-Mat membrane protects the heat mat from hammers and chisels.

I always use a voltage meter to make sure the mat has electrical continuity (meaning that it will work later). I check the mat before I start, after it's installed, and then again after the Ditra-Mat membrane is in. The wires go through a hole drilled in the floor so the electrician can make the connection. The mat comes with complete instructions and a good help line in case it is needed. Now the manufacturer sells a warning sensor that is cllipped on to the lead wires throughout the installation. If a wire is damaged, an alarm will go off.

Keep the wires separated. The heat sensor should be installed as close as possible to the middle of the floor. When running the wire toward the perimeter of the floor, try not to allow it to cross other wires in the mat. A bit of tape helps.

Check the circuit. It's essential to check the continuity of wires in the mat before the area is tiled. Or use a device called an electric fault meter, which sounds an alarm if any wires are damaged during installation.

Q & A

Can I tile *over particleboard or oak flooring?*

Neither *is a suitable substrate for tile. If it's a large floor, I would remove the floor and go down to the subfloor and start from scratch. If it's a small floor, I would go over it with a crack-isolation membrane, but check with the manufacturer.*

TILING A GLASS FLOOR

Ceramic tile can be installed directly over a plywood underlayment, but there's too much expansion and contraction in plywood for glass tile. It will crack. Instead, I start a glass-tile floor with a special membrane called NobleSeal® CIS (for "crack isolation system"), which acts as a buffer between the tile and the plywood below.

Tile for this floor is in three different sizes— 4 in. by 4 in., 4 in. by 8 in., and 8 in. by 8 in.—that will be set in a random pattern. My goal is to have no long, uninterrupted grout lines, but otherwise I will make up the pattern as I go. These tiles have an iridescent coating that sparkles in the light. They are not clear, so I don't have to worry that trowel lines in the thinset cement will show through.

Cut to fit. **A special membrane that isolates glass tile from the wood subfloor is cut to fit the shape of the room.**

Applying the membrane

To apply the membrane, I start with a skim coat of thinset applied with the straight edge of the trowel. I "burn in" the cement, meaning that I push

it firmly into the surface. Keep in mind that to avoid the possibility of too much deflection in the floor and the damage to tile that can come with it, the plywood subfloor and underlayment should total 1⅛ in. in thickness.

After the skim coat, I use a ³⁄₁₆-in. V-notched trowel to spread the thinset, keeping trowel lines going in one direction. Then I roll out the membrane slowly, keeping it straight and flat and pushing it into the thinset as I go. I push out any ripples or kinks and evenly cover the floor. A wood float or a 75-lb. roller will push out any air pockets and even out any high ridges of cement. It's best to wait overnight and give the membrane and thinset a chance to set up before setting any tile.

Apply thinset cement. With pieces of the membrane out of the way, apply thinset to the tile substrate, first with the flat side of the blade and then with a ³⁄₁₆-in. V-notch edge.

Roll it out. **The membrane is bedded in the layer of thinset. For the most dependable bond, make sure that all the lines from the V-notch trowel go in the same direction and are not crosshatched.**

Pushing out the bubbles. Trapped air, ripples in the membrane, or high points in the thinset can be eliminated with a wooden float or a 75-lb. roller.

Installing the floor tile

It's extremely important to use a highly flexible thinset to set glass tile. It helps to accommodate the thermal expansion and contraction inherent in the tile, as well as the differences in rates of expansion between the tile and the wood. The Oceanside Glass Co., which makes this tile, recommends several products for use with it (check product packaging of whatever brand you're using).

With the right thinset in hand and the membrane applied, setting these glass tiles is just like installing any tile floor. The tiles are not perfectly flat, so I use a ⅜-in. notched trowel to apply the thinset. I skim coat the membrane with the back side of the trowel to burn the thinset into the membrane (some experts say this improves the bond strength by 50 percent). Then I comb the thinset on the first area where I've snapped a layout line. With this bathroom, I started with the full pattern against the shower stall, which is the focal point of the room. I was not concerned with the size of the other pieces around the room because with the random pattern I can change the pieces to accommodate the size of the cut. Layout lines help me keep tile lines straight and square.

I spread about 20 sq. ft. at a time, which allows the thinset to stay tacky. Each time I put in tile, I give it a ¼-in. slide to guarantee a good bond. I use a water saw to cut tile.

Grouting is done with sanded floor grout because I used a ¼-in.-wide joint between tiles. These tiles have a rustic and somewhat hand-molded look, so a large grout line complements their character and gives them an Old World feeling. As is the case with other glass tiles, it takes longer for the grout to set before I can wash off the residue. If I wash it too soon, the grout will wash out or drag and become uneven. Seal the tile and the grout with a good impregnator sealer. This tile is very durable and will serve as well as most commercial tiles.

Another layer of cement. After waiting for the membrane and thinset to bond overnight, add another layer of cement on top of the membrane and set the tile.

Setting the glass. These glass tiles are set just like ceramic or stone, but the thinset is a special type that is highly flexible. The ¼-in. gaps between tiles will be filled with sanded grout.

Q & A

The grout *is coming out in different places in the middle of my floor. Is this just a matter of regrouting?*

Probably not. *Usually when the grout comes loose in the middle of the room, it means the tiles are loose. Tap on tiles throughout the room and listen for a clacking sound, which indicates the bond between the tile and the subfloor has been broken. If it's an isolated problem, repairs might be possible in an hour or two. If many tiles are loose, the floor may have to be replaced.*

WHAT CAN GO WRONG

There are many potential pitfalls in setting a tile floor. In addition to the usual concerns about choosing the right thinset and applying it correctly, pay particular attention to the substrate. Too much deflection in the floor caused by inadequate framing or a subfloor that is too thin is a sure recipe for failure. Most tile can be set on a floor with a deflection of L/360 (the span divided by 360 equals the maximum allowable sag in the middle of the floor), but some types of tile need a stiffer floor.

Layout Is Next

It may take 10 minutes or two hours to lay out the floor, but take whatever time you need. Once the first tile goes down, there is no turning back. The tile on this floor is a 12-in. by 12-in. bamboo-green slate from Turkey. It varies in size and thickness and has a shale/cleft facet. The layout has to be perfect and all visual points in the room must be taken into consideration.

Finding the focal point. To begin laying out the tile, I start by identifying the focal point of the room. Here, it's a sliding door on a wall with a great view of the mountains, so tile will be centered on the door.

Establish a center line. Once the position of the first tile is determined, a layout line can be drawn on the substrate with the help of a large square. This tool, which folds up for storage, has legs of 3 ft., 4 ft., and 5 ft.

Some installers start in the middle of the floor and work out from there so the room looks balanced. That's fine if the room is a perfect square or rectangle. In this house, the focal points are the two large windows and the sliding door. This is the area where the eye is drawn first and, at least in my opinion, most frequently. I measured out three courses from the wall and snapped a chalkline to mark the span of tile that would be in front of the door. Then I laid out a row of tiles to see what cuts I would have at the two side walls. I found that if I centered the grout joint of the tiles, rather than the middle of the tile, on the sliding door (which was centered on the wall), I would have an 11-in. piece of tile left on each side of the room.

Compensating for irregularities

The next step was creating a line perpendicular to the first, which I drew with the help of an 8-ft. straightedge and an oversized square based on the 3-4-5 rule (a triangle with legs of 3 ft., 4 ft., and 5 ft., called an A-square in the tile business). This perpendicular line down the middle of the room

A Wet Saw

The water-fed tile saw is by far the most important tool for installing a tile floor, especially now that most floor tiles are ceramic, or porcelain, which is even harder. There are a variety of types and manufacturers. Some saws use glide bars for the cutting table while others have tables with wheels or casters (I prefer the latter). Other saws have a large open face that allows larger tiles to be cut on the diagonal. Target®, Felker®, and MK are three brands that last practically forever and stay accurate. If their settings do get out of whack, they can be adjusted. All this comes at a price—pro level machines cost from $700 to $1,200.

started with a felt-tip marker and was completed all the way across the floor with a chalkline. Even though I knew these lines were square, I took a few measurements from the line to the wall to make sure that the walls were parallel to the centerline. If not, it's reason enough to double-check everything and reevaluate the layout before I start. Here, everything was dead-on.

The last part of the layout phase is to lay out one course of tiles, without any thinset, in each direction. It only takes 10 minutes, but it's invaluable for checking the accuracy of the layout lines I've snapped on the floor. Yes, this can be done with a little bit of math, but with tiles varying in size, I'd rather not make a mental mistake that would have me undoing any of the work or jeopardizing the planned size of the pieces around the room.

Assuming the tiles laid down as expected in this dry run, I picked them up and snapped a series of parallel lines every three courses. This will ensure that all the lines in the floor are straight. A very important rule I follow is to make sure that there is a chalked line in the center of any doorway or main focal point, especially at the top of the stairs.

Snap chalk lines, then double check. Using the line created with the square and straightedge, snap a chalk line across the room. Snap a second line perpendicular to the first at a point three courses of tile out from the door. Double check that lines are square.

Seeing is believing. It only takes 15 minutes to see how tile will actually work on the floor. Lay out dry tile along the layout lines. If you end up with a 1-in. or 2-in. piece on one wall, move the layout line now.

Extending the line. A 10-ft. straightedge used in combination with the square helps get the center line to the middle of the room. Measuring the distance from the straightedge to the wall at each end is a way of checking that the line and the wall are parallel.

Why the lines are important. A long view of the floor makes it obvious why chalk lines are crucial. They are especially important at any vantage point where someone can see along a line, like the doorway at the far end of the room.

What goes first, *the tile or the baseboard?*

The tile *goes first, but many builders are not going to give in to that. On a small floor, I don't think it matters. On a big floor, it is an expansion issue. The floor needs room to expand, and the perimeter should have a ¼-in. space under the baseboard to allow this to happen. With changes in temperature and humidity, the tile and wood can expand or contract. I still can't convince some of my builders, but I do let them know in writing (but very nicely and diplomatically) that they are taking a chance.*

Installing Tile Is the Fun Part

Once the first tile has been set into place, the placement of every tile in this 850-sq.-ft. floor has, in effect, been determined. That's why layout is so important. I set the first tile right at the point where the two perpendicular lines cross. The thinset I'm using is dry-set mortar rather than latex-modified, which is designed for bonding tile to plywood or a similar substrate.

The gridlike top panels of the Ditra-Mat have recessed squares that are dovetailed on the inside. This allows the cement to bond by locking into the holes instead of having to make a direct adhering bond that could be sheared off with movement in the floor. Dry-set thinset is easy to work with and one-third the price of good latex-modified thinset cement. It's also easier to clean up. It does have one disadvantage: It takes an extra day to set up before you can grout it, which is perfectly fine by me.

Because the slate is uneven on the bottom, a ⅜-in. notched trowel is a good choice for spreading thinset cement over the membrane. Use the flat

side of the trowel first to fill in all the wafflelike holes of the membrane underlayment. Then spread the thinset with the notched side of the trowel, keeping trowel lines running in one direction. Spread only enough as that can be covered with tile in 15 minutes. Any longer and it may skin over and prevent a good bond. Keep in mind that warmer temperatures will allow the thinset to dry faster. On a large floor like this, I spread about 30 sq. ft. at a time. Each tile I put in will get a little push and slide when I go to put it in place. This really helps to lock in the bond of the thinset to the tile.

Compensating for irregularities

Not every tile is the same thickness. Some of these slate tiles are quite thick and others are thinner than the rest. So of course I have to butter the backs of some tiles to bring them up to the height of the thicker tiles. I do this by flipping the tile over and using the back side of the spreading trowel to apply enough cement to level off the tiles. Some tiles are so irregular that I have to toss them aside and use them for cuts or in the closet.

Mix tiles as you go. Using tile from three or four boxes at a time helps to blend different shades into an overall pattern and avoid abrupt changes in color.

Each piece varies in shade and color. Any time I use natural store I make a point of working from several boxes at a time. This will help blend all the shades together, which is what makes the natural stone floor so beautiful. If some shades of color are too extreme, I toss the tile and get another.

This floor is in our own vacation home, and to make it more fun for our five children I've included some animal-print decorative tiles. These tiles are very real looking, but they're straight 6-in.-sq. cut tiles. So I cut off the corners and made them irregular. I put them into a cement mixer, added sand and water, and tumbled them for about two hours. Now they look authentic. I used the Gemini Revolution saw to scribe the slate to fit around the decorative tile.

An expansion joint at the door. An expansion joint will prevent a crack from developing at the door—a common problem. A bead of silicone caulk helps seal the joint to the doorsill.

This is it. Of all the tiles that will be installed in this 850-sq. ft. room, this first one counts the most. Its position determines the location of every other tile in the room.

Bed the strip in thinset. The plastic expansion joint is set into thinset cement. Its lattice-like edge will be covered with thinset and then tile.

Match strip with grout. The top edge of the expansion joint is nearly the same color as the grout that will be used on the floor, so the line is unobtrusive.

Q & A

Can I *tile over vinyl?*

Yes, *but it has to be done properly. The floor has to be scarified first and then nailed off with 1¼-in. galvanized roofing nails, just the same way you would nail off a piece of underlayment. I skim coat it with a high-performance thinset and then come back and tile it the next day.*

DESIGN MATTERS

Choose a tile that fits the style of your house: a bear paw print in your cabin, pebbles and shells in a beach house, period tiles in your classic home. This is a great concept we apply in all kinds of homes: empty nests, vacation homes, or for homeowners who have a sense of style and just like to have fun. The choices are endless and always creative.

Adding an expansion joint

On a floor this large, an expansion joint will help compensate for the thermal expansion and contraction of the tile and the inevitable movement of the wood subfloor. A general rule of thumb is to install an expansion joint every 20 ft. to 24 ft. I might have gotten away without one here, but it was better to install one. After all, it's my house and the last thing I want to see is a crack in the middle of the floor.

This expansion joint is also made by Schluter Systems and is installed with thinset cement as I put the tile in. Once I know where it's going to be, I spread the cement, lay it into place, and then tile over it. It's also good practice to leave a ¼-in. gap at the outside walls that will be covered by baseboard. This allows the floor to expand and contract seasonally. During the winter, this room can get very cold. But on a sunny day, the sun can raise the temperature of the floor by more than 70°F between early morning and late afternoon. There will definitely be some expansion and con-

traction going on in this house. (see "About Expansion Joints" on the facing page).

At the sliding door, I used another type of expansion joint. Cracks at the intersection of a tile floor and a doorsill are common because a door is opened and closed so often. The strip I've used here takes the place of the cement joint and will move with the door and always have the appearance of being in place without cracking. Both of these strips come in many colors that can come close to the grout color.

Before grouting this floor, I give it a very good cleaning, not only washing the surface of the tile but also removing any excess thinset in the joints between the tiles. The grout line should be at least 1/8 in. thick. After it is cleaned well, I wipe on the first of two coats of sealer with a rag. I try to avoid getting sealer into the joints. I use Miracle Sealants Porous Plus because the slate can be very porous and also because of the cleft of the surface of the slate tile (see "Resources" on p. 186). It will make it much easier to clean.

A tile for fun. Adding an accent tile, like this bear-claw tile, can make a large floor more interesting. The outline of the accent tile is traced onto a floor tile, then cut with a Revolution tile saw.

About Expansion Joints

For floors more than 24 ft. in length, an expansion joint helps to preclude the possibility of stress cracks caused by unequal expansion and contraction of the tile and the wood subfloor. Although I've used colored sealants in the past, some companies now make expansion strips that are cemented right into the floor as it's being tiled. The tile overlaps the plastic webbing on each side of the joint, and the flexible center core absorbs any movement in the floor.

Adding an expansion joint. To accommodate unequal expansion and contraction of tile and the wood layers beneath it, an expansion joint should be added at least every 24 ft.

Cemented into the floor. Colored sealants are one way of providing an expansion joint, but this type of joint is bonded with thinset cement at the same time the floor tile is laid.

Hardly visible. Plastic webbing along both edges of the expansion joint is covered with thinset and then tiled over.

Clean the grout lines. After the thinset has cured overnight, use a putty knife to cut away excess thinset that would interfere with the grout. Cement should be kept below the level of the tile.

Seal before grout. Sealing the stone with an impregnator-sealer before applying grout is of the utmost importance. On stone as porous as this slate, two coats a few hours apart is a good idea. Use a soft cloth and keep the sealer out of the grout line.

Q & A

Do all ceramic *and stone tiles require a sealer before grouting, and after the floors are grouted does all of the grout have to be sealed?*

All stone tiles *should be sealed before grouting to protect the raw stone from cement residue. Many stones like slate and some limestones require more than one coat of sealer. Some ceramic tiles that have a lot of texture or seem to be porous should be sealed as well. It can't hurt to seal any tile.*

Finishing Up

Grouting the floor is a very tedious task. The tile has a lot of corners where grout must be beveled with the palm of my hand. Even though the slate has been cleaned and sealed, it is still difficult to get all the grout out of the surface. I hold the grout trowel at a 30-degree angle to push the grout deep into the joints and then scrape off the residue by using the trowel at a 60-degree angle. When scraping off the excess grout, I come across the tile and the joint at a 45-degree angle to avoid pulling the grout out of the joints.

Cleaning the tile before applying the last coat of sealer makes a big difference in the overall look of the floor. After the floor is grouted, it retains a slight film that must be removed. If the tile had a glazed finish with a nice shine, I would just bring the tile back up to a shine with a good soft rag, buffing off the cement residue as it starts to haze. But this slate has a flat finish and a lot of irregularities in the surface, so I couldn't get it perfectly clean. I use a good tile and grout cleaner that I can buy at any tile store. If the film is too heavy

and the cleaners won't do the job, sometimes I use a weak solution of muriatic acid. This is a last resort scenario because the acid can weaken and discolor the grout. If the acid is used, the tile should be wetted first. The acid should be mixed to a 6:1 ratio with water (six parts water to one part acid) and the floor should be rinsed twice with clean water after it has been cleaned.

Sealing the tile and grout is like a good insurance policy. Many people think a sealer will prevent the grout from getting dirty, but that is not necessarily true. It does protect the grout and it does keep some dirt out, but if the tile does get dirty you will be able to clean it. The sealer really is there to stop staining. If the floor gets dirty, normal cleaner should work well to clean the floor if it has been properly sealed. The slate, being porous, needs at least three coats of sealer, and the grout needs at least one coat.

Before grouting, I apply sealer with a rag, which helps keep the sealer out of the grout line. After grouting, I use either a sprayer or foam brush to get a really good coat of sealer on evenly.

A little at time. Spread grout over about 150 sq. ft. of floor at a time with a rubber grout float. It will take 15 minutes for the grout to become firm. Excess should be cleaned off the tile within about an hour.

Grouting is tough. Applying grout to such an uneven surface is tedious, but sealing it first makes cleanup far easier than it would be otherwise.

It is important not to leave puddles of sealer on the floor. If you do, the sealer will glaze over and leave irregular shiny spots. The impregnator sealer (Porous Plus from Miracle Sealants Co.) allows the tile to have a natural look, and a flat, honed finish. If I want to have a glazed, polished look, I can apply a top coat or enhancer later.

Use a rag or paper towel to remove excess grout. This helps place the grout on low to high tiles. The less water used, the better.

Wash the surface. The surface of the tile should be washed with water and a soft tile sponge. But don't use too much water: It can wash cement out of the joints and fade colored grout. The rough slate gets extra elbow grease.

Natural Stone

Like nature, stone is easy to live with and blends beautifully with its surroundings. And like stone in nature, which by its very character displays both texture and color, stone tile needs no embellishments. When budget-conscious homeowners substitute ceramic tile for natural stone, they often end up spending more on a poor substitute than they would have on the real thing.

DESIGN OPTIONS

A wide variety in size, color, and texture allows tile to blend with virtually any interior and architectural style. Tile is not only very durable, but also lends itself to expressive designs, even whimsy.

Tile floors are a great alternative to wood floors. In this case, the slate is in keeping with the rustic feeling of the log home. While giving the room an open feeling, the slate is also very durable.

The use of random-size limestone gives this kitchen a soft, old world look.

Setting tile in this entry on a diagonal gives the room its own identity even though the tile itself is the same as what's used elsewhere.

Pinwheel pattern. Using 4-in. and 2-in. tile together in a pinwheel pattern makes a charming design statement, and their size makes them suitable for a small bathroom or entrance.

Texture as well as color. Using a random pattern of 2-in.-sq. matte-finish tile gives this floor great texture while diffusing the impact of grout lines.

Tile

CHAPTER THREE
Wainscot

1 Wainscoting Is a Practical Choice, p. 42

Tile wainscots—sections of wall tile that start at the floor and run about halfway up the wall—have gone in and out of style over the years. Thirty years ago, a bathroom had a wainscot as a matter of course. It was approximately 4 ft. high, tiled with 4-in. tile, and wrapped all the way around the room. The body of the wainscot, called the field, was topped off by a piece called a chair rail, and often there was a border of some sort between the two. The tilework often included a built-in ceramic toothbrush holder, soap dish, and cup holder. But finally the pendulum swung the other way. We tiled tub enclosures; we tiled shower stalls, and we tiled floors. Rarely did we tile a wainscot.

Now we are seeing more wainscots again because they have functional as well as aesthetic purposes, though they don't necessarily wrap all the way around the room. With all the technical advances in the past 30 years, the possibilities are unlimited. Whether you want to use a tile baseboard (called a skirting) at the bottom of the wainscot to create a very classic look, or a whimsical border at the top of the wainscot, choose a design that will look good for years to come. A wainscot is not the place to be trendy.

2 Layout Is Key, p. 45

3 Checking for Obstructions, p. 46

4 Now Check the Horizontal, p. 47

5 Installing the Tile, p. 49

When tiling *a wainscot around the room, do I need to use cement board or will drywall be OK?*

Cement board *is only necessary in areas that get wet, so in most cases, gypsum drywall is just fine. Putting tile on a painted wall is fine too, as long as the paint is not chipping or peeling.*

Shades of white. White and off-white tiles, plus a diagonal pattern below the chair rail, contribute to a clean look that will never go out of style.

Wainscoting Is a Practical Choice

On the functional side, putting tile around the toilet area and behind the sink will make cleaning much easier. It will also increase the lifespan of the walls. Tile stops moist air from permeating walls, and when it's used behind a towel rack it also prevents water damage there. Likewise, tile behind a pedestal sink creates a nice backdrop for the sink and makes it easy to clean up splashed water.

This brings us to the first rule of modern wainscot design: The height of the wainscot depends on the height of the vanity. This height varies. Today, many people are using higher vanities than in the past. A vanity at kitchen-counter height is easier on the back than the older, lower bathroom vanities were, so that's the height many people choose.

Imagine a level line starting at the top of the backsplash at the vanity and going all the way around the room. The line, which would be the top of the wainscot, ties all the areas together and creates a comfortable horizontal focal point. Visually, it ties the walls together by connecting the dots and breaking up large expanses of wall.

A wainscot doesn't have to go all the way around the room. If you have a small, narrow bathroom with the counter on one side and the shower on the other, for example, putting a wainscot on the wall between them will stop your eye and help make the room look wider. It also brings the two sides of the room together. In practice, you might play with the top of the wainscot. Wrap it around the room, but when it goes into the shower, bring it up to eye level and away from the floor to make the border a focal point.

Combining different sizes. Mixing 6-in. and 12-in. squares in this wainscot adds unexpected texture and detail to this wall.

Split-level wainscoting. Although a wainscot often encircles the room, it also can stop at the edge of a shower. Picking up the same checkerboard pattern in an eye-level border helps tie the two elements together.

Tying it all together

Different tiles have different effects. A stone wainscot topped by a classic stone chair rail creates a nice clean look. It will never become dated, and it will match any color or design feature you add down the road. The wainscot also gives you a chance to bring some of the color in the floor back into the walls, giving the room a more cohesive look. For instance, if you had a limestone floor with a white tile wainscot, sandwiching a band of limestone between the chair rail and the balance of the tile will visually bring the floor and walls together. Because of the classic nature of limestone, the design works well with a splash of personality—whether it's a carved decorative piece or three or four rows of small mosaics.

If you prefer a wood wainscot, dress it up with a band of a decorative tile between the wainscot and the wood chair rail.

Installing a Three-Piece Border

Tile used for a wainscot today is far different from what it was. Years ago, we might have added a ½-in. by 6-in. strip and then the cap. It was a clean, classic look. These days, we are more likely to go for something that's visually heavier. We commonly install one-, two-, and three-piece borders in which the top piece is a raised chair rail or rope border. It's important to keep the top piece as straight as possible because the eye picks up inconsistencies so easily. Any little jog will stand out. It may take a few tries to get intricate miters right, but it's worth the effort.

I use a black caulk to hold the mitered piece together.

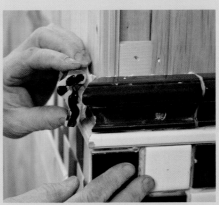

Tiles are pushed together in place on the wall. Excess caulk will ooze out.

Scrape away excess. Because the caulk in the seam is the same color as the tile, no seam will be visible.

Q & A

What height *should a tiled wainscot be?*

Years ago, the standard *height was about 48 in. These days, it's the height of the vanity or pedestal sink, plus 3 in. or 4 in. for the backsplash.*

WHAT CAN GO WRONG

Picture this: You are tiling a bathroom wainscot with a three-piece top border. The layout correctly includes a generous piece of tile where the wall meets the floor, and the side wall pieces look balanced. You use the story pole and lay out the heavy chair rail on the very top of the border to go just under the electrical outlets. In all, it looks like a perfect layout and you start tiling around the room. But as the tile goes through the tub surround, the chair rail runs right into the mixing valve. Oops. It's happened to me more than once over the years. If it does, I insert a flat, blank tile of the same color so the eye doesn't stop at this unplanned interruption.

Making a Story Pole

I'm always amazed at the number of people I meet in the business who have never heard of a story pole. I recall as a child helping my dad, that he made a story pole on about half the jobs he did, usually out of a piece of wood scrap. Growing up with them, I just figured that everyone used story poles.

An accurate story pole makes all of the difference in the world when I'm doing showers, tubs, or wainscots. When tiling a complete room with tile or stone, I do not want to end up with small pieces in any highly visible corners. With a story pole that I make up on a job, I can figure out the complete layout of a whole job in a matter of minutes, thus leaving nothing to guesswork.

Remember that it's just as important to figure the horizontal layout as it is to figure the vertical layout. The last thing a customer wants to hear is, "Well, it just worked out that way." The use of a story pole avoids a poorly laid-out job and an unsatisfied customer.

Making a story pole. Tape measures are good, but story poles are better. Lay out the wainscot on the floor, including the space between tiles, and then mark a piece of wood to show where each tile will fall. Align the story pole with the level layout line, moving it up or down as needed to avoid narrow or oddly shaped pieces at critical areas.

Layout Is Key

It is very simple just to jump in and start tiling on the first straight wall, and many people do. Then, when the job is half finished, they realize that the top of the wainscot is going to run right through an electrical outlet or mixing valve and look awful. Plan ahead: There are a lot of variables to take into consideration. Two jobs we are working on now are perfect examples. Both of them have a three-piece band that sits on the top of the wainscot. On one job, the band has to be below an outlet but above the backsplash. When the wainscot continues through the tub area, the ogee tile runs directly through the plumbing fixtures—a stylistic negative that can't be avoided because there's so little room to make adjustments. In a perfect world (which does exist on rare occasions) the plumbing would be roughed in and built around the decorative tilework.

Every little piece

The other project we're working on is a tile contractor's dream (as long as he likes installing hand-molded decorative tile). There are five bathrooms in a lake house in Maine. Each bathroom has identical tile, though the room sizes vary. The field tile is a 3-in. by 6-in. white tile in a brick pattern. It's topped by a 1-in. by 8-in. white fluted pencil molding, two courses of black and white checkerboard, and another pencil molding, and capped with a 2-in. by 8-in. black ogee-shaped chair rail.

At the bottom of the wall another band begins with a pencil molding and then a white 6-in. square, cut to fit the space. These bottom pieces give the effect of a tiled baseboard. The great thing about this job is that when ordering all these detail pieces we didn't have to be concerned about being short a little in one of the rooms. If

In laying out a wainscot, the trick is keeping intricate borders away from obstructions like electrical switches and receptacles.

we're short any tile we just borrow from the next room. When all is said and done, shortages will only hold up the schedule in one room. We'll make sure it's the least-used room.

The wainscot shown here is in the master bath from the Maine job. In this room, the bottom of the windowsill determines the height of the wainscot. The tilework goes completely around this room and then into the shower. Once the tile enters the shower, the border and trim layout will shift up, so the checkerboard band will be at eye height. (The ogee is eliminated.)

Q & A

I am using *a three-piece border on top of the wainscot. Do I continue it into the shower or tub?*

It depends. *Sometimes we stop the border at the entrance and pick it up again inside the shower at eye level. This keeps the wall from looking like it's been cut in half. If the border contains raised-relief tiles, the end of the first tile will remain exposed if you don't stop it against a wall. You'll either continue the border into the shower, or look at the end of the tile every time you wash your hair. With frameless doors, there isn't room between the door and wall for a raised-relief tile, so stop the border at the door.*

DESIGN MATTERS

Installing tile along with wood bead board gives a refreshing, but timeless look.

Checking for Obstructions

It can take an hour or more to figure out the best layout for a particular room. Keep in mind that once the first tile is set in place, the layout of the whole room is determined. To change the layout after the first piece, you'll have to undo or replace work that you've already started.

Start level lines

Start by snapping a level line around the room that begins and ends with the top of the backsplash. Then make a story pole—sort of a life-sized drawing of the wainscot from top to bottom. Begin with a piece of wood about 4 ft. or 5 ft. long. Put the tiles for the wainscot along the board from bottom to top with all the details and the right-sized grout joints between the pieces. Use another tile, as shown, to mark the edge of the board to show the spacing of the tiles. Now use the stick to survey the room to make sure the top of the wainscot isn't interrupted by obstacles such as sinks, windows, or outlets:

Start at the vanity to see how the tile will finish above it. The entire decorative border should be visible above the counter.

Draw a light level line around the complete room at the proposed final height, using either a level or a laser level. Take the story pole and line it up with the level line. Go around the room, using the story pole to see the size of the piece you will end up with at the floor. You don't want a 1-in. piece where the wall tile meets the floor. These pieces should be at least half a tile wide. Check in several places and anywhere the floor changes heights or levels.

Better than a conventional level. Self-leveling laser levels project a red line all the way around the room automatically, simplifying layout tremendously.

Once you draw the line, take a quick reading to find how other obstacles, such as electrical outlets or switch boxes, fit in the wainscot. A border that's interrupted by a switch plate, for example, won't look as good as one that isn't.

Use the story pole to see how wide the tiles will be where they meet the top around the top of the tub. Anything less than half a tile tall at this point won't look right, and won't be as strong as a larger tile.

If the story pole shows that you have a problem with the layout at any of these points, adjust the top line up or down to solve the problem. Then check everything again—moving the line up or down to solve one problem may create new ones. Keep trying, and keep adjusting until you've got it right. This is the key to a successful wainscot.

Now Check the Horizontal

Once you're satisfied with the vertical arrangement, make a second story pole that shows the horizontal spacing of the tiles, and check to see how the pieces fit across the width of the wall. Avoid small pieces in the corners and on walls that will be a focal point. On this job, which has a running bond pattern similar to brick, it looks best if the tile appears as if it were folded in the corners. If you have a half tile going into the corner on one wall, for example, you should match it with a half tile coming out of the corner on the other wall.

Once you've solved the layout riddle, draw a second level line on the wall—this one marking the bottom of the border. (If there is no border, you can obviously skip this step.) Combined with the first line, which marks the top of the wainscot, this gives you two reference points—the first line you drew keeps the top of the wainscot at a consistent level. The new line keeps the field at a consistent level, thereby keeping the border at a consistent width.

But keeping the tile level is not enough. If you start against a wall that is out of plumb, then the tile will also be out of plumb. More walls are out of plumb than you'd expect, and if you don't plan ahead, they'll turn the job into a complete mess. To avoid the problem, always draw a vertical

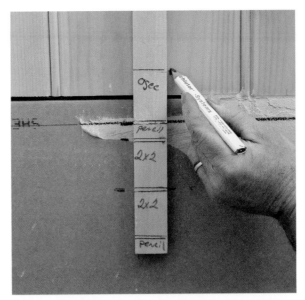

Make a second story pole. The border on this job is complex, so once we've solved all the layout problems we make a second story pole that details where each piece will fall.

I use a level to draw a visible line to keep the tile placement accurate.

plumb line somewhere along the wall. Draw it close to the corner so that you can check immediately while you're tiling to see if the "folded" tiles in the corner are the right size. Draw short horizontal lines across the vertical line to show the location of each tile and each grout line. When you start tiling, start at the vertical line instead of at the corner.

Q & A

When tiling a wainscot, *do I have to use cement board? Also, can I use mastic?*

You do not *have to use a cement board as a substrate when tiling around the outside of the room because it isn't, or at least shouldn't be a wet area. Cement board would be better, but certainly is not necessary. Mastic is fine when tiling wainscot because it shouldn't come in contact with water. I have even used mastic in tub areas, over cement board, it I felt that the bath would get less than average use.*

TOOLS AND MATERIALS

A laser is a great tool for projecting layout lines around the room when you are tiling many walls that must eventually meet. I usually set the laser for the finished height of the tile, shoot the lines, and draw over them in pencil. These devices are self-leveling and very easy to use. They can do horizontal and vertical lines at the same time.

Connect the dots. Follow the story-pole marks to lay out the bottom of the border, which is also the top of the field. The eye tends to travel toward this line, so any irregularities will be easy to see. Make sure it's dead level and continue the lines around the room.

Check for trouble spots. Take the time to lay out the wainscot on the wall to look for potentially awkward transitions. Start with a layout line that marks the top of a prominent part of the pattern, in this case the top of the uppermost pencil molding.

Finding a starting point. Because corners are often out of plumb, draw a vertical line somewhere on the wall and use it as your starting point. Make marks along it with the story pole showing where each row of tiles will go.

Installing the Tile

Tile is installed over drywall (or plaster) with mastic, which has the double advantage of being premixed and tacky enough to keep the tile from slipping while it cures. Inside the shower stall, it's a different story. The shower requires cement backer board and thinset cement, which will not be affected by moisture in this very wet area.

When you're spreading mastic for 4-in. and 6-in. flat tiles, use a 3/16-in. V-notched trowel. If you're using a handcrafted or hand-molded tile, like the ones shown here, use a 1/4-in. by 1/4-in. square-notched trowel. When the tile is extremely uneven, you may have to use a trowel with a slightly larger tooth. When in doubt, pull a tile from the wall and check to make sure that the bonding surface has a full, even coat of thinset. If not, switch to a larger notch. Deeper notches provide a thicker bed of mastic that fills any unevenness in the back of the tile.

Spread mastic in one direction

Always try to spread the mastic in one direction, which will help the tile to sit flat and even. Try not to spread more mastic than you can cover with tile in 20 to 30 minutes. (A pro can lay about 25 sq. ft. of tile in that time. An amateur should plan on laying about half that.)

Applying mastic. Trowel on the mastic, holding the trowel at a slight angle. Leave the layout lines visible so that you can align the tile with them.

Q & A

How do I know *if I should use a water saw or a snap cutter when cutting tile?*

It depends *on the type of tile you need to cut. Almost all stone tiles have to be cut with an electric water saw. Even some of the handmade tiles, because of their composition, have be cut with a water saw. Most ceramic, porcelain, and even some glass tiles can be cut with your average snap cutter.*

DESIGN MATTERS

Wainscoting is an effective way of bringing continuity to a room. A strong horizontal line at the height of the vanity backsplash is a unifying focal point.

If the mastic starts to film over, spread fresh mastic over the old. Be careful not to cover the layout line at the bottom of the border so that you can set tile on it accurately. If the border is too complex and time-consuming, spread mastic for the field first, and lay the border once the field is finished.

Time for tiling

At last it's time to start putting tile on the wall. Start at the top of the wainscot. Generally speaking, you should start at the vertical line you drew earlier. If there is an outside corner, however, it's best to start there so that you can cut the corner tiles to whatever size looks best. Miter the end of the tile, eyeballing what looks like the correct angle. If you make the angle too shallow, you'll get a big fat gap where the pieces meet in the corner. Err on the side of caution—cut the angle so it's too sharp. The adhesive will fill in behind it, and the trim tiles above it will hide the gap.

Safety is a factor

Make sure the end of the tile is on the saw table when you cut, and watch your fingers. A saw is relatively safe—you can hand-hold cuts like this because the blade has no teeth. While you can brush against the blade without getting cut, don't try it. Give any saw too much of a chance and it will cut you. Safety glasses are always a good idea.

Cutting trim tiles—in this case the ogee along the top—is more critical than cutting the field tiles. We make a support jig by cutting square tile in half diagonally. Put the resulting triangle against

Starting installation. Once you've picked a starting point—the top of the border, the top of the field, or at a prominent feature—install the top two rows first. Starting at the top makes it easier to align tiles in an area where mistakes would be highly visible.

Putting up the rest of the tile. When the first two rows of tile are up, work your way down the wall.

Mitering Tile

Cutting tiles at an angle so they meet cleanly in a corner is a job for a wet saw. Making the angle slightly sharper than necessary is better than undercutting it. For cutting narrow molding, a simple jig can help.

Mitering outside corners. If the corner requires a miter, as this one does, apply the mitered pieces first. Put the end of the tile on the saw table, gauging the correct angle by eye, and slide the table to make the cut. The miter won't be perfect, but later work will cover up any gaps.

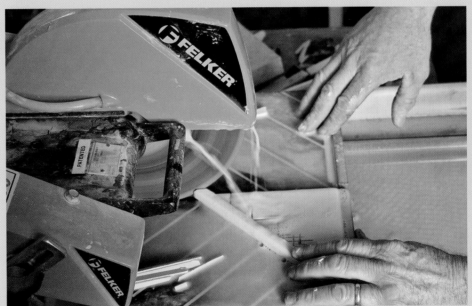

Mitering trim molding. Ogee moldings and pencil moldings like this one need to be mitered precisely so that they will hide any gaps created by miters in the field tile. You can make a guide by cutting a square tile diagonally.

Aligning the ends. Check with a level to make sure the ends of the tiles are aligned and plumb. Any irregularity will be very obvious here.

Q & A

Can I mix *different types of tile, such as stone, glass, and ceramic?*

Absolutely, *we do it every day. Lately, in about half of the large stone jobs that I do, I add some kind of glass inset or border to take the job to another artistic level. When we do a typical six-inch tile tub or shower, we add stone or glass at eye level, and that alone will make a normally simple project much richer, as well as more elegant and interesting. By adding these small details, you get a great-looking bath without robbing the bank.*

DESIGN MATTERS

Skirting handmolded base pieces at the bottom of a wainscot can be pricey. And, in some cases, the exact pieces may not exist. You can make the base pieces look uniform by using a straight field tile starting at the bottom of the wall and then adding a ½-in. by 8-in. pencil trim. You have now created a decorative base effect that is better than the real thing. Changing the color of the pencil will give the wall more definition and may pull more colors into the room. This same effect can be done one tile down from the ceiling. This decorative touch enhances the look of the whole room.

Installing trim molding. Put the trim in place the same way you installed the field tile, but miter both inside and outside corners. Miter pieces for the corners so that they're long enough to look substantial. After installing them, fill in the space between them, trimming pieces to fit as needed.

Installing skirting. Trim the base tiles to width, one by one, and miter or cut to length as necessary.

a stop on the saw, and slide the tile to make the cut wherever you need to make it. Cut right into the support—its sole purpose is to help you make the cuts. Just throw it out when it gets too ragged.

Keep checking

Check both the field and the border for level and plumb every few minutes. Guidelines are just that—guidelines—so put the level across the top and against an edge every few minutes to make sure everything is correctly aligned.

Push a tile into place and then slide it ¼ in. to make a good contact. Work your way across the wall, pushing and sliding each tile into place, checking for level and straightness as you go. You can't check this often enough—it's what the eye sees first. Once you've got a couple of rows in, you can start filling in any way you want—most tile installers install between the vertical line and one corner first, and then between the line and

the other corner. Put in all the full tiles, and then measure the tiles that need to be cut—those along an inside corner, those along the floor, and so on. Often you'll need eight or nine similar-size pieces in the corners. Cut one piece and then test-fit it in each of the openings, in case the size varies slightly.

In the corners

When you've filled the corner, move to the adjoining wall. If you're going for the "folded tile" look, you can cut the corner piece on the new wall to fit. Once it's in place, however, move back to the vertical layout line you drew. Start tiling at the line and work your way back to the corner.

If you're working on an outside corner, tile everything to one side before tiling the other side. If you're tiling an inside corner, tile right up to the corner and butt the tiles together—they don't need to be mitered.

3 Cutting the checkerboard. Cut the 3x6 tiles in half. Set a stop on a tile snapper and cut the tiles with it so that each one will be exactly the same size.

4 Applying the ogee. Build a thick bed of mastic inside the ogee and place the tile on the wall.

5 The ogee tile capping this decorative border must be cut and placed precisely—flaws will be obvious.

6 As you approach an inside corner, miter the tile to fit and apply caulk to seal the joint.

DESIGN OPTIONS

Wainscots are a great way to pull the bathroom together and create a consistent line while protecting the walls behind sinks, toilets, and towel bars.

The dramatic tile pattern of the wainscot is the perfect balance to the cornice that was created at the top of the room.

The classic art deco tile wainscot is not only practical but showcases the sink and mirror beautifully.

Turning tile on a diagonal can give a wainscot a wonderful texture.

The wainscot wraps right around the bathroom and becomes the backsplash over the vanity.

Tiling a

CHAPTER FOUR

Fireplace

1 Design for the Whole Room, p. 58

2 Planning a Hearth and Mantel, p. 58

3 Tiling over the Firebox, p. 61

4 Building a Mantel, p. 64

Whether it's installed for looks or for heat, a fireplace is the focal point of any room. With the introduction of prefab metal fireplaces—which are inexpensive and install quickly—fireplaces have become more popular than ever. It's not uncommon to see a new home that has several. Along with this increase in popularity, we're also seeing increased demand for tiled fireplace surrounds.

Sometimes this amounts to adding a few Delft tiles between the firebox and the mantel; sometimes the entire wall is tile, including the mantel. In the old days—when fireplaces were all masonry—you applied mortar directly to the stone or brick. Metal inserts and modern construction, however, present their own challenges. Part of the surface to be tiled is metal, and part is drywall or plaster, a combination almost guaranteed to crack the tile (see "What Can Go Wrong" on p. 58). Fortunately, there's a solution, and fortunately, it's simple.

Technical issues aside, a fireplace is not unlike a backsplash. It takes up very little space, but it's an important focal point of the room.

Q & A

The beautiful ceramic tile *I have picked does not have a finished piece of trim to go around the inside of the fireplace opening. What do I do?*

There are many *pencil trim pieces that are glazed on three sides—the tip and two long sides. These pieces usually are ¾ in. wide and about 8 in. long. They come in a rainbow of colors and make a beautiful inside trim that can complement absolutely any tile.*

WHAT CAN GO WRONG

Many of today's fireplaces incorporate firebox inserts made of steel. It makes sense because they are faster to install and more affordable than conventional masonry fireplaces. The problem that some tile installers run into is that unequal thermal expansion of the steel and the adjoining gypsum drywall can crack tile that spans the joint. Either the two surfaces must be bridged with a material that protects the tile from this underlying movement, or the tile must stop at the edge of the steel.

Design for the Whole Room

Take the entire room into account when you're tiling, not just the 6 in. to 10 in. around the firebox. Room size and ceiling height are two factors. A dark fireplace works in a large room with a high ceiling, for example, but in smaller rooms the darkness gives the fireplace a massive look. This usually doesn't work unless you're after the "library" look—a darker, more somber color scheme with large, heavy pieces of furniture that balance out the visual weight of the dark fireplace.

If you are going for a lighter feeling, keep in mind the color of the surrounding walls and woodwork. For linen-white walls with white woodwork, think about a lighter tile or a lime-stone surround. This will blend with the walls and open up the room while still giving the area a nice texture and visual interest.

The overall style of the house counts, too. Polished marble is formal any way you look at it. If you're trying to create a cozier, casual feeling, consider tumbled marble or a fun decorative tile. If you have a Mission-style home, then carry the Arts and Crafts feeling right up to the fireplace with handmade tiles.

Planning a Hearth and Mantel

If you have a mantel, the tile you choose depends on how you use the mantel. Decorative tiles surrounding the fireplace are better suited

Tile becomes a rug. The semicircular hearth created with tumbled marble has the look of a fireside rug. Using the same colors in the fireplace surround links the two without overwhelming the picture hanging on the wall above.

Combining wood and tile. A traditional wood mantel looks warmer with the addition of a limestone surround that includes inserts of a darker limestone.

for a mirror or wreath over the mantel. If you have a wonderful painting hanging over the fireplace, on the other hand, tile should complement it rather than fight it for importance. Go with a natural stone—either honed or polished—or with a decorative texture.

Sometimes we'll compromise by putting decorative tiles up the two sides on the outside of the firebox with a plainer tile header across the top. Choose a tile that reflects the style and color of the painting. If you want an image on the tile, try something that relates to the painting.

Delft boats, for example, will fight a beach scene rather than complement it. You might try nautically themed tiles, showing something like sailors' knots. In a cottage, you might want a more whimsical approach: Mimic the style and colors of the painting while complementing it with painted tiles. Try something like tiles with beach grass growing and maybe a blue heron. The header should be simpler, with just sky and a distant seagull flying away for depth.

Hearth considerations

Don't forget the hearth. If this is a traditional fireplace where wood will be stacked on the hearth, use a durable tile or stone able to withstand the weight. If the fireplace is in your bedroom, on the other hand, it may be slightly more formal, and weight may not be an issue.

Flower mural. A summer home is a perfect spot for a tile mural depicting a basket of hydrangea and daffodils.

Q & A

I have an existing *fireplace with a brick face. Can I tile over the bricks?*

Yes, but an extra step *has to take place. The brick facing needs a skim coat of cement to fill in the recessed mortar joints ahead of time. Once filled in, the bricks become a solid flat wall. If this is not done, there is a chance that the joint line could crack the tile as the deeper lines of cement dry at a slower rate than the surface of the bricks.*

Installing Tile over Masonry

When you're installing tile around a fireplace, it doesn't get any simpler than working directly over masonry. The only concern is whether the existing surface is flat. If not, build up the low spots by applying a skim coat of thinset the day before you plan to tile. It's actually a good idea to skim coat any masonry surface—concrete block, brick, or stone. If you don't, the masonry and the mortar holding it together absorb water at different rates and that can cause thinset to crack. Use the flat edge of the trowel and apply a skim coat just thick enough to fill any voids.

If there is any question of the suitability of the masonry, install a layer of stress-crack membrane instead of a skim coat of thinset. On this fireplace, the floor of the hearth posed a problem. Ordinarily, the hearth and the mantel are the same length, and the tiles can run straight up from the end of the hearth to the end of the mantel. The slab for this hearth, however, was poured so that the hearth stopped 6 in. short of each end of the mantel.

Preventing cracks. To keep tile from cracking, cover both the concrete and plywood with thinset and set a stress-crack membrane in the thinset while it is still wet.

Trouble brewing. The concrete for this hearth should have extended further to the right. Tile spanning the concrete and plywood will crack unless you take corrective measures.

Bringing the hearth even with the mantel will mean that the last 6 in. of tile at either end of the hearth will sit on the plywood subfloor. The concrete hearth is part of the chimney foundation and the plywood is part of the wood framing— they are bound to move, settle, and expand and contract at different rates, causing the tile to crack. A true repair would have required extensive work and was out of the question. A stress-crack membrane that isolates the tile from movement, however, would be almost as good, and much simpler.

I spread latex-modified thinset over the entire area to be tiled and put a layer of stress-crack membrane into the thinset. The membrane should be pushed into the thinset with a wood float to remove excess thinset and any air pockets. The solution isn't 100-percent foolproof, but I do feel very comfortable with the process.

There are two ways of approaching the hearth: You can choose a color that seems to flow nicely off the adjacent floor, whether it is carpet or wood. You can also design the hearth as a decorative element, using the same stone on the hearth as on the fireplace, creating a nice, consistent look that may contrast with the floor.

Tiling over the Firebox

People often live with a metal fireplace insert for a while before deciding to spruce it up with tile. Many installers tile right over the joint between the drywall and the edge of the firebox and call it a day. I like to take it a step further.

Until a few years ago, we prevented cracking by bridging the drywall and metal with galvanized wire mesh and mortar. This method is still effective, but it's difficult. Now we bridge the surfaces with a stress-crack membrane. To be honest, it's not a method known to the entire industry, and it hasn't undergone rigid testing, though manufacturers I've talked with say the approach makes sense. There is still a slight chance a crack could develop, but we've never had that happen. Setting tile on a masonry fireplace or around a stove has its own challenges.

Everything is laid out with the help of a story pole. Make sure the lines are both plumb and level—they will guide you as you install the tile as well as when you install stress-crack membrane.

Start with the right thinset

Begin by spreading a high-performance latex-modified thinset over the drywall to be tiled. A ³⁄₁₆-in. by ¼-in. V-notched trowel spreads the right amount. Spread the thinset onto the firebox while you're at it, stopping 1 in. from the

Laying out the tile. A story stick helps lay out the top of each tile. Make the stick by laying the tiles out on the floor with spacers in between. Put the stick next to the layout, and mark the stick to show the tops of the tiles.

Keeping the top level. The eye will be drawn to an uneven or out-of-level surround. Once the story stick tells you where the top of the surround will be, draw a level line laying out the top of the entire surround.

Applying thinset and a stress-crack membrane. The key to preventing cracks is to use stress-crack membrane spanning the wall and the metal band of the firebox. The membrane is applied over a layer of thinset.

Q & A

Can I put *a wood burning stove up against a wall that has been tiled over cement board?*

If it's behind *a wood burning stove, cement board should be installed over noncombustible spacers to keep it 2 in. from the wall. Fire code requirements for the space between woodstove and wall vary from 12 in. to 36 in., depending on the type of stove and the material that insulates the stove from the combustible members in the wall. Check with your fire marshal or building inspector to make sure you follow the rules for your town or county.*

TOOLS AND MATERIALS

A bullnose is a good way of finishing up the inside edge of a fireplace surround. When I'm working with a relatively soft stone, such as limestone, and I have a lot of tile to do, the water-fed profiler in my shop does a good job. But for smaller jobs, I turn to a Flex sander and polisher. It has a 4-in. pad on which I can mount different grades of hook-and-loop sanding pads. After tapering the edge with a tile saw, I use this variable-speed sander to contour the edge until it has a bullnose I'm pleased with (see page 68).

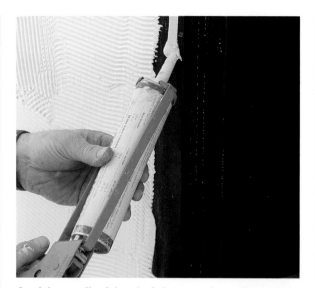

Applying caulk. A bead of elastomeric caulk, made by the membrane manufacturer, is extra insurance when you're applying the membrane to the firebox. Press the membrane into the caulk for a good bond.

inside edge to leave room for a bead of elastomeric caulk.

The caulk—made by the manufacturer of the membrane—is really a last line of defense. It bonds tenaciously to both membrane and metal. If the bond between the thinset and metal ever breaks down, the caulk secures the edge. In fact, because the tile is all on one plane and completely bonded to the membrane, it shouldn't matter if the caulk fails too. The membrane would remain rigid, and the tiles would remain intact.

One very important thing to keep in mind is that while most firebox facings only get warm when there's a blazing fire in the fireplace, some get extremely hot. In fact, some facings get so hot they will melt the membrane. Check with the stove manufacturer to find out whether you can apply a membrane over the particular kind of firebox you have. Avoid tiling any surface that gets to more than 250°F, as the membrane starts getting soft around this point. If the facing gets hot but stays below 250°F, apply caulk where the drywall meets the firebox and let the membrane overlap the firebox by ½ in. You can still tile right to the inside edge of the firebox—the membrane is just to bridge the gap.

Keep the membrane smooth and flat

It's important not to have any ripples or kinks in the membrane. Place the membrane on the wall and gently line it up before applying any pressure. Once the membrane is flat and properly aligned, make sure that the caulk has connected to both surfaces. Then use a wood float to really press the membrane into place. Lean on the float and push from the inside to the outside. This pushes out any air pockets and excess thinset. Don't give the thinset or caulk time to dry out— both have to be very tacky while you're seating the membrane.

On the fireplace shown on p. 61, there was a recess in the floor for a hearth that had never been installed. We filled it with a piece of cement backer board to bring it up to the level of the finished oak and applied a stress-crack membrane over it. The orange membrane you see is a heavy-duty version of the blue one we use on vertical surfaces, but it installs the same way.

Seating the membrane. Press the membrane into the thinset with a wooden trowel to make sure there are no air bubbles between the two. Don't be afraid to lean on the trowel.

TILING AROUND A STOVE

Tiling around a stove has several advantages— it looks good and it protects walls and floors from the heat of the fire. Even units that can sit directly on a wood floor benefit from the mass of the tile, which helps radiate heat into the room. Probably the most crucial part of tiling happens before you tile: Make sure you're happy with the location of the stove. We advise clients to move the stove around the room and to try placing it at different angles to the wall.

Installing a stove surround is like installing a fireplace surround, only easier. We put a ⅛-in.- thick stress-crack membrane in wet thinset applied directly on the floor. Another coat of thinset goes on top of the membrane to hold the tiles down. We install cement backer board on the walls, both as a base for the tiles and to supply more thermal mass. Backer board can be used on the floor as well.

Creating a hearth with visual weight helps ground the look of the wood-burning stove. Check fire codes for spacing between the stove and wall.

Can I use *any type of tile around the fireplace and on the hearth?*

There's bound to be *some tile out there that won't work, but we haven't seen it yet. One thing to keep in mind, however, is that a heavy log dropped on the hearth can chip the glaze on a delicate tile. When in doubt, contact the manufacturer or the Tile Council of America.*

DESIGN MATTERS

Keep in mind what will be hanging over the fireplace or displayed on the mantel when you design a tile surround for a fireplace. If you use decorative tile, you will be limited to displaying something relatively simple, such as a mirror or a wreath, so the two elements don't compete with each other. The same is true when you're using a decorative keystone or center mural. If you have a favorite painting of a beach to display over the fireplace, for example, consider using a limestone keystone, which evokes the feeling of sand without introducing decorative tile. Even a few shells worked into the tile design can accomplish the same thing.

Building a Mantel

On this project, the owner wanted to remove a cold-looking white marble fireplace surround and replace it with a warmer-looking fireplace wall and mantel. He chose 12-in. green slate tile, quarried in China for the wall. For the mantel, he chose handmade ceramic tiles from California. We decided to leave the metal surrounding the fireplace exposed—it's an interesting part of the overall look of the fireplace, and it worked well in the design of the fireplace wall.

The layout of this wall is extremely important. The fireplace becomes the focal point of the room. Everything has to be balanced and symmetrical, with no small, unsightly pieces. The wall is 6 ft. wide, so the 12-in. tiles fit perfectly. The mantel is laid out so that it's three full tiles down from the ceiling and so that the ends of the mantel are each a full tile from the edge of the wall. Given the height of the wall, starting with a full tile at the top of the wall left a band about 6 in. wide across the bottom of the wall. It was

Applying adhesive. If you're building a tile mantel, set a stress-crack membrane in adhesive on top of the mantel to isolate the tiles from potential movement in the lumber that forms the core. Mastic can be used on the face of the mantel.

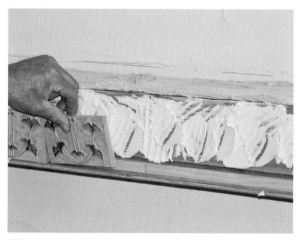

Tiling the front. Screw a small ledger to the bottom of the mantel to hold the tiles in place while the mastic dries.

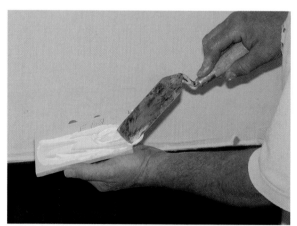

Back-butter the tiles. On handmade tiles with irregular surfaces, such as these, apply adhesive to the back of the tile as well as to the substrate to make sure there aren't any voids.

Applying trim. Tile the top of the mantel and then set the trim pieces, using spacers to ensure an even gap.

unavoidable, but it was better to have the band across the bottom of the wall, mimicking baseboard, than it was to have it sit awkwardly across the top.

Doing the prep work

Now the prep work can begin. Begin by skim coating the entire surface to be tiled with thinset, using the straight edge of a trowel to apply just enough to cover the surface. (I always apply a skim coat of thinset to drywall after priming it to ensure a good bond).

Once the skim coat dries, you can make the core that will support the mantel tiles, and it's easier and neater to skim coat the entire wall now without the obstruction of the mantel. This is a two-part process—first comes a core built up of 2x4s, and then comes a plywood casing for stability. The length and depth should be a multiple of the tile size, including grout lines. The height should be a multiple of the tile height plus the trim piece, including the grout lines. The trim pieces are mitered together at the corners; the full tiles butt at the corners. If you're at all in doubt about the proper size, make a trial run on a shoe box and measure the finished sizes.

Build up 2x4 layers

Once you know the proper size for the core, start by applying construction adhesive to a 2x4 and screwing it to the wall. Then apply construction adhesive and screw another 2x4 over the first. Repeat, screwing and adhering a third 2x4 in place before using lag screws to attach the entire assembly to the studs. Next, provide a stable surface for the tile and build the mantel to the proper height and width by screwing plywood to the top, side, and ends of the 2x4s. Temporarily screw a piece of wood under the mantel so that it sticks out ½ in. This lip will support the tiles when you apply them. You can

Mitering Small Pieces

Tile saws sometimes come with a guide for cutting a miter. But if you're like me, it will get lost or just won't be there when you need it. If the miter is small and hidden, you can often cut it by resting one end of the tile on the table under the blade, lifting the other end, and making the cut. This method won't work if the miter is going to be seen, like the ones in the trim pieces on this mantel. In the worst of cases, the two corner pieces will only be at roughly the same angle, and the difference will be both noticeable and objectionable. For accurate angles, cut a piece of 12-in. tile on the diagonal and use one half as a miter guide. Hold the piece against the guide, slide the table, and continue the cut through the piece and into the guide. At the end of the day your guide will be pretty ragged. Throw it away and make a new one.

Use two hands and make sure both pieces are held tightly. This ensures an accurate cut.

remove it once the tiles are up and the thinset has hardened.

Third and last, apply a stress-crack membrane to thinset on top of the mantel. There are three boards on edge below the plywood, and without the membrane the top may crack as the wood

Q & A

Can I use mastic *to install the tile around my fireplace?*

You can, but *thinset is far better. When a fireplace gets too hot, it can dry up mastic and cause it to break down. A high-performance latex-modified thinset, if used properly, will hold up well.*

Tiling the wall. Tile the top of the wall first to avoid having a partial tile against the ceiling. To support the tiles, measure one full tile up from the mantel, including grout lines, and screw a level ledger to the wall. Tile from the ledger toward the ceiling.

TOOLS & MATERIALS

When making a bullnose by hand, I use a right-angle polishing sander. It has a 4-in. Velcro® drive pad that allows me to switch sanding papers as I increase the grit. I start with lower grit paper (80 or 120) to remove enough stone to round the edge to where I want it. I then use higher grit paper (240 to 600) to achieve the finish and shine. I also have hand pads that do a lot of the same work.

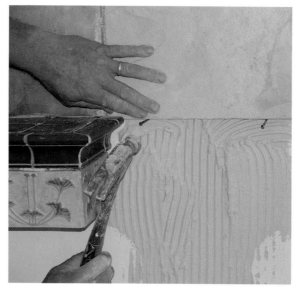

Getting support. The mantel supports the tiles directly above it, but tiles to the side are unsupported and will slip. Drive a couple of nails in the wall to support them.

expands and contracts. Trowel on the thinset with a ³⁄₁₆-in. V-notched trowel and press the membrane into it with a wooden float, removing bumps and voids. Let everything set until the next day before applying any tile.

Tiling the mantel

You could start tiling on either the mantel or the wall. We like to start with the mantel. Having it in place when we do the wall tiles lets us choose tiles that bring out the color in the mantel.

You can apply the tile in any order. In this case, we started with the front, tiled the top, and then put the trim pieces in place. We saved the end pieces for last, setting them after the wall tiles were in place. It's easier to cut ogee or chair-rail pieces off square and butt them into the wall than it is to scribe the wall tile around these profiled trim pieces.

Making a Picture Frame

"Picture framing" is a way to highlight a decorative tile by setting it into surrounding tiles. The process really starts before you put any tile on the walls. Place four tiles side by side, positioning them as they will be on the wall. Center a fifth tile on top of them and trace around it. Cut along the lines with a tile saw, and set the four outer tiles in place first. Apply a thick layer of thinset to the fifth tile so it will sit proud of the other tiles. This makes the inset tile more pronounced and noticeable. It also camouflages imperfections in the cut edges of the frame tiles.

Picture framing. Cut away parts of four tiles to create an opening and inset a full tile for a decorative effect.

Tiling the wall

Normally, you would start tiling a wall from the bottom and work your toward the top. In order to get the three full tiles above the mantel to work out perfectly, however, it was best here to begin with the upper section of wall. But begin-

ning at the top is also working against gravity: All the tiles you put up will want to slip down the wall while the thinset dries. We use a variety of tricks to hold the tile in place—ledgers, the mantel, a trestle, even a couple of nails.

Q & A

Can I install *the stress-crack membrane over any metal fireplace facing?*

No. *Some units get quite hot, and you should never install a membrane over anything that heats up to more than 250°F. Every unit has different specifications; check with the manufacturer to make sure you can apply a membrane over the fireplace you're thinking of tiling.*

WHAT CAN GO WRONG

When tiling the face of a fireplace with heavy stone or porcelain tile, you need to use spacers to hold the tile in place and maintain a consistent grout joint. I use the x-shape spacers but stick them in sideways to hold each course of tiles in place above the course below, rather than setting the spacers into the joints at the intersection where tile corners meet. When the tile is set, I remove the spacers and use them on the next job. If the bottom course of tile is level, I maintain straight, level tile on the whole wall by using these uniform spacers between each course.

Begin by screwing a level ledger to the wall so that the top edge is one full tile above the mantel. Lay a course directly on the ledger and then scribe the course above that to fit below the ceiling and install it, too.

After about three hours you can remove the ledger and install the course directly above the mantel. The mantel will support most of this course, except for the two outside tiles, which aren't directly above the mantel. Support them by temporarily driving a couple of nails along the bottom edge of each tile.

Once the top three rows are properly placed, you can work from the floor up with gravity on your side. Measure and trim the bottom course to the right height (remember that because the wall ends at the ceiling with a full tile, the bottom course will have to be trimmed to fit) and install the two outside tiles. Then work your way toward the fireplace—in this case there's only one more tile between the wall and the fireplace opening—and cut the last piece to fit, as needed. The idea is to set the full tiles at the ceiling and at the outside edges first, and then work toward the point where

Beveling the tile. If you need to cut tiles to fit, the cut edges will look out of place. Bevel them with a grinder to give them a finished edge.

Keeping the tiles aligned. It's very easy for the tiles immediately above the opening to get misaligned. Draw a guideline to make sure the tops of the tiles are in a straight line.

tiles will have to be cut. We bevel the edges with a grinder to give them a finished look.

When the first course is in place, set the second course, third course, and so on. Draw a line to show where the row above the fireplace should be, and then trim tiles to fit around the opening. As these tiles are unsupported, they'll want to slip. Build a trestle to support them (see "Supporting Tile from Below" on the facing page.

When the wall is done, lay the hearth. We like to change to a diagonal pattern for two reasons—the look is warmer, and lining up the grout lines in the wall and the floor isn't quite as crucial.

Apply two coats of a very good sealer to the tile before grouting the wall. The slate is very porous, and the grout would set up on the surface if enough sealer were not applied. A lightened natural gray grout seems to complement the different shades of green and yellow that are in this slate. Once the grout dries and it is cleaned, apply a final coat of sealer.

Supporting Tile from Below

When tiling the face of a fireplace, I may use temporary spacers to hold the tiles in place as the thinset cement cures. But over the middle of the firebox there's nothing to support the bottom edge of the tile. I use a three-piece fixture made of wood to create a bridge that will support the weight of the tile temporarily.

Simple fixture for tile support. Over the center of a fireplace opening, tile can be supported by a temporary wood brace while the thinset cement cures. One screw in each upper corner is all the brace needs.

Floor support. Legs of the supporting structure rest on the floor, preventing tile over the opening from sliding downward.

Move the legs. Should the hearth also need a tile covering, the support legs can easily be moved inside the firebox to clear the area of obstructions.

DESIGN OPTIONS

A fireplace, like a backsplash, is limited square footage with a big impact. Keep in mind what you will be hanging over the mantel so it won't compete with the artistry of the tile around the fireplace.

Focal point for a room. A fireplace is often the dominant visual element in a room, presenting an opportunity for emphasis and elaboration with tile.

White on white. A combination of moldings creates beautiful columns and a mantel for this fireplace.

Complementary colors. The deep tones of the tile in this surround draw out the rich color of the wood around it.

Reducing mass. A light shade of limestone makes this large fireplace seem less massive and helps it blend with the rest of the room. Varying tile sizes and patterns adds texture.

Feel of the sea. The blue and white tiles in this surround evoke a nautical theme that is emphasized with the display of sailboats on the mantel.

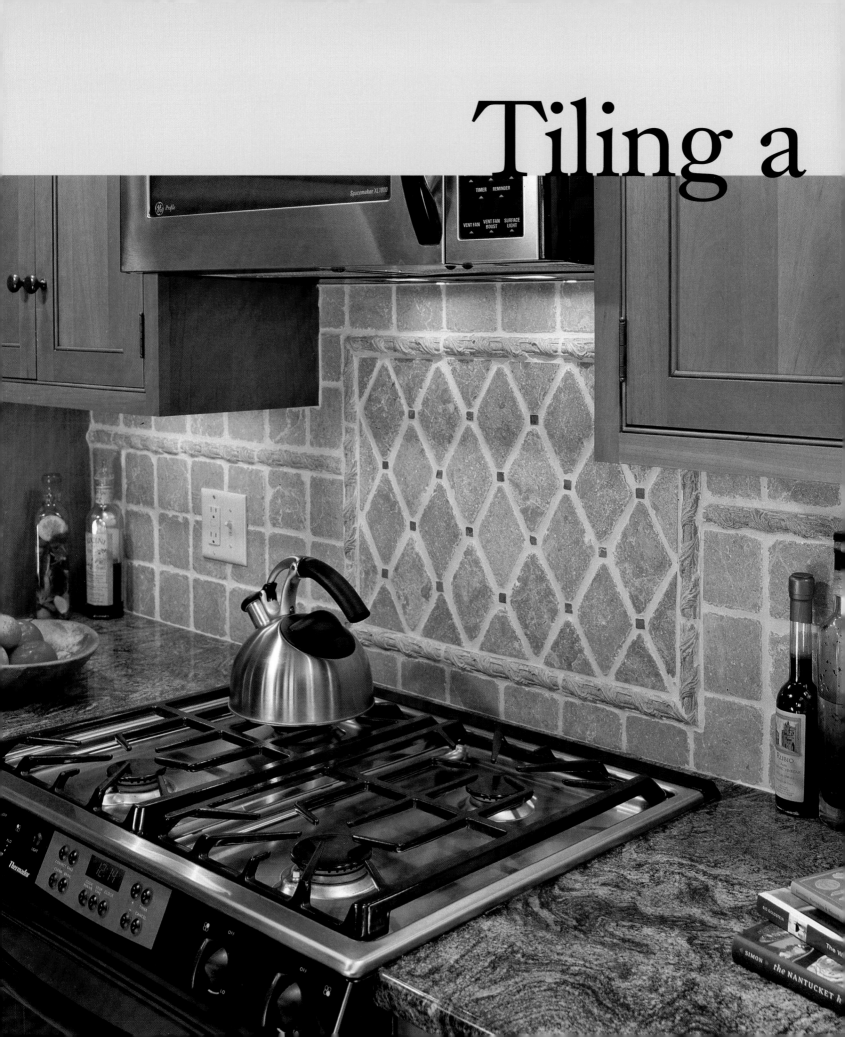

CHAPTER FIVE

Backsplash

1 Color, Patterns, and Accents, p. 74

2 Installing a Tumbled Marble Backsplash, p. 76

3 Sealing and Grouting, p. 81

O f the five or six estimates we do every Saturday morning, at least two of them are for kitchen backsplashes. Some backsplashes are in new kitchens that need a distinctive touch along the narrow band of wall between the countertop and the upper cabinets. Others are in older kitchens, where a good backsplash brings a tired kitchen back to life without costing a small fortune. Whether the kitchen is new or old, the backsplash represents a great design opportunity. It's a place where you can express color, creativity, boldness, subtlety, and craftsmanship.

Tiling a kitchen backsplash is a great starter project if you're new to tiling work. You don't need a large quantity of material, so it's an affordable job even if you splurge on some special tile. The backsplash doesn't get the hard use a countertop does, so you can focus on decorative treatments; it's an opportunity to have some fun and be creative. And despite the project's small scale, there are quite a few important skills involved: design, layout, cutting, grouting, sealing, and protecting surrounding areas from damage (see "Design Matters" on p. 76).

Q & A

What if the countertop *already has its own short back-splash?*

It usually looks better *to have a tile backsplash run all the way down to the countertop surface. But this isn't always possible, since some countertops come with a built-in 3-in. or 4-in. backsplash. If you can't easily remove one of these short backsplashes, design a tile backsplash that's compatible with it.*

WHAT CAN GO WRONG

Layout is a key factor in installing a backsplash. It's easy to start on one long wall and just start setting tile. But when the backsplash meets a focal point in the kitchen, such as the tiled area behind a stove, odd-sized pieces or any misalignments stick out like a sore thumb. The answer is to start in the area behind the stove and work outward in both directions.

Matching the look. White means bright, which was the goal in this kitchen. Hand-painted accent tiles add visual interest.

Color, Patterns, and Accents

Because a backsplash won't be exposed constantly to water, you can make it from almost any type of tile. Tumbled marble tile, featured in this chapter, has become one of our favorites for backsplashes because each tile's unique texture and irregular edges give the finished backsplash plenty of character.

The color and texture of backsplash tiles should play off other visual elements in the kitchen: countertops, cabinets, portable and fixed appliances, and even dishes if you have cabinets with glass doors (see "Blending In" on the facing page). With all these elements in place, try different sizes, colors, and spacing intervals in the backsplash area. If you're considering hand-painted decorative tile, tape up the jacks, queens, and kings from a deck of cards to get an idea of what these colorful tiles will look like. Sample tiles also work, of course. Tape them in place with double-sided tape, and move them around until you like the way things look.

Satin or matte reduces glare

Look also at the amount of natural light that you have coming into the kitchen. If there is a great deal of sunlight streaming in, you may get an unpleasant glare off glossy tile, so stick with a satin or matte finish, which reflects less light. If, on the other hand, the kitchen is dark, the reflective property of shiny tile will brighten it and is probably your best choice.

Every backsplash has at least one focal point. In most cases, the focal point will be over the stove or over the sink. Your view of the backsplash in these areas is unlikely to be blocked by a coffee-maker, toaster, cookie jar, or other countertop clutter, so this is where you might want to do something special. Options include adding extra color or accent tiles or changing the pattern. Hand-painted tiles are also a very popular accent. Take your time and have fun planning the design.

If there's room, add accents

If you have generous stretches of space, think about incorporating a border or accent strip in your backsplash design. In tiling terminology, an accent strip is sometimes called a "listello." It can be boldly different from surrounding tiles, identical in color and texture, or anything in between. It all depends on the look you're after. But here's something important to remember: Like the horizon line in a landscape painting, the border shouldn't run across the center of the backsplash, cutting it in half. Instead, it's better to run the border three-quarters of the way up the backsplash. This brings your border line above a toaster and the wall outlets.

You can also create visual interest by introducing more than one pattern. As shown in the photos of the tumbled marble backsplash, we like to switch from horizontal and vertical grout lines to diagonal ones in focal-point areas. Still another way to add visual interest is to insert small accent pieces—diamond-shaped pieces where the corners of larger tiles meet, for example. These decorative strategies can be used separately or together to create the overall design of a backsplash.

Laying out accents. Knowing where to place accent tiles can be a challenge. Tape a few playing cards in place to help you imagine what the finished wall will look like. Move them around until you find a pattern you like.

BLENDING IN

Even the most beautiful backsplash in the world will look terrible in the wrong kitchen. The design of the backsplash has to work with the rest of the kitchen. Most kitchens have a focal point, something that the eye automatically goes to. The focal point of this kitchen, for example, was the big stainless-steel stove. But you want people to walk into the kitchen and say, "What a beautiful kitchen," not, "Oh, I love your new stove." So rather than just throw industrial-looking white tile behind the stove, making it look even more massive, we complemented it with a metallic-finish tile. When you design a backsplash, at least one of its major colors should draw on colors found elsewhere in the room.

Matching the surroundings. The stainless-steel range is the centerpiece of this kitchen, and the metallic finish on the backsplash tile builds on the high-tech theme. Smaller accent tiles add color and interest.

Q & A

When tiling around *existing outlets, do I have to have an electrician move all of the electrical boxes out in order to be flush with the tile?*

No, just replace the screws *that hold the outlet or switch in place with longer screws so you can pull the outlet or switch out. When installing the tile, slip the edge of the tile behind the metal "horns" that hold the screws; that way, the outlet or switch is steady and won't rock when used.*

DESIGN MATTERS

We often tell customers not to worry about installing the tile backsplash until they've moved in and arranged things on their countertops. People like to say they'll keep counters cleaned off, but the reality is that most of us have a coffeepot or toaster on the counter. So until you've had a chance to live in the kitchen, you may not know where to put your favorite decorative tiles. A kitchen needs to be functional as well as decorative.

Installing a Tumbled Marble Backsplash

Tumbled marble makes a beautiful backsplash. Most people envision a highly polished surface when they think of marble. But when marble tiles are tumbled together—a process that originally involved an old cement mixer, some sand, and a lot of noise—the result is a tile that shows off a coarse, natural texture. This can contrast nicely with a smooth, shiny kitchen countertop.

The design also incorporates a border made from 1-in. by 8-in. ceramic tile pieces that look like stone. Installing a backsplash like this isn't complicated, but it is time consuming. The decorative pattern above the stove must be laid out carefully, and it's often necessary to fine-tune the spacing between tiles because this type of tile is not uniform in size.

Protecting the work area

It's critical to protect appliances, countertops, and other finished surfaces when you're tiling in a kitchen—even if it's just the backsplash. Tile chips can easily be ground into a countertop if you're not careful. On the installation shown here, we put down a rubber shower-pan liner and cardboard to protect the countertop and floors. The rubber liner is great because it can take some impact if something is dropped on it. Also, it doesn't slip around like a drop cloth.

The tile saw poses another problem. Because of the mess it makes, it's set up outside, but water dripping from a freshly cut tile or grit on the bottom of your shoes can easily cause floor damage. To avoid this, we usually protect the pathway from the wet saw to the work area with sections of rubber membrane or drop cloths.

Laying out accents. Create accents by cutting small squares from a contrasting tile. Trace around the accents onto the surrounding tiles and cut along the lines to create space for the accent tiles.

Preassembling patterns. Test-fitting the diagonal pattern on a flat section of countertop is the best insurance that installation on the wall will go smoothly. A framing square and straightedge help keep the assembly square.

Layout: It's like making a road map

Except for the area behind the stove, the layout of this backsplash is fairly simple. There are three courses of 4-in. by 4-in. tile, topped off by a narrower border and a filler piece that reaches the bottom of the upper cabinets. The difficult part of the layout is the patterned area behind the back of the stove. This must be dead-on accurate and perfectly centered on the area above the stove.

Over the years we've found that doing the layout on the wall doesn't work very well, especially with tumbled marble and other handcrafted tiles that can vary in size. Shifting tiles around in wet mortar to get the layout exactly symmetrical gets messy very quickly, and if the customer walks in the room, you don't look very professional.

First try a dry run

Instead of working on the wall, we draw the outline of the patterned area full-size on a nearby horizontal surface and test-fit the tiles there. Cut all tiles as needed so they fit into the outline the way they should fit on the wall. Don't start to set tile on the wall until the test-fitting is complete (see "What Can Go Wrong" on p. 74). This ensures accuracy and eliminates the mess you encounter when going back and forth between the work area and the tile saw.

There are also some layout considerations elsewhere on the backsplash, in the regular areas where grout lines are simply horizontal and vertical. For example, when there is a window in the middle of a wall, we like to arrange the layout so there's a full tile on each side of the window. This extends the symmetry of the window trim and looks much nicer than having unequal-size tiles on either side of the window.

Q & A

How wide *do I make the grout joints?*

It depends on the type *of tile and also the look that you want. Handmade tile varies in size, so with this tile, go with wide joints—¼ in. or wider. If the tile is uniform in size, you can use a normal ¹/₁₆-in. grout line, as you would for bathroom wall tile.*

DESIGN MATTERS

When installing any type of natural stone or hand-crafted tile that varies slightly in color, always take tile from three or more cartons at a time. If you simply lay your tile from one carton at a time, your backsplash will probably have clusters of light- or dark-toned tile grouped together.

Tiling Around an Outlet

You can't tile a backsplash without contending with electrical outlets. You may be able to move the outlets to better positions during new construction or major remodeling, but sooner or later, you'll have to tile around them. A symmetrical layout looks best. This usually means cutting out equal amounts of tile on opposite sides of the outlet. If doing so jeopardizes the layout or symmetry of the rest of the wall, however, we settle for what we can get around the outlets. You can buy switches, receptacles, and cover plates in colors that complement the tile. If you can't find the right color, camouflage it with paint.

Laying out the opening. Trace around the cover plate before removing it to make sure there will no gaps when the job is complete. Tile should extend about ¼ in. beyond the layout lines.

Cutting in around the outlets. Mark the tile to make sure the cut will accurately fit around the outlet and at the same time will also be ¼ in. inside the outside border of the cover plate.

Installing the tile. When you install the cut tile, make sure you slide it behind the ears of the receptacle. You may need to get longer screws to hold the outlet in place.

Start at the bottom. Work from bottom to top, laying up diagonal tile, accent squares, and border pieces as you go.

Plan for partial tiles

Of course, you may need to have partial tiles somewhere over or under the window. There are no rules here: Plan the size and location of partial tiles (called "dutchmen") to please the eye. Layout is also important with regard to electrical outlets. Like it or not, outlets need to be design elements in your backsplash. (For tips on how to deal with outlet boxes, see "Tiling Around an Outlet" on the facing page.)

Laying up the tile

Whether you start your work with the tricky part of the project (in this case, it's the backsplash behind the stove) or with the easier section of the backsplash, the process is basically the same. Begin by spreading either all-purpose mastic or thinset on the wall using a trowel with ¼-in. by ¼-in. notches. In this case, we used all-purpose mastic because the stone is dark and dense. With white or translucent stone tile, we would use a white thinset to avoid spotting or darkening the tile.

You can sometimes lay the tiles diagonally if you're working in a small area and have precut the tiles to fit, but as a rule of thumb, lay the bottom course first and work your way up the wall course by course.

Don't rest the tile directly on the countertop, in case the countertop has to be replaced sometime in the future. Leave a space of about ⅛ in. or so between the counter and the first tile. It's small enough that the counter won't cause the grout in the space to crack, but big enough for the work space you'll need to get in a new counter.

Irregular tiles have uneven lines

Elsewhere, the joints between tiles are ¼ in. wide, but it's important to realize that because these tiles are irregular, joint sizes may vary slightly. Instead of relying on spacers to establish the joints, shift the tiles as the different sizes require. As you install each tile, press it tightly against the wall about ¼ in. from its final location, and slide it into place to ensure a tight bond.

Q & A

Do I seal *the tile before I grout?*

Natural stone tile *(like tumbled marble and limestone, for example) and tile that has a crackle glaze should be sealed before grouting. Most other tile doesn't need to be sealed first. One exception is tile that has some sort of relief profile. Sealing this decorative tile before grouting can help prevent grout from getting stuck in crevices. When presealing tile, I use a clean cloth dampened with the sealer. This helps keep sealer out of grout joints.*

WHAT CAN GO WRONG

If the grout cracks between the field tiles, it's usually a sign that either the tile is loose or the wall was not grouted properly. Tap on the tiles one by one. If you hear a hollow sound, the tile is loose and should be replaced. If the sound is solid along the cracked area, then the grout is failing. Cut out that joint with a utility knife and re-grout.

Because this backsplash is only four courses high, it's fairly easy to keep grout lines plumb, level, and straight. But just to be safe, lay a 2-ft. level on top of the third course to make sure the top edges align. When seen from a distance, a couple of high tiles can make a wall look very uneven.

On the main sections of this backsplash, border tiles are installed between the third and fourth courses of regular tile. We like the border to stand slightly proud of surrounding tiles. This is a subtle way to create more visual interest, and it's not difficult to do.

Before installing each border piece, build up the back with some mortar or mastic, whichever you are installing the tiles with. Then press the piece into place.

To finish installing tile in the main sections of the backsplash, cut tiles to fit against the end walls and upper cabinets. We like to allow for little or no joint, since grout is most likely to crack where two different materials meet.

The sequence for installing the diagonal pattern above the stove is the same. Remember to cut the tiles and create the full pattern before installing anything. Then work from bottom to top, inserting the tiny square accent pieces as you lay up the

Building up the border. To make the border pieces stand proud of the field tiles, apply some extra mastic to the back of each border piece. Miter the border pieces where they meet at corners.

Leveling the pattern. After laying up the topmost diagonal pieces, check the top of the pattern for level.

Applying grout. A rubber-backed float is the tool of choice for spreading grout.

larger diamond-shaped pieces. Put the level to work again at the top of the pattern, after laying up the triangular pieces that abut the border.

Sealing and Grouting

Grouting tumbled marble tile is a little more difficult than grouting standard glazed tile. Tumbled marble tile has irregular edges that tend to "catch" grout (see "Seal Porous Tile" on p. 83). The slightly higher border in this project also demands careful attention.

Once you've got the tiles on the wall, use a clean cloth to wipe a good-quality impregnator sealer on the marble and ceramic tiles. This helps protect the marble and works as a grout release.

Because of the wide joints between tiles, we always use a sanded grout with tumbled marble. Sand combines with the portland cement to add body and strength to the grout.

Mix a stiff but workable batch of grout, and float it on generously, as shown in the photo above.

Tools and Materials

Backsplash tiles can slide out of position before the mastic or thinset holding them to the wall has had a chance to cure. Plastic spacers support the tile until the adhesive can do its job. X-shaped spacers are a good choice for tumbled stone and handcrafted tile. Plastic spacers are much easier to extract than homemade spacers made from cardboard or some other porous material.

The level serves as a ledger board to hold up the tiles.

Q & A

Can I grout *the tile same day that I install it?*

No, wait until *the next day. The mastic needs air to dry out well, and grout application will prevent this.*

DESIGN MATTERS
Picking the right grout

When picking grout for a stone tile or a stone look-alike tile, you need to decide if you want to use the standard gray or white grout or if you want a more natural color grout to complement the tile. I always try to let the tile be the main visual element and to use the grout as the visual "glue" that gives the whole a cohesive look. I avoid high-contrast grout that would make the tile look like a grid.

Clean tile after grout sets

Let the grout set until it is firm to the touch, and then wipe down the walls with a grouting sponge dampened with clean water. Don't use too much water because this can wash out some of the cement in the grout. Pay attention to rough indentations in the marble tiles and relieved areas in the border tiles; you may need to wash more aggressively in these spots.

Once the grout has set up for about 15 minutes (or sooner, if room temperature is warmer than normal), use a clean towel to wipe the haze off the surface of the tile. This is also the time to use a putty knife or trowel to tidy up the grout in corners, along perimeter walls, and along other intersections where you want to see a clean, straight grout line.

Do the final cleaning the next day with a good tile cleaner. Make sure to protect the countertop, stove, and sink, because some cleaners may have a corrosive or staining effect on these surfaces.

Extra sealer is needed in kitchen

A day or two after cleaning, you can finish the job by applying sealer to the tile and grout. (If the tiles are stone, and you sealed them before grouting, seal them again anyway so that the grout is protected, too.) We like to apply the sealer with a disposable foam brush, giving the backsplash behind the stove a couple of extra coats to protect the tile and grout from grease and sauces.

Cleaning up with a trowel. Use a narrow trowel to cut clean grout lines along all corners and edges.

Seal Porous Tile

Some types of tile used in backsplashes, like this tumbled marble, are extremely porous. Failing to seal the tile before applying grout can make the surface difficult if not impossible to clean completely once the installation is finished.

Seal before grouting. Before applying grout, seal the surface of porous tile with a good impregnator sealer. Two coats will be needed on very porous materials. Try to keep the sealer out of the joints.

Then seal again. Once the tile is grouted, it's equally important to seal the surface again. Apply a liberal coat of sealer over the entire surface and then wipe off the excess. Wait a few hours and apply a second coat. A foam brush makes a good applicator.

DESIGN OPTIONS

A backsplash is probably the smallest amount of square footage you will design, but some of the most important and visible tile in your house.

Having the wave splash up and over the faucet frames the faucet while not losing the design behind the fixture.

The space behind the stove can be the perfect focal point for a mural. Keep in mind that you'll be looking at it four seasons of the year.

The carved black granite frames the area over the stove while balancing the dramatic hood and cabinet detail.

The large area over the stove is the perfect place to add a dramatic element and can be enjoyed while cooking or sitting at the island.

The tone-on-tone backsplash creates a wonderful texture, giving the homeowner the ability to change other colors in the kitchen at anytime.

The combination of tile and stone creates a beautiful richness in this bar area backsplash.

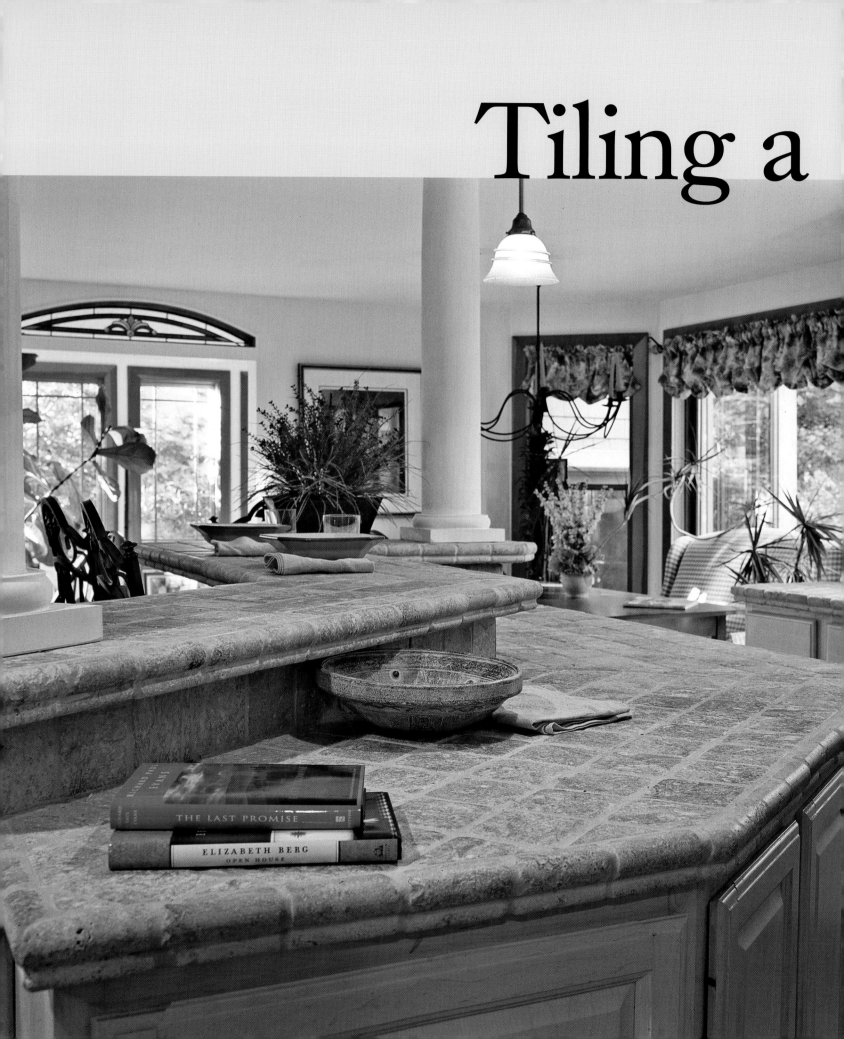

CHAPTER SIX

Countertop

You can put many of the same tiles on a counter that you can put on the wall, floor, or ceiling. Each has its own personality, along with its practical pluses and minuses.

Tumbled marble has wonderful veining and color variation within the stone. You can lay the tile in uniform rows, for a proper, elegant look, or combine sizes and mix patterns for a more decorative effect. There are a variety of chair rails, pencil profiles, and other trim pieces you can use to customize the edge of the counter. On the practical side, you can sand the edges of the tile to ease any sharp corners.

Ceramic tile gives you the chance to add a decorative color or pattern to your counter. In addition to the world of color that ceramic tile introduces, it is also available in many different finishes, such as glossy, crackled, or matte. On a practical level, some glazes are not as durable as others and may scratch or chip, but don't let this discourage you. Just make sure you check with your tile dealer for the proper grade of tile. As for the front edges of the counter, the number of trim tiles available for ceramic tiles is even greater than for stone.

1 Keeping It Clean, p. 88

2 Getting Started, p. 90

3 Cut the Tiles First, p. 92

4 Adding Edge Trim and Grout, p. 93

Q & A

Do tilesetters *really use a 1-in.-thick wire-reinforced mortar bed as the base for counters in California?*

Yes. *The old-fashioned mud jobs common in California and elsewhere are still the best method, as far as I'm concerned. But is it necessary? In a few cases, perhaps, but generally, no. Modern installation materials are far superior to those of the past and result in a good solid counter.*

TOOLS AND MATERIALS

The Revolution saw (made by the Gemini Saw Co.) is a tool that can be used on almost any countertop installation because it cuts perfect inside and outside radius curves in virtually any material, including glass. Its 10-in blade is a ½-in. circle band, much like a bandsaw, which allows tile to be weaved in and out for cutting almost any radius. It makes less noise than other saws, generates almost no chatter vibration, is lightweight, throws very little water, has a slide table, and will make straight cuts in porcelain tile. On big floor jobs, however, I stick to my regular pulley drive tile saw for straight cuts.

Laying a Counter over Laminate

Counters in existing kitchens are often finished with laminate, such as Formica. Rather than ripping out everything, prep the existing counters and then tile over them. This saves a lot of time, mess, and money. Start by making sure that the laminate is well bonded and the counter is structurally sound. Prepare the surface with a grinder and a rough diamond blade. Rough up—tilesetters call this "scarifying"—the surface to allow the thinset to bite into the surface.

Although you could tile right over this substrate, we use a thin membrane. By spending an extra $50 for the product and about a half-hour of labor, you get a counter that is bulletproof and should last forever. There is one important thing to keep in mind: When you're bonding membrane or tile to laminate, you must use a high-performance thinset.

Using laminate as a base. Laminates on existing counters make a good base for tile. Scarify it so the thinset can bond with it, and cover with a waterproof membrane for good measure.

Floor tiles are also make great countertops. They give you the ability to build a counter that matches the floor, creating an open, uninterrupted feeling. It goes without saying that floor tiles are among the most durable, and they come in a variety of styles. On a practical level, however, you may not be able to get trim tiles that you need along the edge of the counter. Use a wood edge that matches the cabinet finish instead.

Keeping It Clean

One thing that discourages homeowners from tiling a kitchen counter is concern about keeping the grout clean and good-looking. While it's a legitimate concern, grouts and sealers have improved by leaps and bounds in the past few years.

The grouts are stronger and denser, with chemical additives that resist stains. Impregnating sealers used to treat grout are unimaginably better than the simple silicone sealers of years ago. They penetrate into the pores of the grout, sealing it from the inside out. When purchasing a sealer, get the best you can. Sealers are the insurance policy on your investment. This isn't the time to look for bargains.

Epoxy grout usually unnecessary

We're also often asked whether epoxy grout should be used on a countertop. The answer is generally no, although it might be a good idea in commercial and very active residential kitchens. It is not recommended for most stone tile or for any handmade tile. If in doubt about whether epoxy works with a tile, check with the manufacturer. Epoxy grout is more expensive than conventional grout, and it's harder to work with. We also rely on thinset cement to set tile on counters, not mastic.

Most counters have at least one sink, and the type of tile you use may depend on the sink. Undermount sinks—which have edges that are completely covered—require special trim pieces. Incidentally, trim pieces create a lot of grout lines right around the sink, so make sure that area is very well sealed.

If, on the other hand, you are considering a decorative top-mount sink as a focal point, then maybe you want to put the money into the sink rather than the counters.

Tile, generally speaking, is far less expensive than a solid stone counter.

What Can Go Wrong

A few years ago, I tiled a countertop in limestone with a 14-in. overhang. Although I told the builder from the beginning that the overhang needed support, he insisted that two layers of ¾-in. plywood cantilevered over the edge of the counter would be enough. Wrong. The moisture from the thinset alone caused the plywood to warp. The builder added brackets that should have been there in the first place, and I repaired the problems caused by the warping plywood. Any overhang more than 10 in. wide needs brackets for support. When the substrate bends or warps, grout and tile may crack.

Overhangs greater than 10 in. should be supported by brackets.

DESIGN MATTERS

Unlike a tiled backsplash, a countertop is seen from above. We often use a decorative strip as the bullnose or edging at the front edge of the counter because it will be highly visible. We don't usually use a lot of decorative tile in the counter itself, since it is a work area, a food preparation area, and a place where appliances and other decorative objects may be positioned. If there are decorative tiles on the counter, they are interspersed in areas that are strategically visible.

Wood edging. Counter edges do not have to be finished with tile. A wood edge can be used if tile is not available with coordinating edge trim or when a counter is designed to look like a piece of furniture.

Have some fun. Large, irregular pieces of tumbled limestone with inserts of beach glass give this bathroom vanity counter a sense of adventure.

Q & A

Does the front facing
always have to be tiled?

No, *sometimes you get a more elegant and softer look with a finished wood edge. If you're getting new cabinets, have them make up some counter edging, too, so that the finish will match the cabinets.*

TOOLS AND MATERIALS

When I want a radius at the edge of a stone countertop, I give the thinset a day to set up and then use a grinder to round over the sharp edge of the tile. Fitted with a slightly ribbed diamond wheel, the grinder eats right through the stone, and I take down as much material as necessary to make a smooth curve. I follow up with a sander to make the finish nice and smooth. Start with 80-grit paper and work your way up to 600 grit, depending on how much of a shine you're looking for. Make sure you use safety glasses when working tile with abrasives.

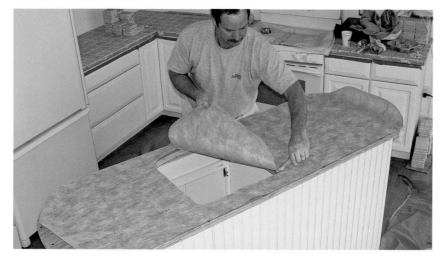

Cutting the membrane. A waterproof membrane protects the plywood substrate from water damage. Use the counter as a template to cut the membrane to size.

Spreading the thinset. The membrane sits on a thin coat of latex-modified thinset. Spread it with a ³⁄₁₆-in. notched trowel.

Getting Started

We often tile a kitchen countertop as a way of giving new life to an old kitchen. Tile can even be applied over an existing laminate surface (see "Laying a Counter over Laminate" on p. 88), and it can be applied on counter overhangs—provided there's enough support to prevent a sag (see "What Can Go Wrong" on p. 89).

In this case, the kitchen is in a new house on Cape Cod. The stone tile we're using is a 4-in. square in gray-blue tumbled marble. The counters against the walls are simply a straight pattern with a backsplash that has diagonal tiles after the first course. The island, which we'll focus on here, has diagonal tiles, surrounded by a border that is parallel with the edges. Each end of the counter is a half circle, which will add a little difficulty to the tile installation—and a lot of character.

A counter begins with its base. Have the carpenters install a double layer of ⅝-in. plywood and glue and screw the layers together. This is firm enough to prevent movement, and you could install the tile directly on it.

We always like to go a step further, however. We install a waterproof membrane that will stabilize the bond between the tile and counter and prevent moisture from penetrating into the plywood. Like everything else in life and tiling, there are other options—plywood topped by cement backer board, or even a full mud bed. We've found that the firm structure of the wood, combined with the waterproof membrane, is easy, reliable, and very efficient.

Tiling a Rounded End

Creating the curved end of a countertop requires cutting angled edges on the tile. If edges aren't angled, grout joints will be larger on the outside of the curve than on the inside. Cut each tile on a slight angle (here, it's roughly ¼ in. on the inside to zero on the outside). Do this on both sides of the tile and the grout line will be even. Plan on some trial and error. It is not uncommon to go back and forth to the saw to get the angle just right. Sometimes you have to cheat and make one tile narrower than the others, or open the joints a little bit to get the layout to work out. But given the curves used in construction, the taper is almost always somewhere between ¼ in. and ½ in.

Trimming tiles around the sink. At the sink, you'll have to cut tiles to fit around the opening. Hold the tile in place and mark it from below.

Line them up. Keep cutting pieces until all the tiles fit in a smooth curve. Grout lines should be even.

Number tiles for reference. Once the dry run is complete, number the backs of all the tiles. Then apply thinset cement to the substrate and re-set the tiles in order.

We use Schluter Systems Kerdi® membrane for counter work (see Resources on p. 186), laying it out and cutting it right on the counter. After cutting it to size, remove the membrane temporarily and spread a layer of latex-modified thinset on the plywood with a ³⁄₁₆-in. V-notch trowel. Lay the membrane into the thinset while the thinset is good and tacky and flatten it out with a wood floating trowel. Push out all the air pockets to insure a 100-percent bond. Apply a thin coat of thinset to the edge of the plywood and allow everything to sit until the next day.

Q & A

Are tile countertops
practical?

Yes and no. *Maintenance is the primary issue. There is no doubt that a solid surface counter is easier to keep clean. When choosing to do a tile counter, it has to be the right kind of tile in the right place. If proper sealing and the right kind of grout is used, the tiled counter can be practical in many places, but not all.*

WHAT CAN GO WRONG

When installing a complicated island counter with a radius curve like the one we show in this chapter, it pays to do a dry layout first. I lay out one row of tile the length of the counter and one row the width of the counter. At that point I cut in the curve cuts. By doing a dry layout, I avoid putting the tiles down in thinset and then picking them up again to make adjustments. The radius cuts sometimes have to be cut a few times to accommodate the right size pieces to make the full radius. Once the tiles on the radius and the sink have been cut, I spread half the counter with thinset and transfer the pieces to the dry side so they are close at hand when installing.

Cut the Tiles First

Installing a countertop like this can be quite a production. The best way to approach it is to cut and piece the tiles together before you put any thinset on top of the membrane. Start with the tiles that form a border around the edge of the counter. The two straight stretches are pretty simple, but the curves at the end make up for it. Each tile has to be tapered on two edges to follow the radius of the counter, and there's no way of knowing how big a taper to cut (see "Tiling a Rounded End" on p. 91).

Mark each tile. To swing around the corner evenly, tiles must be cut to fit. Cuts can vary as the radius of the curve changes, so some trial and error is usually part of the job.

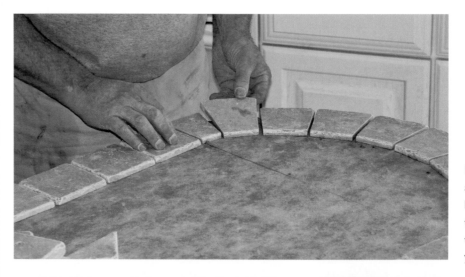

Make a trial run. For a complex pattern like this, lay out the tiles to make sure they will fit before you apply any thinset.

Cutting a curve. To cut along a curve, feed the tile into the blade and cut about halfway around the curve. Then back the tile out and finish the cut from the other edge.

Cutting to fit. To lay out the curve where the tiles meet the radius ends of the counter, hold the tile in place and sketch the curve with a permanent marker. Take off the bulk of the waste and then make a second cut to smooth out the curve.

Leave a small overhang, about ½ in., so that you can tuck the tiles on the edge of the counter underneath those on top. With the border in place, start cutting a series of tiles in half diagonally. Place them around the border and piece the diagonal pattern together.

Adding Edge Trim and Grout

Installing the front trim piece requires a little trick to keep the tiles from succumbing to gravity. Keep the trim pieces aligned and in place by screwing a temporary strip of wood, called a ledger board, to the bottom of the counter. Position it to extend out beyond the edge of the counter so the tiles can rest on it.

Make a point of applying mortar to the back of each tile—called back-buttering—to ensure a perfect bond. These tiles will get bumped a lot, and you want to make sure they will not fall off in years to come. When the last of these pieces are in, it's time to do a thorough cleaning of all the tile and the joints. Clean the tile with a damp sponge, and rag on a coat of sealer to protect the tile and to

keep the grout from sticking to the face. This is also the time to ease any sharp edges on the corner and polish them smooth. (see "Tools and Materials" on p. 90).

Grouting tumbled marble is not hard, but it does require some attention. With tumbled marble, try to use a grout that matches the color of the stone. Natural marble has a lot of little imperfections and indentations. No matter how hard you try, grout is going to get into some of them, and no matter how hard you try, you won't be able to get it all out. Sealing the tile before you grout helps a great deal. A grout that matches the tile remains more or less invisible if it gets stuck in the pores. Once the grout is in, wash it down as best you can without removing the grout.

A week later, when the thinset and grout have dried, apply two more coats of impregnator sealer to both the tile and the grout for extra protection. Clean and reseal the counter every year. Kitchen counters take a lot of physical and chemical abuse on an everyday basis. With a natural stone, wear and tear can actually improve the overall look over the years, as long as the stone isn't stained or dirty.

Back-buttering the tiles. Edge tiles get a lot of abuse. For a good bond, this tile is back-buttered, or coated with mortar on the back. Apply the mortar with a trowel and make sure you work it into any irregularities in the surface.

Attaching the ledger board. As long as the mortar is wet, the edge tiles slide down unless supported. Screw a ledger to the bottom of the counter to hold them in place.

DESIGN OPTIONS

Tile counters can be a wonderful alternative to traditional solid surface counters. Not only can you add a decorative touch with color and texture, but you can get a terrific end result for a fraction of the cost of other surfaces.

Tumbled marble is a good choice. One advantage of using tumbled marble on a counter is that the front edge can be eased with a grinder and orbital sander to create a finished bullnose.

Adding a decorative flair. A V-cap has been added to the front edge of this counter. Decorative touches on a counter edge are always visible, while those on the work surface may be hidden by appliances or kitchen clutter.

Coordinating cabinets and counter. The front edge of this counter has been finished with wood that matches the cabinets and the trim piece above the glass-tile backsplash.

A coordinated look. Tile used on this kitchen floor also makes a good countertop and backsplash, giving the room a neutral and pulled-together look.

Decorative band. A band around the top edge of this counter frames the vessel sink beautifully.

Tile, not a slab. The addition of a chair rail on the front edge of this marble counter makes it look thicker than it really is, and the profile adds a pleasing design element.

Tiling a Tub

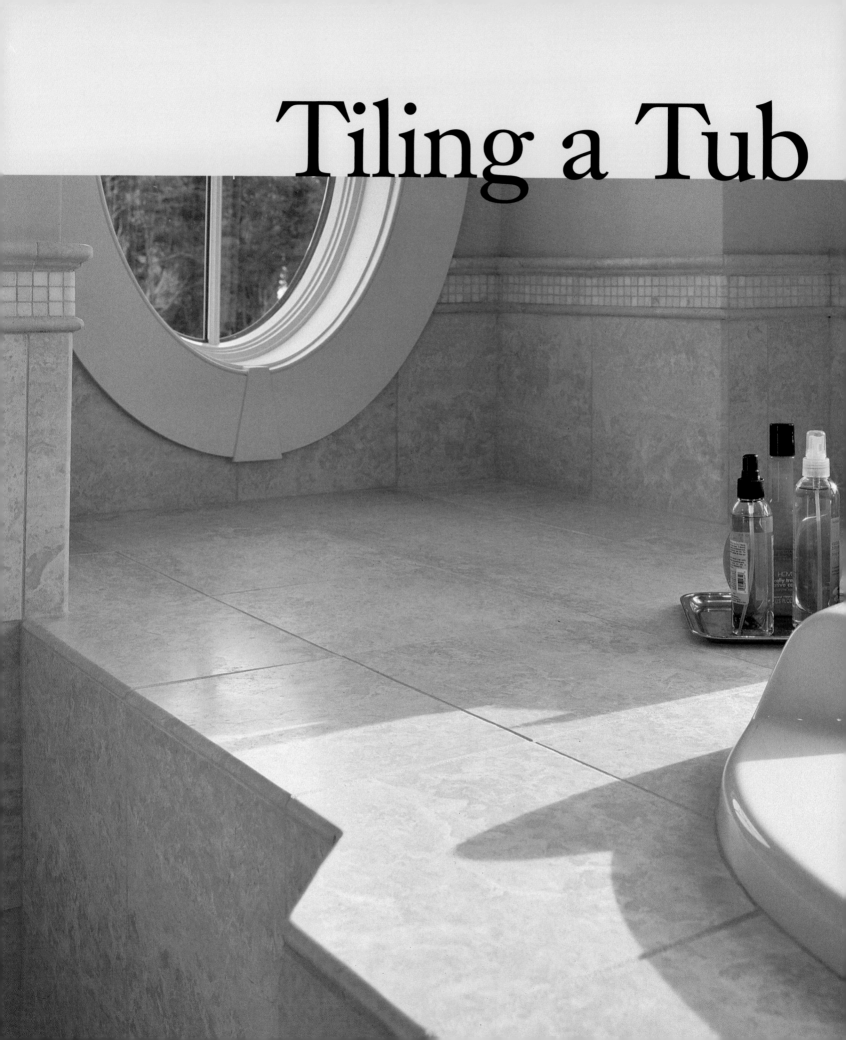

CHAPTER SEVEN

Surround

1 Check for Plumb and Level, p. 99

When you're tiling the area around a tub, the first thing to consider is just what kind of tub it is—a conventional tub used as a shower, or a soaking tub? If the surround is for a shower tub, the tile will probably be hidden most of the time by a shower curtain. You may want to add a band of decorative tile high on the wall—so it can be seen even when the curtain is pulled closed—but keep most of the surround relatively simple. If wainscoting is being used, it's best to continue wrapping it right through the shower. Not only will the wainscoting add a design element to the room but it has practical advantages as well. It can be difficult to finish off the end of a chair rail cleanly as it meets the edge of the shower.

If the tub surround is for a soaking tub, you should consider access for the complex plumbing that often goes with it. No one wants to hear that there may ever be a plumbing problem on a new tub, but if that's the case the plumber will need a way to fix it. We usually design the front of the tub so it has a wood panel matching the cabinet doors of the vanity. If you can get access to the plumbing through a closet or other hidden area, then tiling the front face gives you the chance to introduce a step or a decorative front edge.

2 Use a Story Pole for Layout, p. 99

3 Planning the Installation, p. 102

4 Now for the Installation, p. 104

5 Finishing Up Corners and Edges, p. 105

6 Finishing Up, p. 107

Q & A

What do I do *if the tub is quite a bit out of level?*

When the tub *is out of level by more than a little bit, plan the layout so you have good-size pieces where wall tile meets the tub. This will allow you to make up the difference by cutting each tile on a slight angle at the bottom. If the tub is out of level by only ⅛ in. or so, you can hide the variation in the grout joint.*

TOOLS AND MATERIALS

The most important tools for installing a tub surround are your levels. Always make sure they are accurate. I buy Stabila levels, which I think are the best. Never buy a bargain level. The levels I use are guaranteed for life, but I still check them occasionally for accuracy. They come in many different sizes. In a normal tub enclosure, I use a 2-ft., 3-ft., and 4-ft. level, plus 58-in. and 32-in. sizes. They all come in handy.

Soaking tubs need more room

Soaking tubs should be designed so they are easy to use. Give yourself a little edge around the tub surround so you have a place to sit as you swing your legs in or out of the tub. Then consider the splash around the tub. As a general rule this area is approximately 12 in. high. If you are running a decorative border you'll want to bring the design up just a bit so you can enjoy the pattern. Keep in mind that a soaking tub is a top-mount with a rim that will visually interrupt the view of any decorative band right along the tub deck.

Before You Start

A tub surround is not the most difficult tiling job you'll encounter, but it can present some challenges. If the tub and ceiling are out of level, or the walls are out of plumb, even by less than an inch, it can be difficult—even for a professional.

The goal is to keep tiles plumb and level and to end up with cut pieces that are not too small. Layout is the key, because once the first tile is set, the final outcome is determined.

Another concern is protecting the tub from damage during the installation. The first thing I do is to clean the tub perfectly to make sure that there are no chips or scratches. If there are, I inform the owner or builder before I start working. If I don't, the problem is mine. It's always a good idea to put a drop cloth or a piece of cardboard in the tub and tape some cardboard to the top edge of the tub in case you need to stand on the tub while tiling the top of the enclosure.

As is the case in any wet area, the substrate for the tile is cement backer board. It will not deteriorate or harbor mold (gypsum drywall will). Backer board comes in different sizes, but 3-ft. by 5-ft. pieces are great for tubs. The cement board cuts mostly like drywall, although it's a little more work to use. I nail it with 1½-in. galvanized roof-

Off the deck. The decorative border has been brought up to start after two rows of 3-in. by 6-in. tile so it's high enough to be seen and enjoyed.

View to soak by. The surround for this large soaking tub is a whimsical mural of a mountain retreat, giving bathers the feeling of being in the woods as they enjoy a soak.

ing nails every 6 in. Once it's in place, I use mesh tape and thinset to seam the joints.

For a detailed explanation of how to install backer board in a wet area, see p. 116.

Check for Plumb and Level

The first thing I do is to find out whether the tub is level and the walls are plumb so I know where adjustments will have to be made in laying out the tile. It's not unusual for either the walls or tub (or both) to be out of whack.

If the walls are out just a little, I can sometimes disguise the problem by adjusting tile spacing slightly and using some of the ¼-in. space where tiles meet in the corner. On side walls, I start at the outside edge of the tub and work my way into the inside corner. If that wall is a little out of

plumb, I can make up the difference by cutting pieces that go into the corner.

When the tub is off level, there is no forgiveness. I have to open up the joints between tiles just a bit, or cut the tiles that follow the top edge of the tub. Once I have determined the status of plumb and level on the walls and tub, it's time to lay out the job and decide where tile and grout lines will fall.

Use a Story Pole for Layout

The surround will look best if pieces in all corners and along the top edge of the tub are not too small—my goal is to end up with no cut tiles smaller than half their full width. I use a story pole to check what size pieces will go on each wall (see "Making a Story Pole" on p. 44).

Q & A

What do I do *if the lip of the tub forces the backer board on the wall outward and makes the tile sit at an angle?*

If the angle is significant, *soften it by tapering the bottom of the backer board with thinset the day before you set the tile. But trimming the back side of the tile along the bottom edge with a wet saw is usually enough.*

TOOLS AND MATERIALS

Another tool essential for tiling a tub with standard 4-in. and 6-in. bathroom tile is the basic Superior snap-cutting machine. It is very quick, accurate, and easy to use. It also has a guide that locks in place so I can make many tile cuts that are the same size. The cutter works like a glass cutter. Tile is scored with a carbide wheel mounted on the handle. A quick, light pop splits the tile neatly.

Start at the seat. A story pole showing the location of each tile in a row makes it easy to see where wall tiles will fall when they are aligned with the edge of the seat, and how the course will end at the far corner.

Lucky layout. The layout on the back wall allows a full tile in the corner. Any piece over a half-tile would have been fine, but this outcome is better.

Mark the center of the wall. Rather then drawing a plumb line at the seat to start tiling, use the story pole to mark the middle of the wall. If tiles vary in size, or the side wall is slightly out of plumb, the problem will be easier to control from the center.

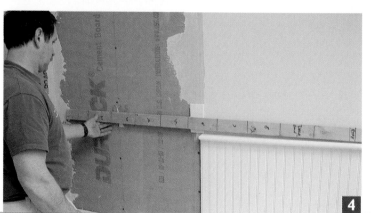

Keep cuts in the corner. On the side wall above the seat, a full tile will start at the outside edge of the tub wall. Cut tiles will go in the corner where they will be less visible.

There are times, of course, when small pieces are unavoidable, but the problem can be minimized with a little effort and imagination.

I use the story pole on each wall and determine my layout from left to right (or right to left). On the back wall of the tub, which is seen first and is highly visible, I like to center the tile on the wall and have pieces of equal size in both corners. On the side walls, symmetry is not as important.

I usually run tile right to the ceiling. I'd rather not end up with a small piece at the ceiling, but I also want a full tile at the tub, so determining the size of each course can require a little compromise. If it looks as though the course of tile at the ceiling will be too narrow, I try reducing the size of the pieces on top of the tub. Also, if the tub is way out of level, a line of cut tile at the tub line will make the problem less obvious.

Waterproofing a Tub Seat

Cement backer board and a slight pitch by themselves are not enough to prevent horizontal surfaces in a tub or shower from leaking. A thin, waterproof membrane applied over the backer board will help keep water out. I have been called on too many jobs to troubleshoot a leak in an area where there is a tiled seat. Any horizontal area in a shower or tub should be treated like the shower pan. Even though there is cement board on the seat, water will still be absorbed and eventually make its way into the room or space below. Remember: Concrete and cement board are porous.

Waterproofing the seat. A few minutes of work and $12 worth of materials will guarantee a leak-proof seat. I start by spreading latex-modified thinset with a 3/16-in. notched trowel.

Take it up the wall. Thinset cement and waterproofing membrane should extend at least 1 in. up the wall for a complete and trouble-free seal.

Clip and fold the corners. Running the membrane slightly past the edge of the seat allows me to clip and fold the corners and fully protect the edges from water intrusion.

Flatten the membrane. After pressing this thin waterproofing membrane firmly into the thinset, I use a steel trowel to push out any excess cement and eliminate any air pockets. More thinset and tile will follow.

Q & A

Should I tape the joints of the cement board, and can I use drywall joint compound?

Yes, you should tape all seams to avoid cracking. And no, you should not use taping compound designed for drywall, but the same thinset you use to bond tile. And choose fiberglass mesh tape, not the paper tape used for gypsum drywall.

WHAT CAN GO WRONG

Once the starting point in the middle of the back wall has been determined, I draw a level reference line all the way across the wall. The temptation is to start setting tile immediately, without taking the time to draw a second line—a plumb line perpendicular to the first. But without this plumb line, tile can start to drift off course. And once that happens, you're fighting a losing battle. All you can do is cut your losses, take that area down, and reset it after plumbing the wall properly. My dad always said, "The longest way is usually the shortest way."

Finding the starting point. A level line that crosses the back wall about one-third of the way up will define the starting point for setting tile. With the tub slightly off level, tile at the bottom of the wall will have to be cut to fit.

Completing the thought. Continuing the level reference line around the corner and across the two side walls ensures that tile will be level all the way around.

Planning the Installation

One highlight of this installation is a seat at one end of the tub that could be used as a shelf for plants, shampoo, and soap. Whenever there is a horizontal area in a showering area, however, it must be waterproofed. (see "Waterproofing a Tub Seat" on p. 101).

It's a simple procedure and takes just a few minutes. This bathroom also has a decorative band of tile just above eye level (see "Design Matters" on p. 106). It's rather inexpensive, yet this gives the tub surround the detail found in a high-priced bathroom.

This tub is out of level by about ¼ in. from end to end (which is very common). I will make that up by cutting the bottom row of tile. One advantage of making the adjustment here is that it allows the bottom course to line up evenly with the seat at the far end of the tub. Even without the seat, it's easier to compensate for an out-of-level tub by making a gradual adjustment in tiles on the bottom row.

Adjust for irregularity

I would typically center the tile on the back wall, but in this case the tile would not line up exactly with the full tile and trim piece on the seat. So rather than center the tile, I'll move it slightly so it aligns with the seat. That may complicate cuts for the corners, but it's a better look overall. In this case, the seat determines a good part of the layout because it's so visually dominant. Everything should line up nicely.

Now that I know what the layout is going to be, I use the story pole to locate center lines on the back and side walls. By drawing level and plumb lines in the middle of the back wall, I can be assured that the wall will be straight and true. Even if the tiles vary in size, they won't affect the overall appearance of the wall.

Critical reference line. A 5-ft. level makes a long plumb line in the middle of the back wall. This is the wall that will be viewed straight on, so tile must be set very accurately.

Starting on the wall. Working from the level reference line down, I spread thinset with a ¼-in. notched trowel. I try to keep all the trowel lines going in one direction, which will help keep tile well bonded and flat.

Q & A

Can I use *ceramic tiles and stone tiles in the same tub surround?*

Sure. *You may find a great accent band or border in stone that really complements the ceramic tile very well. Just keep in mind that any stone installed should be sealed before grouting. The sealer works as a grout release and helps to make grouting and cleanup much easier. Don't worry about getting sealer on the ceramic tile. Just towel off any residue.*

TOOLS AND MATERIALS

For all straight cuts, a basic snap cutter works quickly and makes a perfectly clean cut. If the cuts are difficult, small, or L-shaped, it may be better to use a water saw.

Now for the Installation

Installing the tile is the fun part. I start with the lower part of the back wall, spreading thinset cement with a ¼-in. square-notched trowel below the line I've drawn, about one-third of the way up the wall.

I always spread an ample amount of cement in order to get a full bond rather than skimping and leaving a few voids on the wall. When there's a good coating of thinset on the wall, I comb it with

First tile, front and center. The starting point for setting tile is at the intersection of plumb and level reference lines.

the teeth of the trowel in one direction. This makes a big difference in achieving a complete bond. If trowel lines all go in one direction, coverage can be more than 95 percent. It will reduce the possibility of voids in the thinset behind the tile.

Depending on the weather, I have about 20 minutes before the thinset starts to scab up. If the thinset has some tack to it, I just freshen it up. But if it is starting to harden, then it must be removed from the wall and replaced with fresh material. The thinset does not have to be latex-modified if the tile is being bonded to cement backer board or a concrete slab. Plain thinset cement (dry-set mortar) and water is easy to work with, and the cleanup is minimal.

Setting the first tile

On the middle of the back wall, where my two lines meet (one level, which is horizontal, and one plumb, which is vertical), I set the first tile and slide it ¼ in. to ensure good contact. Then I install a double row of tile and check it with the level.

When I continue to install the tile, I follow down the plumb line, which I can just barely see through the thinset. If I can't see the layout line, I use a 2-ft. level to make sure I'm setting tiles

Checking progress. After the first two courses have been set, it's a good idea to use a level to check that they are level and perfectly straight. This is the time for adjusting any tiles that are out of line.

accurately. By doing this I keep the tile straight and the joints don't start stepping out of line. (see "What Can Go Wrong" on p. 102).

Fill in all but cut tile

Now it's just a matter of filling in the field until there is nothing left but cutting the tile in. With each tile that I put in, I push the tile into the cement and give it a ¼-in. slide to achieve a good bond.

Finishing Up Corners and Edges

Cutting and fitting tile in the corners on the back wall is easy because I know that tile on the side walls will fill any minor gaps. As I mark the tile, I know that I have about ¼ in. of play. The tile I am cutting here is a basic 6-in. by 6-in. ceramic tile. I use a regular score-and-snap cutter.

If I need to make any angle cuts (to compensate for an off-level tub), I just angle the piece a little and then cut the same way as I do the rest.

I usually do the lower half of all three walls first before I tile any of the upper walls. In this way I can check with a level that wall tiles are running at the same height and that joints will line up in the corners.

Bottom half is the hardest

The bottom half of the tub area is by far the hardest because of all the cutting that has to be done at the tub line and also the importance of establishing a level row of tile across the wall. The upper walls are very easy as long as the tile already set is dead level. If so, all I have to do is start from a plumb line in the middle of the wall and work toward the corners.

The short walls at either end of the tub start with a full tile cap or bullnose at the outside

Keeping cuts to the bottom. The second-to-last row of tile on the back wall ends up at seat height. Tile below this will be cut to fit. If a full course of tile had been used at the bottom, unattractively thin pieces would have been needed above the seat.

First the seat, then the wall. After tiling the seat, which is pitched slightly toward the tub, I use a level to establish a plumb reference line on the short wall above it.

Q & A

How often *do I have to re-grout a tub surround?*

In new construction, *most settling occurs in the first six months. Occasionally, the vertical seam in the corners and the seam at the tub line will need re-grouting. In general, in New England we find that grout should be checked every two years or so. That may vary in different parts of the country. Avoid using acidic cleaners— they can break down the cement in the grout.*

DESIGN MATTERS

It doesn't take much to turn a simple tub enclosure into an elegant surround. A decorative border at eye level can make a world of difference and change the whole look of a bathroom. In this one, plain 6-in. square field tile on the walls is capped by a row of decorative scallop-shell tiles that alternate with blank tile. A line of 1-in. by 6-in. braided rope tile completes the border, followed by one more course of field tile and a 2-in.-wide cap. The added cost is only about $200, but the decorative tile triples the value of the bathroom.

Topping out the wall. Tiling the upper portion of the walls is the easy part. Early vigilance means tiles are level, so Tom only has to follow a plumb line as he works upward and outward.

Affordable decoration. Scallop-shell tile, alternating with plain field tile followed by an accent of braided-rope tile near the top of the wall, adds interest but not a lot of cost.

Last check. With the wall complete, Tom uses a level as a straightedge to make sure there are no clearly visible highs or lows.

Saw first, then nippers. Rough cuts can be made with a tile saw, but the final shape is achieved gradually with tile nippers.

corner. The only time I would not start with a full tile against the trim cap is when the cut piece in the corner works out to be one inch or less. For the most part, the piece is buried in the corner and is not obvious when one first walks into the room.

To make any right-angle cuts—tiles cut to an L-shape—it's usually easier to use the water saw (this installation doesn't have any pieces like that, but it's not unusual). Enter the tile from both directions, discarding the piece that's left over.

When cutting around pipes or a mixing valve, I use tile nippers. The trick to using the nippers is not to squeeze down on the handles but to grab a small piece of tile and bend the nippers downward. This allows me to take off little pieces one at a time and work the cut to go around any area that needs it. It takes a little bit of time to acquire the skill, but then again, what doesn't?

Finishing Up

Grouting basic wall tile is done with nonsanded wall grout because the joint is less than an ⅛ in. wide. Even though the grouting is a very standard grout job, it still has to be done

exceptionally well because it's a wet area. My dad used to say, "A good grout job can make an okay tile job look great, and a bad grout job can make a great tile job look bad."

I spread the grout and let it set for about 10 minutes. As it is setting up, I use a grout stick with a rounded point (the back side of a Sharpie® marker works well, too) and strike all the grout joints, packing the grout in and establishing a nice, even joint. I then wash all the walls down with a sponge to clean and remove any grout residue. About 20 minutes later a haze will appear on the surface of the tile. I use a clean rag to buff the tile to a shine.

Wait a week, then seal

Sealing the grout takes place about a week later with a good impregnator sealer. I apply it with a foam brush and then buff it dry with a clean rag. I typically use grout, not caulk, on the joint between the tile and the tub. It may need re-grouting after the house has settled (see Q&A on the facing page), but I hardly ever have to go back and do it again.

DESIGN OPTIONS

When tiling a tub surround, there are a few things you need to keep in mind. One major consideration should be access to plumbing. In many cases, this will determine whether it makes sense to use wood on the front panels allowing easy access should your plumbing need repairs.

The height of the splash will also be dictated by the height of the counter. Think of it as though a transit (or revolving laser) is placed in the middle of the room and a line is shot around the room keeping everything level by eliminating all the different heights of the vanity, tub, benches, etc. Keeping all the practical aspects in mind, remember that the tub is the focal point; use it to pull the room together by making the height of the backsplash in the tub the same height as the top of the vanity.

Pebbles and stone. Mesh-mounted pebbles used on the tub deck and on the floor in front of the tub give the installation a beautiful flow. Natural stone used on the face of the tub help to unify the design.

Simple accents. If a shower curtain will block the surround most of the time, consider adding a decorative border high on the wall. Extending a chair rail right through the tub area is another simple design addition.

Extending the floor. The 4-in. glass tile that flows from the floor right up the front façade of the tub gives this bathroom a large, uncluttered feeling.

Plumbing was accessible from a bedroom closet, allowing the face of this soaking tub to be tiled.

The decorative element of the tub front was repeated at the top of the wall, giving the room an unexpected texture as well as continuity.

The combination of glass block and granite tile gives this bathroom a rich and elegant look, which only increases when natural light reflects off these com- plementary materials.

Tiling

CHAPTER EIGHT

Showers

1 Out with the Old, p. 113

2 Installing a Pan and Backer Board, p. 116

3 Story Sticks Guide Layout, p. 118

4 Cutting Tiles to Fit, p. 121

5 Installing a Glass-Block Shower Wall, p. 122

Tile for a shower should be considered in the context of the entire room. Depending on where the shower is, you may not see much of it until you're actually using it. A shower door or curtain can either give you a window into the shower or obscure the view. Tile design should be planned accordingly.

If the shower tile is being replaced for aesthetic reasons or because of needed repairs, there's the question of blending the new tile with the old. Even if it's a patch job, it should look as though you designed the bathroom this way from the beginning.

First-floor bathrooms are the most likely candidates for later modification to make them handicapped-accessible. They may require lower thresholds in the shower or extra blocking for grab bars in the shower walls.

A bench is also a great addition. This could be as small as a little corner seat (for a woman, a handy place to prop a foot while shaving your legs), or a long built-in bench for relaxing.

Where are you putting the soap and shampoo? A niche, a corner shelf, or wire baskets all work, but make sure that you tell the installer what you are planning from the beginning. I like to put the niche or shelf on the same side of the shower as the showerhead so it's not directly in the stream of water.

Q & A

If I'm doing a demolition or rip out of a tile job, what do I do if I hit a pipe and it starts leaking?

Of course the answer is to turn off the water main immediately and call a plumber. If you're unsure about the location of pipe in a wall and worry about puncturing a pipe during demolition, find out where the water shut-off is before you start tearing out; don't wait for an emergency to start looking for the shut-off. Another tip: If you do cause a leak, on your way to turn off the water main, open the faucets in the kitchen to reduce the water pressure.

DESIGN MATTERS
Something new to look at

Removing an old fiberglass shower unit and replacing it with tile means that shower walls will be much more appealing to look at. If you plan to use a shower curtain, it may be closed much of the time and you won't be able to enjoy the tile installed below the curtain rod. In that case, pay attention to the upper portion of the wall, which will be visible even with the curtain closed. If you're adding a glass door instead, the entire wall will be on display. So plan the design accordingly.

Plan around showerhead, valve

The placement of the showerhead also helps determine the layout of the tile. We generally tile right to the ceiling and find that 6 in. to 12 in. down is the perfect place to add decorative tile or a band of tile, but some adjustment may be necessary so the band doesn't run right through a mixing valve, showerhead, or extra water jets.

We usually do not tile the ceiling unless it's in a steam shower. With new code requirements for bathroom ventilation, moisture that might damage a ceiling should be exhausted, and a tiled ceiling can give the shower a more boxed-in, heavy look.

As for the size of the tile, anything goes. It all depends on the finished look you are trying to achieve. We often use 12-in. limestone on the floor and extend it right up the walls. In contrast, 1-in. glass tile adds a wonderful texture to a wall. As a rule of thumb, we prefer 6-in. tile rather than 4-in. tile in showers for a clean look with fewer grout lines.

Reviving a Bathroom with Tile

Putting in a new shower usually means taking out the old one. These days, showers are usually made from fiberglass. These fixtures were developed during the 1970s as an inexpensive and more reliable alternative to installing tile over gypsum drywall.

In the project shown here, the master bath (and two other bathrooms in the house) had fiberglass shower surrounds. The homeowner wanted to dress up the master bath, but he didn't know how to deal with the old fixture. Fortunately, taking out a fiberglass shower stall is not a major production. You cut the unit into pieces and remove

them one by one. The plumber spends a few hours installing a new drain and mixing valve. After that, you can build anything you want.

Choosing the right tile

These owners decided on something that would relate to the tile already in the room. The stall itself is white 6-in. tile, which complements the discontinued white 6-in. by 8-in. tile used on the whirlpool tub across the room.

To kick it up a bit and give the shower some character, we added a three-piece band of color at about eye level. It is made of 2-in. by 6-in. white-

Avoiding trouble. Before you start, check walls that back up to the shower to see if there's any wiring there. Proceed carefully: Even if there are no switches or outlets visible, wires going to other rooms could still be hidden in the wall.

Removing an old surround. A reciprocating saw cuts quickly, but remember that there's a wall behind it, and possibly plumbing and wiring. The sawblade may be longer than the wall is thick, so hold the blade at an angle when you cut.

rope tile sandwiched between two ¾-in. by 6-in. blue pencil moldings that pick up the color of the main floor. The 2-in. by 2-in. tile on the shower floor is also in the same color family. None of this breaks the budget.

The back wall of a shower is always the focal point. It is seen first and most frequently. Plan the tile layout with that in mind. Center the tile horizontally to give the wall symmetry and balance.

The two corner rows should be the same width and at least a half tile wide. As you look at the layout from bottom to top, the design should call for a full tile on the bottom and a half tile or more at the ceiling.

Completing the tile plan

The side walls start with finished trim pieces on the outside edge, followed by a row of full tiles. When the space at the corner is smaller than a full tile, cut to fit. If you put tile on the ceiling, as

we did in this stall, install it diagonally. It's a great look, it's easier than it looks, and it takes away the regimented geometric feeling. We do about 95 percent of our ceilings diagonally.

Another option when installing tile showers is to use glass block for shower walls. They are installed on top of a threshold on the floor and can be designed so no shower door is needed (see "Installing a Glass-Block Shower Wall" on p. 122).

Out with the Old

Start the job by turning off the main water valve in the house, then disassemble the plumbing—the mixing valve, the showerhead, and so on. They all come apart somewhat differently, but it's usually a matter of starting at the outside and working your way in.

With the preliminaries out of the way, put on your safety glasses and your dust mask. Demolition is dirty work, so close the door, open the window,

Removing the Drain

The hardest part of removing an old fiberglass tub or shower unit is breaking the unit away from the drain assembly. Fiberglass in this area is thick and the drain fitting is tight, making it difficult to gain any leverage to pry pieces away.

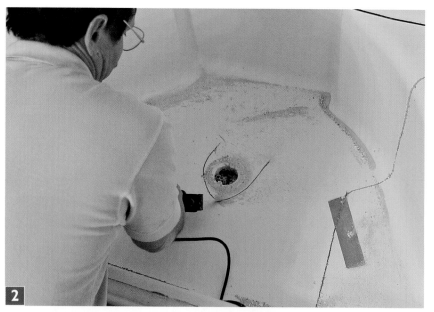

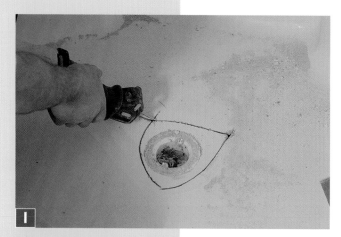

1, 2 The fiberglass tub is cut out in pieces. The drain requires more detailed work. It is cut loose with a wire saw (see photos 4 and 5 for wire saw details). A new drain assembly will be installed for the shower pan installation.

3 Cutting into the corners and then cutting back out into the field weakens the structure. The back corners and the area around the front of the tub must be cut out before the pieces will give way and you can pull them out. The more cuts you make, the easier the unit will release from the framing.

4, 5 Once the fiberglass has been cut out around the drain, I use a wire saw to cut the PVC drain pipe. A wire saw is simply an 18-in. piece of rough wire with a plastic handle at each end. By pulling the wire back and forth, it will cut through most PVC pipes. Once the unit is ripped out, a professional plumber should put in a new drain assembly.

and put a box fan in it to keep dust from spreading through the house. The temptation is always to start with the big stuff, but you'll be better off if you start by scoring the drywall along the outside edge of the unit with a knife. There's a flange behind it that's part of the shower stall, covered by two or three coats of joint compound. If the knife won't cut through the seam, work gently with a hammer and chisel.

Once you've removed it, pull the nails holding the flange to the wall. This part of the job is a little tedious, but it prevents damage to the drywall that remains. Your goal should be to work so precisely that you will not have to do any repair work to the outside walls once the tile job is done. The less damage you do, the less time you'll spend repairing it.

Once you've scored along the edge of the stall, you can begin to cut the fiberglass unit into five or six pieces. Start at the top of the surround, and work down, making the cuts with a reciprocating saw (see "Tools and Materials" on p. 120).

Tips for removing the old unit

Check for electrical lines before you start cutting, and then drill or poke a starter hole in the stall. Put the blade in the hole, and angle the saw up or down as you cut so the blade doesn't go through the other side of the wall (see "What Can Go Wrong" on p. 116). It's not a difficult cut, but it does help to have someone hold some of the loose pieces, which tend to vibrate furiously as you cut through them.

The hardest piece to remove is the floor immediately around the drain (see "Removing the Drain" on the facing page). Be patient. Cut a circle around the drain and then cut small pieces out of the rest of the stall floor. Cut away enough that you can reach down and undo the drain assembly with a wrench. (If it's a plastic drain, you

Installing the pan. The shower pan is a project in itself and should be installed before you put backer board on the walls. For more on installing showers see Chapter Nine, "Installing a Shower Pan," on p. 128.

may be able to cut through it.) Remove the assembly, and keep cutting until you've carted the whole stall away.

There's always some plumbing involved when you install a shower. At the very least, you'll need a plumber to repair the drain. If the shower is replacing a tub, the plumbing can be more complicated.

The plumber has to move the drain to the center of the shower, maintain the proper slope of the line going back to the existing pipe, make watertight joints, and install the trap properly so it keeps out sewer gas.

The plumber will also replace the mixing valve with one designed for showers and raise it to the proper height. Talk to the plumber in advance to see what's involved.

Q & A

Is it expensive *to take out an average fiberglass unit and make ready for a new tile shower stall installation?*

Not really. *For an average professional, demolition takes a couple of hours. Then a plumber moves or changes the drain assembly and the height of the mixing valve or faucets. A tile person or a carpenter can repair the plywood floor and put in three 2x4s for the threshold. At this point it's like starting a new tile job. This prep work usually costs $600 to $700.*

WHAT CAN GO WRONG

Cutting what you don't want to

y biggest concern when removing a fiberglass shower or tub is that I'll inadvertently slice through hidden plumbing or electrical wires as I'm cutting the tub or shower into pieces. It's not possible to know exactly what's behind the fiberglass. I always turn off the water main for that hour when I'm cutting the unit into pieces, and I check to see whether I'm working near the main electrical panel. If so, I'm more careful than ever because wires are more likely to be concentrated here. If you have real doubts about the location of wires and are unsure about working around them, contact an electrician.

Reinforcing the joints. The spaces between two sheets of backer board are reinforced with thinset and mesh tape. Apply the thinset first and then the tape. Smooth out the joint with a trowel once the tape is in place.

Installing a Pan and Backer Board

The first part of a new shower to go in is the shower pan. A proper pan is installed between two layers of cement. The first layer goes under the pan and provides pitch towards the drainage weep holes. The second coat, which is much thicker (2½ in. to 3 in.) goes into the pan and provides the base for the shower floor. I install the cement board on top of this coat of cement so I won't have to work on top of the pan liner. Some installers put the cement board in before and hold it 1½ inches off of the bottom of the pan floor. To do this, use a 2x4 laid on it's side as a gauge and to hold it at the right height off the floor of the pan. This will also stop moisture from wicking up the wall and darkening the tile or stone. Building a shower pan is also covered in chapter 9.

I usually start with a full piece of board right on top of the cement. If the builder wants to do the sheetrock ahead of time, I tell him to start on the top and leave the last piece out until I install my pan. The pan liner has to go partially up the wall behind the cement board. It is recommended to use a membrane such as tar paper or plastic behind the cementboard and let it over hang into the shower pan. I prefer tarpaper.

Avoid small pieces

Backer board sheets come in various sizes. When you install the board, use the largest piece that will fit on the wall. Cutting and fitting lots of little pieces together is a good way to get rid of scrap, but it isn't as strong as a single large piece. Cut the pieces so any vertical seams will meet in the middle of a stud. The horizontal edges don't need support.

Secure the sheets well. If you use screws, use special screws made for backer board. We use nails because they are a bit more forgiving. Houses settle; studs expand and contract with changes in weather; some studs warp or twist after they're installed. Nails will flex to accommodate the change. Screws won't. We like to use 1½-in. galvanized roofing nails and nail the pieces every 6 in. to 8 in.

It is very important that you do not nail or screw into the backer board any lower than 2 in. above the top of the curb at the entry to the shower. Nails below this point will poke holes in the liner, and it will leak if the shower ever floods.

Keep backer board out of the water

It's equally important that you keep the backer board 1½ in. above the floor of the installed pan, not counting the thinset and tile you'll add later. Many of the tiles and stones today are very porous and water can seep through them.

The vinyl liner usually catches the seepage and directs the water toward the drain. If the backer board is sitting anywhere below water level, however, water can wick upward and actually darken the tile from moisture.

Wherever two pieces of backer board meet, the joints have to be taped and seamed. This is done with mesh tape and thinset cement. I apply a layer of thinset first, then roll out a 2½-in.-wide band of fiberglass mesh tape. I flatten out the tape and wipe off any excess thinset with a flat steel trowel. In the corners, I wrap the tape so half is on one wall and the other half is on the other wall. Once again, I apply the cement and make sure the whole installation is smooth and without ridges.

Making an Opening

When cutting around the valve, both the tile and the cement board should be cut to within ¼ in. of the temporary plastic guide. The finished trim pieces that the plumber installs sometimes do not have a lot of play. A loosely cut tile may leave a small gap that can lead to a leak down below.

Making an opening. Trace around the shower valve you're installing and make an opening for it by breaking through the backer board. Cut away the mesh with a utility knife once the opening is the right size and shape. When you tile, trim the tiles to the size and shape required by the opening.

Q & A

Do I have to use cement board in a shower stall?

It is highly recommended that some type of cement board is used in all wet areas. You can use a waterproof membrane over sheetrock, but in this day and age of legal problems with mold, I'd rather not use drywall as a base. And of course there is always wire and cement (a mud job) which is still the best.

Making a story stick. A story stick is more accurate than a tape measure. Make one by laying tiles on a board, spacing them as they will be when installed. Draw lines showing the location of the grout joints.

WHAT CAN GO WRONG

Always shut off the water at the main. Cutting through a line when the water is on upstairs will cause some serious flooding downstairs. We've never cut *through* a pipe, but we have managed to drive a nail through one. You'll know you've done it when you hear a hissing sound behind the wall.

Story Sticks Guide Layout

You can never trust a wall to be straight or plumb, so start laying tile from plumb and level guidelines that you draw in the middle of the wall. Lay out the lines with the help of two story sticks you'll use like big yardsticks. One should be a bit shorter than the stall is tall. The other should be a tile shorter than the stall is wide.

To make a story stick, put a 1x4 or other scrap board on the floor. Lay tiles on the board with spaces the size of grout joints between them. Mark where the joints fall, and number the tiles in between them.

Now for the layout lines: Start with the back wall because it's the most visible. Laying it out first lets you make sure the tiles will be centered, and that the tiles you cut to fit against the corners will be the same width at each end of the wall. Put the tall stick in place and make a mark on the backer board at a grout joint about halfway up the wall.

Laying out the tile. Keep the layout plumb and level by working from lines drawn on the backer board. Start by making a mark at a grout joint about halfway up the wall.

Making a Shampoo Niche

We normally include a built-in shampoo niche in our showers, but in the shower we chose for this chapter there were too many water and vent pipes between the studs. This niche is one I did for another shower.

When building a shampoo and soap niche in the wall, don't cut the hole in the cement board for it until your story sticks have told you exactly where the tiles will be. Then lay out the niche so that the edges are along the grout lines. Cut out the hole in the wallboard with a grinder, and then cut 2x4s to frame out the top, bottom, and sides of the opening. Put them in place with construction adhesive. Add extra strength by screwing through the backer board and into the 2x4s.

To waterproof the niche, apply thinset to the surfaces and then line it with NobleSeal TS membrane. Let it dry, and then spread more thinset and apply tile.

For a ready-made niche, the NobleSeal Co. and the Bonsal® Co. both make ready made inserts for you to tile over. They work very well but come in standard sizes that may not meet the needs of a particular job.

Making a shampoo niche. With shampoo, conditioner, and all the other hair and soap products we use today, the shower can get pretty crowded. We cut through the backer board to build a recessed shelf to hold everything.

Making soap shelves. Soap dishes aren't as popular as they once were, but many people like small shelves to hold soap and shampoo. The shelf fits on top of a tile, and the next tile up is notched to fit over the shelf.

Q & A

What types of tile *are recommended for use in a shower stall?*

Any type of tile *can be used in a shower. Some ceramic tiles are easier to install and clean. Even marble and limestone tiles when sealed properly have no problems in a shower. If very small tiles are used, there will be a lot of grout joints so extra sealer should be applied. On shower floors, use smaller tile to help pitch to the drain.*

TOOLS AND MATERIALS

Reciprocating saw

The most useful tool for removing a fiberglass tub or shower is a reciprocating saw. Its relatively narrow blade is available in several lengths and tooth configurations. I use a 5-in. blade designed for cutting rough lumber. The key is to hold the saw on an angle so you're not plunging the blade to its full depth. This saw is great for getting into corners and other hard-to-reach places.

Centering the tile. Put the top of the shorter stick on the mark, and move the story pole back and forth to center it between the walls. Make a mark at the grout joint closest to the center of the wall.

Drawing guidelines. Draw a plumb line through the mark you made with the shorter stick and a level line through the other mark. Start laying tile at the intersection of the lines and work your way out to the walls and down to the floor.

Now hold the short stick horizontally at the mark and move it back and forth until the space between the ends of the stick and the walls is equal at both ends. Make a mark at a grout joint near the middle of the wall and draw a plumb line through it. Draw a level line through the other mark. The story sticks will also help determine where to install a shampoo niche if you plan to include one (see "Making a Shampoo Niche" on p. 119).

Ready for tiling

Now, start tiling. Begin by spreading thinset below the horizontal line. Try to spread it in one direction to help the tiles sit flat and even. Give each tile a ¼-in. slide in the thinset in order to achieve a secure bond.

Work your way from the center, where the layout lines cross, to the edges of the wall, where you'll cut the tile to fit. Then go back to the layout line and lay a new row below the existing one. If you want to add a soap dish in the corner, it should be worked in as you go.

When you've tiled your way down to the floor, go to the side walls. Draw a horizontal level line across the middle of each wall, aligning it with a grout line in the back wall. It looks best if any cut tiles are in the back corners, so, working one wall at a time, start in the front with a trim tile and lay full tiles back toward the corner, cutting the last one to fit.

With the bottom half of the shower done, start on the upper half, beginning with the back wall. The upper half of the wall is actually much easier to install then the lower half. The tiles simply just follow the bottom half of the shower wall and it's just a matter of keeping grout lines level and plumb. When you finish the back wall, do the side walls.

Tiling the second wall. Once you've tiled from the line down on the first wall, draw lines on the adjoining walls with the level. Start at the line by putting up the trim tile along the outside edge, then work toward the back corner.

Dressing up. This three-piece border, made of a rope tile and two pencil moldings, adds color to an otherwise all-white shower.

Cutting Tiles to Fit

Cutting tile at the ceiling takes a bit of patience. Ceilings are often out of level and may be slightly wavy. If this is the case, scribe the tiles to fit. The eye is naturally attracted to the point where the ceiling and wall meet. If you don't scribe the tiles so the grout line at the top of the wall is uniform, it's going to be an eyesore.

Installing the border also takes a little patience. It's very important that it be perfectly straight. When we install the pencil moldings, we pack a little extra thinset on the back so that they'll stick out a little beyond the other tiles. A three-part border that sticks out a bit from the plane of the wall makes a stronger statement than a narrower, flat border.

Putting in the shower threshold, dam, or curb (it's known by all three names) is a very important part of the shower installation. The threshold must be level left to right so the shower door works correctly and must be pitched $\frac{1}{4}$ in. to the inside to allow water to drain back into the shower stall.

After we have tiled the inside and outside parts of the threshold, we cap it off with tile or a 6-in.-wide piece of Corian® solid surface material with edges sanded and rounded. Building the curb itself is part of installing the shower pan, and I go into it more thoroughly in Chapter Nine.

Laying the shower floor is just like laying any other floor and was the easiest part of this job. Here, tiles are simple 2-in. squares with a matte blue surface. Lay out the floor so that there is a full tile against the back wall, the part of the floor you see as you enter the shower. Center the tiles between the walls the way you would on any floor, so that the tiles on each side of the floor are the same width.

Q & A

Can anyone install *glass block?*

No, not really. *It takes a little more patience and skill. The first thing I would recommend is to get the proper instructions from the manufacturer. I also would suggest not to take on a large project the first few times you install glass block. With common sense and experience it becomes an acquired skill.*

WHAT CAN GO WRONG

When installing a glass-block wall, it is extremely important to prevent the blocks from going out of plumb even a little. Because glass is 100 percent non-porous, it takes a while for it to set up and it tends to shift. I install only two or three courses at a time, then come back a couple of hours later and do many minor adjustments before it finally sets up. Installing glass block is time consuming and cannot be rushed. If you come back to the job the next day and the wall is out of plumb, you start over.

Installing a Glass-Block Shower Wall

Glass block is one of those materials that seem to go in and out of vogue. I may go six months without a single installation and then get four jobs in a row, and it takes a while to get back into the groove. Setting glass block is not a job to rush.

In this installation, which is typical, glass block is used to complete a shower stall whose two back walls are tiled. Block is installed over a tile threshold with a 28-in. gap left to serve as a doorway (it won't need a shower door). Specialized products such as mortar, interlocking spacers, and panel anchors (perforated metal strips) all make it easier to install glass block, and if I have any technical questions, Pittsburgh Corning's technical staff can supply the answers.

Panel anchors and bands of rebar make it possible to build freestanding walls. If the block wall is contained between two structural walls, I'm not as concerned that it will stay in place. But I still use panel anchors at the base and a soft joint (elasticized caulk or silicone) where the glass meets the outside walls, to allow for expansion. Soft foam also can be used to absorb any movement. The foam comes in strips ¼ in. by 4 in. by 24 in., which I usually tack in place with a staple gun.

Layout is key

The first and most important step in installing glass block is to take accurate measurements to make sure the block will fit, because unlike tile, glass block can't be cut to fit an odd opening. The key is to measure in block-size increments. In this case, the 8-in. increment includes an allowance for the grout joint. I also allow for a joint at the wall where I start.

The block will sit on a 5-in. high wall (known as a shower dam or threshold) that extends out from one wall, makes two 45-degree jogs, and returns to the other wall. The center section of the threshold is not very wide so here I'll use smaller block. Specially shaped block will help the wall turn the two 45-degree corners.

Lay out the block first. Before setting glass block, lay it out on the shower threshold to make sure it fits. Then trace the outline on the threshold to make a clear layout line.

Rough up the tile. To guarantee a good bond, I use a grinder to scarify the surface of the tile on the threshold.

Two layers to start. I use two coats of cement to bond the first and most important course of block, beginning with thinset mortar and following with a layer of glass block mortar.

Keep the block level. Because the tile threshold is pitched inward, the first course of block must be shimmed level with a wedge.

Before I actually build the threshold, I lay the blocks out on the floor to see how they will fit. It can take less than ½ in. to foul up a layout, so I mark the threshold location carefully. Once I see how the blocks will sit in the middle of the threshold, I can proceed with the tile installation, including the threshold.

Initially, I'm leaving off one vertical row of tile where the block will meet the wall. That will allow me to set panel anchors or wall tiles right into the studs and lock the wall into place. Tiling the threshold is also important. It must be level from side to side but pitched slightly from the outside toward the inside of the shower.

Setting the block

Before setting the first row of glass block in place, I use a grinder to rough up the surface of the base cap on the top of the threshold so the thinset cement will adhere properly. I also use a panel anchor to connect the block to the threshold firmly. Because the top of the cap is on a slant, I have to shim the first course of blocks on the inside to make sure they are plumb. I allow this first course to set up completely before going any further.

Butter it up. As I install each block, I butter the side that will butt up to the last block in place. When I tap the block home, some mortar will squeeze out, letting me know there's plenty of cement and no voids.

The mortar is mixed to a slightly stiffer-than-usual consistency to keep the blocks firmly in place. The interlocking spacers not only make mortar joints even but also lock blocks in place as the mortar cures. Later, the tabs are knocked off with a stick and a rubber mallet.

Panel anchors are used every two or three courses to fasten and lock the glass wall to the existing structural wall. They can also be used to reinforce the middle of the wall. Finally, there is a

Q & A

Do the joints *of the blocks have to be the same color as the mortar that they are installed with?*

No, you can use *any color sanded grout that you like. Of course, you would use light colors that would complement the glass block and maybe the tile around it. The key is to clean and recess the joints between the blocks each day while the mortar is somewhat fresh. Also, use a white mortar to install the blocks. Gray would darken or shadow the background of the glass.*

THE TILESETTER'S CHECKLIST

• The first course has to be set level. After that, level and plumb have to be maintained.

• Extra levels are great to have. I lock one in place with a couple of large clamps to form a permanent vertical ledger board.

• I install wall ties every two courses to ensure the block wall never separates from the supporting wall.

• Use a rubber mallet to tap each block in place. If one block sits too high, it will throw out succeeding courses of block.

Strengthen the wall connection. At the end of a freestanding glass-block wall, a wall panel anchor will reinforce the mortar bond.

Trick for keeping walls plumb. Clamping a 6-ft. level to the first course of block is a great way of keeping subsequent courses straight and plumb.

Spacers at every intersection. These spacers hold blocks in place while regulating the width of the grout joints. Panel anchors also reinforce the joint.

double band of thin rebar that can run the full length of a course every two or three courses for additional reinforcement. All these materials are available from glass block suppliers.

After the base course sets up, I install two courses at a time. I'm sure some installers do more than that, but I like to let two courses set up for an hour or two while I work on another project. Once the mortar has firmed up, I make sure they are dead-on accurate.

With each course, I lay out a layer of glass-block mortar into which I will press each block. As I put in each block, I butter one side of the block that I'm about to put in. I then press that block up against the last block that was put in and tap it with the rubber mallet. The rubber mallet allows me to tap the block and imbed it tightly into the cement. The process continues, course after course.

Finishing up

Cleaning the joints should be done after the cement has set up a little. It's best to clean up the mortar the same day, but if I have to wait until the next day to do the cleaning, I wet down the wall with a good amount of water to soften the cement a little. The harder the cement gets, the greater the chances of chipping a block.

Grouting goes more easily if the blocks are cleaned thoroughly. I use a sanded grout that picks up the base color of the glass (here, I used a color called Silverado).

Once I spread the grout, I let it set at least a half hour (longer if the weather is cool) before washing off the excess. After I have washed the wall down without using too much water, I wait for a dry film to form before bringing the block to a shine with a buffing rag.

If the film won't rub off, I use a very light acidic wash the next day. A few days later I give everything a good coat of an impregnator sealer. One thing about sealers: Use the best. It's worth every penny.

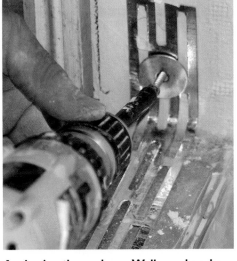

Add plenty of mortar. With spacers and wall anchors in place, I trowel mortar on the top of a course of block so it stands a little proud. When I press the next blocks down, there is some give for adjustment. But too much mortar makes blocks hard to control.

Anchoring the anchors. Wall panel anchors are tied into wall framing with screws and flat washers. Anchors bend easily to form an L-shape and should be connected with two screws at each juncture.

Reinforcing rods add to strength. In addition to wall panel anchors, these reinforcing rods will help strengthen the wall. Once the rods are positioned, I add spacers and then mortar.

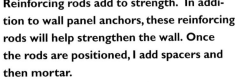

At door openings. At the doorway, I finish off the wall with finished-end blocks. On the very top, I install a corner block finished on two sides. Glass-block walls can even be capped with limestone or tile with a bullnose edge.

DESIGN OPTIONS

The shower can be the perfect sanctuary to start the day, and the focal point that makes a statement for the rest of the bathroom.

Unbroken wainscot. A colorful wainscot wrapping the entire bathroom lends consistency while making the room seem more expansive. The effect would have been lost had the shower been hidden by a curtain.

Adding glass. The addition of glass tile in this limestone bath provides contrast, color, and shimmer. The glass accent is more powerful inside the confines of the shower, yet doesn't overwhelm the rest of the room on exterior shower walls.

Shower with a view. An all-glass shower enclosure makes it easy to appreciate this decorative band of tile. Turning tile above it on the diagonal adds texture and breaks up an otherwise uninterrupted wall of tile.

Changing shapes for added texture. The 6-in. glass base tile in this shower goes to 3-in. by 6-in. tile in the main field and then to a band of 1-in. square tile, adding texture. The reflective quality of the glass also brings variations in color.

Installing a

CHAPTER NINE
Shower Pan

The floor of a shower is called the shower pan, and tile installers make or break their reputations on the quality of a pan. In the past 10 years, we have installed well over 1,000 pans. Only two have leaked: One belonged to Lane's parents, the other to our dentist.

Needless to say, we made both repairs immediately, especially since I was about to have two root canals. As it turns out, both leaks were the result of faulty drain assemblies. Honest.

The point is that when it comes to shower-pan design, pretty counts, but not as much as construction. A leaky pan will let water drip—or pour—into the space below it. The first sign will be water stains on the ceiling below the shower.

The next sign will be pieces of ceiling sitting on the floor. With time, the floor framing that supports the shower will begin to rot. It's also likely to attract carpenter ants, termites, or both.

It will probably be a matter or years, but sooner or later, you'll have to take out the shower and replace the framing. Better to get it right the first time.

1 Start with the Subfloor, p. 130

2 First Layer of Mortar, p. 132

3 Installing the Waterproof Membrane, p. 135

4 Attaching the Drain and Liner, p. 137

5 Installing Backer Board and Tile, p. 140

Q & A

I have a leak in the shower stall in my home, and we don't know where the water is coming from. How do I track it down?

Look for obvious spaces between tiles where grout has fallen out or worn away. If it's not that, repeat your initial test for leaks in the shower pan. Remove the two screws and the drain cover, and put in a 2-in. expansion plug. Fill the bottom of the shower with water, mark the height, and wait. If the water level doesn't drop, you've eliminated the worst case. Be happy, and start checking the walls for empty joints.

DESIGN MATTERS

Keeping the tile on the floor of the shower as close in color as possible to that of the rest of the bathroom floor gives the room a more expansive look. If you're using a stone tile, such as limestone or marble, it may be available in 2-in. by 2-in. mesh-mounted squares for the floor. If not, cut the main floor tile into 3-in.-sq. or 4-in.-sq. pieces to create your own. Many ceramic tiles are available in this size for just such a purpose.

Getting It Right

A well-made shower pan is a combination of plumbing, mortar, tile, and a flexible chlorinated polyethylene (CPE) lining called a membrane. (In the days before CPE, the liner was a thick lead pan made onsite. The lead is gone, but the term "pan" remains.)

The plumbing consists of a drain designed especially for shower pans. It has a flange that clamps to the membrane to prevent leaks, and weep holes that collect any water that works its way through the tile.

The pan itself begins with a mortar bed that slopes toward the drain on the subfloor. The membrane sits on top of the mortar bed, and on top of it is another layer of mortar that, once dry, provides a sturdy base for the tile.

Coordinate the color

Tile for a shower floor should be as close in color as possible to the main floor, and preferably made by the same manufacturer (see "Design Matters" at left). This will help the room appear larger.

If it isn't possible to match floor colors, then the tile should complement the wall tile. If the walls are perfectly white or bland, you can bring some designs or patterns into the floor. The tiles themselves should be 4 in. sq. or less (3 in. is better).

Tile this size, combined with the grout joints, provide traction and also are small enough to conform to the mortar bed. Larger tiles would be too slippery. Because of the grout lines, you can even use a small shiny tile, but a textured or flat finished tile will give you better traction.

If you're considering a stone floor, marble and granite are fine as long as they are cut to 3-in.

Contrast in color. Just because the tile is inexpensive doesn't mean you have to compromise on style. These 2-in. ceramic tiles aren't costly, but contrasting two colors gives the bathroom a striking look.

pieces. Of all the stone options, limestone is the easiest to work with and has the most traction. Either limestone or tumbled marble can be cut to any size to create a design. For dimension and character, we often put a row of tiles around the perimeter of the floor and fill in the field with tile placed on the diagonal.

Start with the Subfloor

Before you install the pan, clean the subfloor and the shower area thoroughly and inspect them. The subfloor should be ¾ in. thick—check in the area around the drain to make sure that it is. Stand on the floor and bounce a little—if it feels spongy, the floor is not sound.

If the floor is old, check to see if there is any water damage. If it's bouncy, add a layer of ½-in. plywood before the plumber sets the drain assembly (but real structural damage, including any rot, should be repaired before going any further—covering it up with more plywood won't help).

Generally speaking, the plumber roughs in the plumbing before you put in the new subfloor and installs the drain after the subfloor is in. He'll install the first part of a three-part drain assembly. It's a flange that sits under the liner; you'll install the other parts later. Talk this over with the plumber, however.

Once the plumber is done, look for anything that might punch or wear a hole in the membrane in the future (see "What Can Go Wrong" on p. 138). Use a hammer and nail set to sink any nail heads that are in the lower 6 in. to 8 in. of the wall framing.

The plumber usually puts a nail plate in the framing along the floor. The plate, designed to keep builders from driving nails through the pipes, has sharp corners. Put an extra piece of membrane over it to make sure the metal corners don't puncture the membrane.

Building a shower curb

There is more than one way of building the shower threshold (also called a dam or curb), the small step at the shower door that keeps water from flowing into the rest of the bathroom. However it's done, the threshold is a very important detail that must be complete before the shower pan is formed with mortar and the waterproof liner.

Some installers are very adamant about building it from poured concrete, blocks, or a wire form filled with concrete. These are great methods to be sure, but not the ones I use.

The carpenter screws in 6-in.-long screws to lock all three pieces of lumber together to form a curb.

Sealing the floor. Apply a skim coat of thinset to the floor before you apply your first layer of mortar and put a seal in the drain, so that once the liner is installed it can be tested for leaks.

Q & A

If I am not *comfortable with the difficult threshold work, are there any pre-formed systems?*

Yes, *a few companies make thresholds from dense foam that has been chemically treated. They work well, don't leak, and are easy to install.*

First layer of mortar. After shoveling mortar into the pan, smooth it by pulling a level across the surface. The bed should slope up and away from the drain, rising about ¼ in. per ft.

Mixing Mud

Tile installers mix their own mortar for shower pans with roughly three or four parts sand to one part portland cement. Make the mixture in a 3-ft. by 5-ft. mixing tub. For an average 36-in. by 42-in. shower pan, the bottom layer requires four shovels of sand to 1½ shovels of portland cement.

The top layer will take about 12 full shovels of sand to half a 94-lb. bag of portland cement. Put the sand in first and then shake the cement over it. Mix thoroughly with a mason's hoe. It usually takes two "pulls," meaning that you pull the hoe the width of the box, row by row, until you have hoed the entire width and length.

Then add water. How much is enough? On a normal day, it takes about half of a 5-gal. pail of water for a batch this size, but this varies. If the sand is dry, it takes more water; if the sand is soaked, add less initially and more as you mix. The proof is in the pudding. Pull the wet mix-

Mixing mortar. Mortar that will form the shower pan can be mixed in a shallow wooden box with a hoe. It consists of three or four parts of sand to one part portland cement and water.

ture through three or four times, adding most of the water on the first pull. You'll know the mixture is right when it holds together in the grip of your hand. If it's too dry, add more water. If it's too wet, add more of the sand and portland mix, keeping it at a 3-to-1 ratio.

The bottom line is that the threshold must be totally waterproof on top and where it meets the side wall. It also has to be level from side to side and pitched to the inside of the shower stall.

There should be no nails on the inside wall of the threshold, and if there are any nails on the top they should be within 1 in. of the outside edge. I prefer no nails on top.

I build the core of the threshold from three 2x4s that are stacked on top of each other, glued and nailed together, and secured with 6-in. screws (see drawings on p. 142). When the shower pan goes in, the liner should cover the top of the dam and extend up the wall where the threshold meets it to protect this joint. As the wood shrinks, this is the joint that would open up.

First layer of mortar

Once the plumber has the drain in place, install the drain plug that you'll use to test the shower for leaks to keep stray mortar out of the pipes. Apply a layer of latex-modified thinset about ⅛ in. thick to the floor. This is just a skim coat, designed to keep the plywood from sucking all the water out of the mortar.

Traditionally, tilesetters used tar paper and wire at this point—the wire for strength, and the tar

Cutting the pan liner. Sketch the shape and dimensions of the shower pan on a piece of paper, and then draw it full-size on the liner. Lay out a second line, adding at least 7 in. along the walls. On the edge that meets the curb, add enough liner so that it can wrap all the way around the curb.

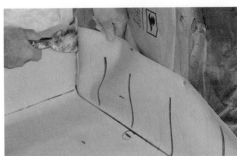

Install the liner. When the mortar forming the bottom of the pan has set, put in the liner, folding it as needed to fit into the corners. Push the excess back behind the framing with a putty knife.

paper to keep the wood subfloor from absorbing moisture in the mortar. Manufacturers say that for this application, modern mortar mixes are already strong enough, and the thinset takes the place of the tar paper—it's formulated to go over a wood subfloor without drying out too quickly.

Mix your own mortar and spread it on top of the thinset while the thinset is still wet. The top of the mortar should be flush with the top of the clamping ring and rise ¼ in. per foot as it moves toward the shower walls. If you want to be precise, you can draw a line on the wall framing, but most installers just eyeball it. This layer of mortar does not have to be dead-on accurate. The first layer is not as thick as the second coat.

Let the mud dry overnight and cover it with a layer of 15-lb. felt paper the next day. The felt paper protects the vinyl membrane that you're about to put over the mud from any grit that could abrade it. The felt paper also isolates the finished shower pan from any movement that might occur in the subfloor and cause cracks. When you lay the felt paper, pay particular attention to the area around the drain. Cut the paper for a tight fit.

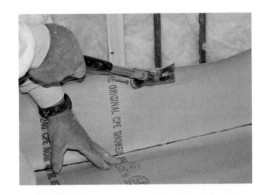

Don't nail too low. Nail the liner into place, keeping the nails above the height of the curb. This keeps water from working through the liner should the drain clog, though, let's face it—your floor's going to be soaked.

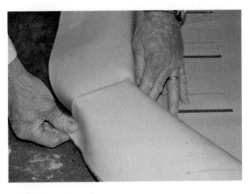

Waterproof the curb. Wrap the liner completely around the curb, folding it as needed to get a neat job that won't get in the way of the next layer.

Nail at the corner. Fold the front corner tightly and nail it into place. Try to keep the fold as tight as possible, but don't drive any nails in below the curb, where they could cause leaks. Nails should be on the outside of the threshold, not in the shower.

Joining a Shower-Pan Liner

Because shower-pan liners come in 4-ft, 5-ft., and 6-ft. widths, it's often necessary to join two pieces together for a large shower. You should check the manufacturer's specifications, because techniques vary from company to company. We use the Chloraloy® liner, and here's what's involved in joining two pieces.

Begin by cutting the pieces to size, adding 2 in. to each piece for the seam in addition to 7 in. you'll need to roll up each wall and whatever you'll need for the curb. There are two ways to join the pieces together. Chloraloy makes a solvent that essentially melts the two pieces together, but this method is being replaced by an elastomeric caulk that bonds pieces together. I think the caulk is superior. The caulk provides firmer contact between the sheets, and you don't have to worry about air bubbles the way you do with a solvent. Put the caulk in a caulk gun and cut off the tip, leaving a hole about ⅛ in. in diameter, and poke through the seal, which lies within the tip, at the point where it meets the tub of the caulk.

Overlap the pieces approximately 2 in. at the seam. Apply a ¼-in. bead of sealant ¼ in. from the edge of the bottom sheet. Apply a second bead ¾ in. from the edge of the bottom sheet. Keep the beads parallel and continuous. Gaps along the length of the bead could lead to leaks. Overlap the sheets and press them together, applying pressure along the entire seam by leaning on a trowel or a specially made hand roller. The bond is firm enough that you can actually pick up the piece and move it immediately. I let the caulk cure overnight first, just to be safe.

When the liner is too small. Some shower floors may be bigger than available widths of liner. A double bead of elastomeric caulk seals the 2-in. seam between sheets.

Press in place. After applying the caulk, bring the seams together and press the two pieces of liner together.

Firm pressure. A wood trowel or roller should be used along the seam to ensure a good bond. The liner can be moved immediately.

Installing the Waterproof Membrane

We use a membrane called Chloraloy, made by the Noble Co., for our shower pans (see "Resources" on p. 186). You can buy a 4-ft. by 50-ft. roll for under $400 or a 4-ft. by 6-ft. section for about $50. In larger showers, two or more pieces may have to be joined (see "Joining a Shower-Pan Liner" on the facing page).

Roll out the membrane on a clean floor and get ready to lay out the pan with a felt-tip pen. The membrane needs to be the size of the shower floor plus 7 in. on each side or 2 in. above the top of the curb, whichever is higher.

To get the overall size, measure the length and width of the floor and add at least 14 in. to each dimension. Lay out the outer edges, using two edges of the membrane as the edges of the pan. Measure in 7 in. from each edge and draw another set of lines showing where the membrane will turn and go up the wall. These lines will help you position the membrane in the shower. Always double-check the lines before cutting, and then make the cut with tinsnips or scissors.

Work liner into place

If you haven't already removed the drain barrel from the clamping ring, do so now. Turn the top part of the two-part clamping ring so that it clears the bolts and then remove it and set it aside. Leave the lower part of the ring in place on the floor. Put the membrane over the bottom part of the clamping ring and align the lines you drew with the edges of the floor.

Once in place, the membrane will bunch up against the blocking in the corners. Push it directly into the corner with your finger. Pinch the excess material between your thumb and finger and then fold it to form a pleat. Push the pleat against the

Folding the Corners of a Waterproof Membrane

The plastic liner that makes a shower pan waterproof is folded at the corners and nailed to wall framing before concrete backer board is installed. The trick is in folding corners compactly so they will not push the bottom of the backer board outward and create a curve at the bottom of the shower wall.

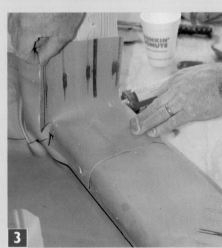

Folding the corner. Before nailing the plastic liner in place, fold the corner carefully so there is no stress on the membrane.

Tuck the fold aside. After nailing the upper edge of the liner into the corner, attach the bulky corner fold to the side of a corner stud. This prevents the liner from creating a bulge in the cement backer board.

Beef up the threshold. An extra piece of liner, about 6 in. by 12 in., helps to protect the vulnerable spot where the threshold meets the wall. Seal the reinforcing piece in place by running a ¼-in. bead of elastomeric caulk around the edge on the back side.

What goes in first, *the cement board or the main mud base?*

Either. *If you are very careful to protect the shower pan, you can do the board first and then the pan. We like to put the pan in first and do a 24-hour water test. When the test is over, we immediately pour the concrete before anyone does any more work in the shower stall. No human being ever sets foot on the membrane. It only takes stepping on one nail or tile chip to cause a leak.*

TOOLS AND MATERIALS
Caulk gun and ratchet

When you're installing a shower pan, two essential tools are a caulk gun and a ratchet wrench. The caulk gun is used to shoot a bead of elastomeric caulk into the area where the membrane forms the seal with the drain assembly. A caulking gun is the only way to reach in and get an even ring of caulk around the flange. The wrench—another tool you might not automatically associate with tiling—is used to tighten the four bolts that secure the top ring of the drain assembly. Each bolt is tightened a little at a time to keep the pressure even.

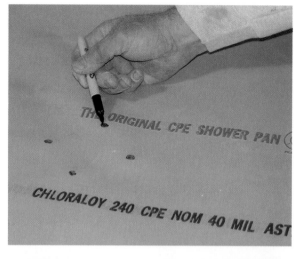

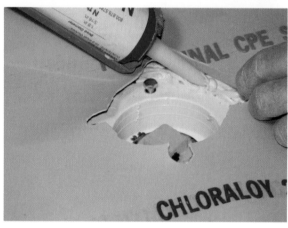

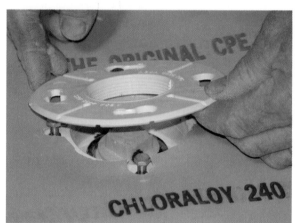

Installing the liner around the drain. Make a mark where you can feel the bolts in the drain assembly through the liner, and cut around the bolts and the drain opening. Keep the tip of the knife pointing down and toward the plug so it won't slip.

Seal the joint with caulk. Once the liner has been trimmed, seal the space between the liner and the drain with caulk made by the same company that makes the liner. Then put the retaining ring in place and tighten the bolts evenly.

The Layers of an Effective Shower Pan

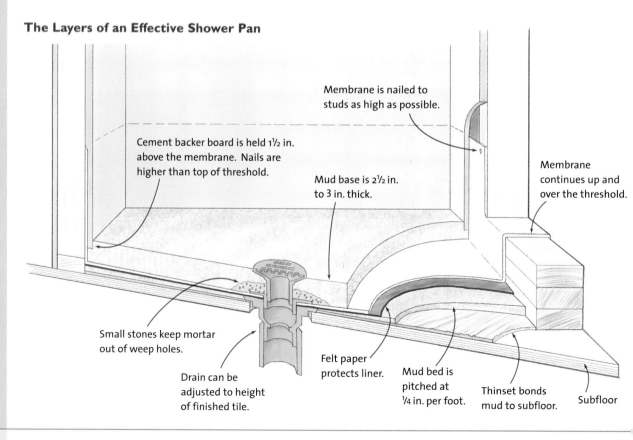

Membrane is nailed to studs as high as possible.

Cement backer board is held 1½ in. above the membrane. Nails are higher than top of threshold.

Mud base is 2½ in. to 3 in. thick.

Membrane continues up and over the threshold.

Small stones keep mortar out of weep holes.

Drain can be adjusted to height of finished tile.

Felt paper protects liner.

Mud bed is pitched at ¼ in. per foot.

Thinset bonds mud to subfloor.

Subfloor

framing and nail it tightly into place to prevent bulges in the backer board that will be applied over it (see "Folding the Corners of a Waterproof Membrane" on p. 135).

Work your way to the next corner, nailing the upper edge of the membrane to each stud as you go. Keep the edge of the liner parallel to the floor and make sure you don't pull it off the floor or stretch it too tight.

Lately, we've been asking carpenters to omit the blocking along the floor. It allows us to tuck the liner inside the studs instead of folding it into the corners. This eliminates the bulges, which force the corners of the backer board out of alignment. It's a tremendous time-saver and assures a neater-looking job.

Attaching the Drain and Liner

One of the most crucial steps in building the pan is cutting and connecting the membrane to the plastic drain assembly. If the seam isn't tight, the pan will leak.

Start by making marks on the membrane to show where the heads of the drain-assembly bolts are. Then put a fresh blade in your utility knife, make a small slit at each bolt, and push the membrane down over the bolts. Guide the knife in a circle around the inside of the drain, cutting from bolt to bolt. Always cut toward the center of the drain to avoid slipping with the knife and cutting into the floor area of the membrane.

Because the seal between the membrane and the drain is such a crucial part of a leak-proof assembly, always lift the membrane at this point and make sure the bottom clamping ring is clear of dirt and grit. Apply the adhesive as directed by the manufacturer.

Conducting the water test. Make sure the drain plug is tight, fill the pan with water, and wait a day to see if there are leaks.

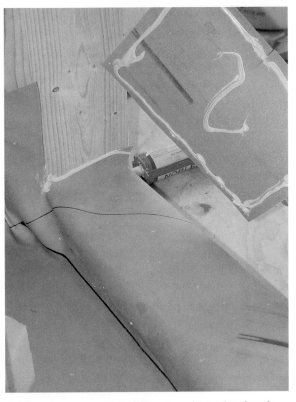

Adding a corner patch. The area where the threshold meets the wall is vulnerable to leaks and should be reinforced with a patch of the liner. It's bonded with elastomeric caulk.

Can I patch *a hole in the membrane?*

Absolutely, *as long as the membrane isn't covered with concrete. If you can seam and join two pieces together, making a patch is a piece of cake. For small leaks like nail holes, we cut a 4-in. patch and apply the manufacturer's elastomeric caulk liberally to the membrane. Press the patch firmly into the membrane with a clean trowel. For larger leaks, cut a patch big enough to extend 2 in. beyond the leak in all directions. For multiple leaks, or very large ones, it's safer to replace the entire membrane. Test it again.*

WHAT CAN GO WRONG

Plastic shower-pan membranes will last forever if they're installed correctly and protected from damage during construction. But until they are tiled, the membranes are very vulnerable. That's why I place mortar over the liner only after I've tested it for leaks and before anyone has a chance to step on it. If one nail is dropped on the shower floor and goes unnoticed (which I see all the time), all someone has to do is to step on it. The side of the head will put a crescent-shaped cut in the liner that's hardly noticeable. If it's not caught in time, and the pan is tiled, it may leak.

The makers of Chloraloy recommend a heavy bead of NobleSealant 150, an elastomeric caulk, between the sheet and the bottom clamping ring. Once the appropriate sealant is in place, press the bottom ring and the membrane together and then put the top ring in position. Tighten the bolts slowly, applying equal pressure on each bolt (see "Tools and Materials" on p. 136).

At the threshold, I cut the membrane along the framed opening, fold it over, and nail it to the

Oops. If you have a leak, this is what it looks like. Better to find out now than after you've put the tile in place. Check the liner for leaks. In this case, the problem was a nail that hadn't been set deeply enough and poked a hole through the liner.

Forming the mesh. Wire mesh holds mortar in place on the threshold. Bend the wire over a piece of 2x4 so that it takes the shape of the curb.

threshold framing. To seal the cuts, I fold and glue 6-in. by 8-in. pieces of membrane into the corners with the recommended cement.

Testing the pan

At this point, you should test the pan for leaks. To do this, put an expandable rubber drain plug into the drain. There's a heavy-duty metal washer on one end of the plug and a knob at the other end.

Twisting the knob pulls the washer toward the knob, forcing the plug to get wider in the middle. Turn the knob until the seal is tight, dump in enough water to fill the shower pan with 2 in. to 3 in. of water, and let the pan sit overnight. The next day, check to make sure the level of the water hasn't gone down. Check for wet spots in the ceiling directly below the stall, too.

If you find a leak is in the middle of the pan and not in a creased corner, cut a round, 4-in. patch and hold it in place with two beads of elastomeric caulk, just as you would if you were seaming two pieces of liner together. If the leak is in a corner, you may have to replace the entire liner.

Adding backer board. You can simplify the job a bit by nailing cement backer board to the outside of the curb. Without doing as much work, you get a flat surface that works just as well as mud.

Once the membrane passes inspection, take out the drain plug and let the water drain. Make sure that no one steps into the shower pan until you have poured the mud base over it for the tile. Put a protective layer of felt paper over the membrane to protect it from big clunky feet until you're ready to put in the next layer of mud. Put tape over the drain opening to keep mud from falling into it.

Wrap the curb in wire mesh

Instead of nailing cement board on all three sides, I wrap a piece of prefolded galvanized wire mesh over the complete dam. When I measure and cut the wire, I hold it off the bottom of the shower floor about 1½ in. so there is no chance of puncturing the pan liner.

I form the wire around a 2x4 straddling two buckets. Then I pinch the two side walls inward so the wire will fit like a tight glove when installed over the 2x4s in the threshold. The only nails I use are on the outside wall, toward the room.

When I place the mud base inside the shower pan, which is at least 2½ in. deep, the mortar will lock in the edge of wire on the inside of the threshold (and no nails are needed). I then cover all the wire with a thin coat of mortar. The next day I apply a fresh coat of cement and tile the shower threshold. It may be thinset or mortar, depending on the thickness.

Thick mud makes a sturdy base

Once you're sure the pan doesn't leak, it's time to put a layer of mud on top of the membrane. With a level, draw a level line on the studs where a 2-in.- to 3-in.-thick mud bed would meet the wall. Double-check to make sure the line is level. Put the barrel back in the drain and adjust it so that it and the line on the wall are the same distance above the membrane. Pour a couple of

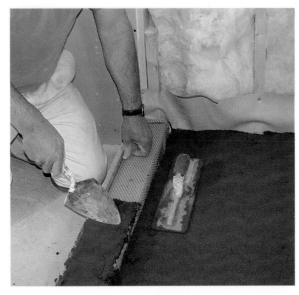

Add mortar to the mesh. Build up a layer of mortar along the side of the mesh and level it with the top of the backer board. Pull a piece of screen along the top to roughen the surface to help the thinset stick to it later.

handfuls of ¼-in. stone in the weep holes to keep them clear of mortar. As a final step before you mix up the mud, round over the corners of a steel trowel with sandpaper. A square corner could slice or puncture the membrane.

Mix another batch of mortar using the same proportions as before. Dump a good amount into the pan—the weight of the mix keeps the membrane from creeping. Pack the mud in place with a wooden float, connecting the line on the wall

Q & A

When the builder *put in the shower pan, he ran the cement board all the way down to the floor and nailed it one inch above the bottom floor of the pan. Will it be OK?*

No, *take off the cement board and cut it so the top will be above the shower pan. Nails that are only 1 in. above will have punctured the membrane, so rip it out and replace it. Don't try patching the holes—in order to get a good patch, you need to work on a flat surface and apply a patch that overlaps the holes by 2 in. in each direction. The wall isn't that kind of place.*

TOOLS AND MATERIALS

New to the tile industry is a two-level set made just for tile installers (Stabila™ Inc.). The longer level is 58 in. and fits nicely in any 5-ft. tub, even after the cement board has been installed. The shorter level is 32-in. long, which works well on the side walls of any tub or shower. These levels are easy to clean and made to be used with cement and mastics. These levels make tilesetting go faster and give more accurate results.

with the top of the drain as best you can. The surface should be pitched toward the drain, ¼ in. per foot.

Once you've got the mud in place, clean up the slope with a straightedge. We use a level, because we can check the perimeter of the pan for level as we work, but any straightedge will do. Rest one end of the straightedge on the drain and put the other end on the line you drew on the wall. Pull the straightedge across the mud to flatten it, and then smooth out the resulting surface with a flat steel trowel. Keep working the surface to elimi-

nate any voids or low spots that will collect water once the tile is installed. When the mud layer is smooth, evenly pitched, and level around the perimeter, let it sit overnight, or tile right away.

Installing Backer Board and Tile

There are two ways to install the cement backer board. One is before the second layer of mortar is placed in the pan. In this case, the cement board is held 1½ in. off the membrane in the

A second layer of mortar. Put the drain barrel in the drain assembly and adjust it so the top will be flush with the finished surface of the tile. Then add a second layer of mortar over the liner. Keep the perimeter level, and smooth the surface to slope to the drain.

bottom of the shower pan (a 2x4 laid flat is a good gauge of height).

The other method is to install the backer board after the second layer of mortar has been placed over the membrane, in which case the backer board can sit directly on the mortar. I do this because I can assure the customer that no human being has set foot on the membrane after it was tested and before the mortar was poured. Both methods are correct.

The idea is to keep the bottom edge of the cement board out of any standing water in the bottom of the liner (see "The Layers of an Effective Shower Pan" on p. 136). If it does, moisture can wick up into the wall, creating a variety of problems. Also, the lowest nail in the wall should always be higher than the curb. If the drain ever clogs, water would leak in around any nails placed below the curb. Finally, sheets of backer board must meet over a stud. If not, they will flex, causing cracks in the tile job. Don't forget to use a membrane such as tarpaper or plastic behind the cementboard and let it overhang into the shower pan. I prefer tarpaper.

At this point, the stall is ready to tile, and doing so is the same as any other tile job. Do the walls first so that any mud that falls on the floor won't hit the finished tile.

At the transition between the wall and floor you can either install a cove tile or simply bring the floor tile against the wall tile. Leave a small grout joint between the floor and wall and grout it but don't caulk it. The floor is plenty watertight even without the grout, and in our experience, latex caulk eventually turns black and silicon caulk generally peels off.

Tiling the threshold

I start with the outside face of the threshold and cut the tile so it's higher than the threshold core

Finishing the top of the threshold. Once the mud on the curb dries, apply thinset to hold the tiles in place and shovel in more mud, leveling it with the top of the tiles.

by about ¾ in. This creates the proper pitch in the top of the threshold toward the inside of the shower. It also provides a generous bed of mortar to cap the wire and skim coat applied the day before.

It's very important to keep the front face of the threshold perfectly level from side to side. This will make it possible to install a shower door without any problems.

On the inside of the threshold, I tile that wall but keep the top ¼ in. lower than the outside. I have now established a perfect pitch to the inside. With this pitch, any shower spray will drain right back into the shower. I have run across many jobs where the dam is pitched the wrong way, or just flat level. This just causes problems.

With both the interior and exterior walls done, I float the cavity between the two with mud (three parts sand to one part portland cement). If it is ¼ in. or less deep, I just fill it in with thinset. This finish coat will give the top of the threshold a flat, even coat that can be tiled any time.

Q & A

Can I make *a handicapped shower stall in an existing room without major construction?*

Yes, *but the question is whether the floor can be pitched enough. The floor needs to slope toward the drain. With a very low pitch, flooding would occur very quickly if the drain were to become clogged. For an existing floor, that means you need to build up the outside edges, which usually creates a step that interferes with wheelchairs. Some special membranes, however, let you build up a thinner bed that will do the job.*

WHAT CAN GO WRONG

I have often been called in to fix a problem caused by an installer who installed cement board directly on the floor of the shower pan and then poured cement over it. Usually no one discovers the problem until about a year later when moisture at the bottom of the pan wicks up and darkens the bottom few rows of tile. Fixing this problem is a major repair that essentially requires ripping out the shower pan and rebuilding it correctly. If the cement board had been held 1½ in. off the bottom of the pan, this would not have happened.

Minimizing grout joints

There are two choices for covering the top of the threshold. Either I can tile it with the same tile I used on the sides, or I can use a slab of stone or solid surfacing (such as Corian). I prefer using a slab because it is one solid piece with no grout joints, and it looks elegant and rich.

On this job, I asked the people who installed the counters and tub deck to make pieces of Corian or marble of the same color for the threshold cap. To get a good bond, I scarify the bottom of the Corian with a grinder and then set it with latex-modified thinset the day after the mortar has set.

Laying the foundation. A curbless shower uses a true mud bed. Tar paper isolates the bed from movement in the floor, and wire mesh reinforces the mortar.

Building a Shower Curb

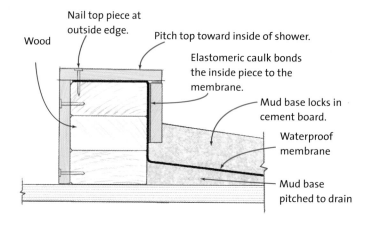

Wood

Nail top piece at outside edge.

Pitch top toward inside of shower.

Elastomeric caulk bonds the inside piece to the membrane.

Mud base locks in cement board.

Waterproof membrane

Mud base pitched to drain

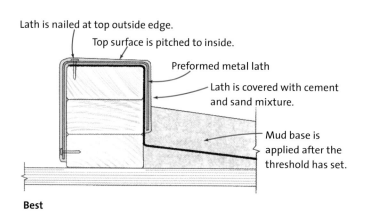

Lath is nailed at top outside edge.

Top surface is pitched to inside.

Preformed metal lath

Lath is covered with cement and sand mixture.

Mud base is applied after the threshold has set.

Best

There are two sound approaches to building a shower threshold. In both cases, the waterproof pan liner should extend up the inside wall of the threshold and over the top. No nails should be used on the inside top or inside wall of the threshold, to prevent possible damage to the liner.

Building a Curbless Shower

We used to get asked to install a curbless (or handicapped-accessible) shower once or twice a year. Now it's at least once a month and sometimes more. Part of it, no doubt, is our aging population. Because there is no curb, these showers are wheelchair compatible. But a good part of it is fashion. Curbless showers are large, and they don't need a shower curtain. They are true "walk-in" showers.

They are not, however, jobs for the do-it-yourselfer. Installing a curbless shower is not just a matter of putting in a waterproof membrane, as in a regular shower.

A floor of many layers

A curbless shower requires building up a large section of the floor with mortar and leveling and pitching it without building up the grade of the floor too high. In fact, it's an old-fashioned mud job that includes tar paper, galvanized wire, and mortar.

This creates a dilemma. You can't create the slope without the mud job, but the mud raises the floor and creates a step that a wheelchair can't get over. To solve this problem in new construction, the shower floor may be framed a bit lower than the rest of the bathroom.

If you're retrofitting an existing shower, however, you're not about to reframe the house. We solve the problem with a Schluter Systems membrane (see "Resources" on p. 186), which goes on top of the mud bed instead of between two layers, as shown elsewhere in this chapter.

The shower here is 6 ft. wide by 12 ft. long. The drain and shower are on the left, on the 6-ft. wall. The doorway is in the middle of the

Screeding the floor. Flatten the floor by pulling a straightedge across it—most tilesetters use their levels. After you create the general slope, pack the mortar down with a steel floating trowel and smooth it with the wood floating trowel.

Putting down the membrane. The membrane is installed with thinset cement. Once the sheet is laid in place, use a steel trowel to push out any voids or air pockets to ensure perfect contact with the concrete base.

Q & A

When tiling the threshold, can I just nail the cement board over some 2x material to create a base for the tile?

You can get away with driving a few nails on the outside face of the threshold and along the outside edge of the top. Driving nails on the inside face is asking for leaks. Some installers try to get away with putting a few nails high up on the inside face, but it's not recommended by the Tile Council of America. I have found the easiest and best way for me is to wrap the threshold with a piece of galvanized wire mesh and build up the surface with mortar.

WHAT CAN GO WRONG

Water is wicking up the wall from the bottom of the shower pan. Whoever installed the shower set the bottom of the cement backer board on the top of the pan. There is always some water in the bottom of the shower pan below the tile (that's why there is a pan) and it's making its way up the wall. The only repair is to rebuild.

Overlapping corners. This wall has a strip of membrane on it that is cut and folded at each corner. The strip along the adjoining wall will also be folded in the corner, giving the wall extra protection in a weak spot.

12-ft. wall. The job starts with tar paper, spread across the floor to isolate the mud bed from movement. Next come some sheets of wire mesh. They overlap by 1 in. wherever two sheets meet and are nailed down with 1¼ in. roofing nails every 6 in.

Forming the mortar bed

The mortar I use is a mix of one part portland cement and three or four parts of sand (I usually go with four). The best way to create a flat surface is to pull a straightedge across it, usually a level. (Don't try to get the floor level; just try to get it flat.) Smooth out the surface left by the straightedge with a steel floating trowel and

wood float. The goal is to create a slope that directs the water from around the room toward the drain. I usually extend the slope at least 1 ft. beyond the point that spray will reach.

Two areas are especially crucial—the doorway and the toilet flange (or any other piping that comes up through the floor). Make sure that the floor slopes away from them. On this job, we created a slight (½-in.) ramp in the doorway to keep water in, making the thickest part of the bed 1½ in. thick. From about 5 ft. out, we started pitching the mortar toward the drain, which will be ¼ in. to ½ in. above the subfloor. This didn't give us a lot of pitch, but enough to make the shower work.

Tiling the floor. When the membrane is down, you apply thinset directly over it. This lets you build a thinner bed, which won't require you to step up to get into the shower.

Adding the membrane

After placing the mortar, we installed a membrane called Schluter Kerdi, wrapping it up the wall to create a liner—in essence, a small wading pool. There's a lot of floor, so you have to overlap pieces to cover everything.

We made the overlap 4 in. wide and cemented the pieces together with thinset for a waterproof seam. In corners, the membrane is overlapped from two different directions with different folds. The drain assembly has a flange made of membrane material. A coat of thinset creates a waterproof seal between it and the rest of the floor membrane. I recommend using the Kerdi membrane up the walls to the height of the shower head. It's a better way to waterproof the complete showering area.

When it comes time to tile, use the same thinset to attach the tile to the membrane. Use the smallest tile possible, so that it will follow the pitch and roll of the mortar base.

DESIGN OPTIONS

Don't just think of it as a shower floor. It is an extension of the main floor. It can hold many of the same decorative elements as the walls and floors and feel wonderful under your feet.

Repeating patterns. Running the same herringbone tile on the wall and the floor adds a dramatic element to this shower without becoming overwhelming.

Simple touches. A shower floor is a perfect place to add a simple element of design, like this border of mosaics. Interior tile is set on the diagonal.

Limestone shower floor.
Limestone is available in a variety
of colors, and it's relatively easy to
cut into 1-in., 2-in., or 3-in. squares
suitable for a shower floor.

Integrating shower and floor.
Because there is no threshold on
this shower, floor tile should be
consistent from the shower to
the rest of the bathroom.

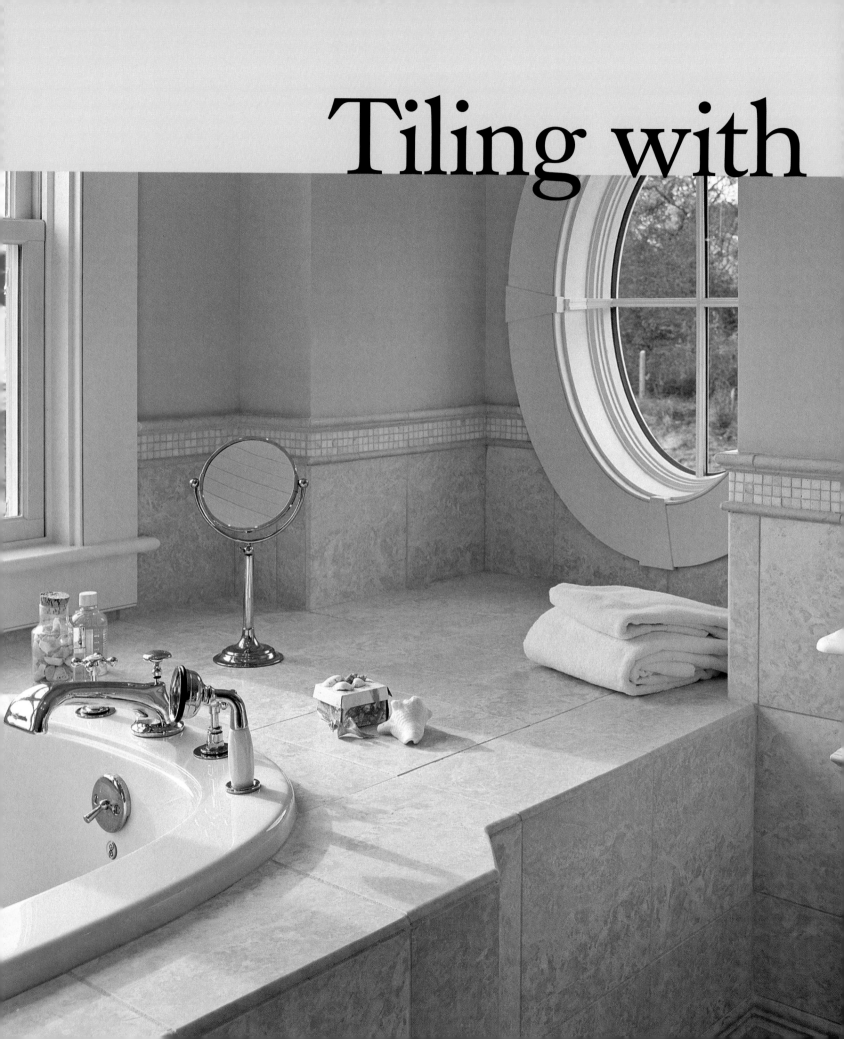

Tiling with

CHAPTER TEN

Stone

1 Choosing the Stone and the Look, p. 150

2 Cutting and Installing Stone Tile, p. 153

3 Stone Should Be Sealed, p. 158

Have you ever looked out a window and thought, "I wish the leaves on that oak tree were a different shade of green?" Probably not. Colors in nature just seem right. It's when we try to mimic natural colors with glazes that they seem more contrived.

And so it is with stone tile, a natural material that can be used to create a look that never goes out of style and can be combined with many accent colors. No two stones are ever exactly the same, which is the real beauty of stone tile (see "Design Matters" on p. 150).

Decorative stone tile can be pricey, but plain field tile isn't necessarily expensive. Slate and some kinds of limestone, in fact, are quite reasonably priced.

Slate can cost roughly the same as many ceramic tiles. Now consider that you won't need any decorative tiles, and you'll realize that real stone could come in at a lower price than ceramic tile.

Our customers are quite often surprised that a tumbled marble backsplash costs less than if they did the same area with ceramic tile and then added decorative tile to bring it up a notch.

Most stone is available in a variety of sizes, but it can be cut to custom sizes and smoothed with abrasives for a completely finished look.

Q & A

When grouting polished marble or limestone, can I use colored grout?

Carefully, but test a small area first. The tile has to be presealed and the grout should be made a little stiff. Do not make the grout too loose. It will bleed into the pores of the tile and stain the edges.

DESIGN MATTERS

Stone's natural variations are one of its main attractions for people who choose it over ceramic tile. You don't have to make stone into something that it isn't. When adding decorative tile to a stone installation, keep it simple and understated so the natural beauty of stone shines through.

Naturally beautiful. Stone is a warm and welcoming floor surface that needs no elaboration or embellishment.

Old is good. Some of these reclaimed tiles are well over 100 years old. Many are brick or terracotta pavers made close to the chateaus from which they were salvaged. Some reclaimed limestone tiles are much older.

Choosing the Stone and the Look

When we are tiling a bathroom and want to use the same tile on the main floor and the shower floor, a natural stone makes that easy. The stone can always be cut down to 3-in. or 4-in. squares to accommodate the pitch of the shower floor and give the room an overall larger look.

Adding a bullnose edge isn't difficult, and the stone can be brought to whatever level of polish is needed with diamond pads. Think about how useful that is for finishing a shower edge or threshold or the inside of a fireplace surround (see "Making a Custom Shampoo Shelf" on p. 157).

The Big Three

Three types stone are commonly used in residential construction: limestone, marble, and slate.

Thanks to a variety of excellent protective sealers and maintenance products, stone tile can be used in many different areas, from foyers and bathrooms to backsplashes and floors. One exception is polished marble, which should not be used in high-traffic areas.

Reclaimed antique stone is not as well known, but it's becoming increasingly popular. Some of it is well over 1,000 years old.

Although it's not really stone, reclaimed terracotta tile taken from chateaus in Europe also is available. It's often a couple of hundred years old (give or take a decade or two). These tiles can be extremely beautiful, rustic—and expensive. Thickness can vary by more than ½ in., so installation is that much more difficult.

I install a limestone master bath at least once a week. Limestone is great to work with. Unlike polished marble, it's very forgiving. If I have a high corner or a scratch on the surface of the stone, I can hit it with two different grits of sandpaper (80 grit and then 120) and the problem is solved.

I can do the same thing with slate, but with polished marble I have to go a few grits higher to get that polished shine back. With ceramic tile, I have to lay out my walls for factory-made cap or bullnose. With any type of natural stone, I can do a finished bullnose on any size piece (see "Tools for Installing Tile" in Chapter One, p. 15).

Tune in to color and texture

Different shades of color make the stone look natural. It is important to work from three or four boxes of tile at the same time to blend color and textures, rather than to work from a single box at a time and risk abrupt transitions.

Three shades of stone. The three types of stone tile used most frequently include, from left, slate, marble, and limestone. Each comes in many different colors.

Limestone is made of seashells and skeletons of sea creatures that accumulated over eons in the sediment on the ocean floor. Some of that limestone encountered tremendous geological heat and pressure, crystallizing and transforming it into marble.

Stone can be use in conjunction with glass tile, glass block, and ceramic tile. Different types of stone also can be mixed on the same job, while borders and decorative inserts offer other ways of being creative with this material.

A neutral stone also can be an effective backdrop for a decorative tile mural (see "Adding a Custom Mural" on p. 156). To install a mural, I start by laying out the pieces dry on the floor and taking accurate measurements of its dimensions. Then I transfer the dimensions to the wall, which in this case is limestone.

The limestone has been set with uniform ⅛-in. wide grout lines and designed so that a 2½-in. border will frame the outline of the mural. The

Q & A

I have *a couple of scratches in the middle of a limestone floor. How can I take them out?*

You can't really *remove the scratches, but you can sand the area around them, which will remove part of the stone and make them disappear. Just use the right grit paper to get the finish to be the same as the rest of the tile.*

TOOLS AND MATERIALS

An important tool for working with stone is a sander/polisher, useful for adding a quick bullnose or just an eased edge at the doorway. If there is a high edge in the middle of the room, this tool will sand it down and polish the tile back to a shine if needed. The 4-in. pads are attached with a hook-and-loop system, making it easy to switch between different grits of abrasives. If I have to really grind some stone down, I can attach a cup grinder with diamond abrasives that will eat through any stone quickly.

warm, soft, tones of the limestone are a perfect setting for the bolder colors of the mural, which sits at the end of a bathtub near a window with a view of a marsh.

Combining different kinds of stone also can produce some dramatic effects, as shown by the green slate and yellow-gold limestone used in the shower in the photo at right. The floors and the bench seat also will be tiled in green slate for an elegant contrast.

Just before the top course, I will install another piece of green slate in the form of a decorative band. All of the other walls here are going to be made of glass block. The block wall will start on the threshold and follow the full radius of the curb.

Choosing Thinset and Trowels

When you're installing stone tile, it's important to use the proper kind of thinset cement. Natural stone can be either soft and porous or hard. I use the best grade of thinset across the board. Stone tile is more expensive than most other types and it may have veins that make it a little fragile until the cement sets. For this reason, I also skim-coat the back of the tile as I'm setting it. For any light-colored limestone or marble, white thinset should always be used (see "What Can Go Wrong" on p. 154).

If gray thinset is used, it has a very good chance of darkening the tile, an effect that won't change as the thinset dries. When in doubt, use white thinset, even with dark stone (it can never hurt).

Using the right trowel is always of the utmost importance. Although some tilesetters wouldn't be so fussy, I think 95 percent of the tile should be coated with thinset.

Mix and match. Natural stone can be combined easily with other types of tile and stone. In this bathroom, bamboo green slate is teamed up with a gold-colored Jerusalem limestone. Decorative tiles on the wall help unify the design.

For help with this, follow the instructions of the "Trowel and Error" video produced by the National Tile Contractors Association (see "Resources" on p. 186).

On most of my stone floors, I use a ¼-in. by ⅜-in. U-notched trowel to apply the thinset. When tiling walls, I use a ¼-in. by ¼-in. square-notched trowel.

Once again, with any soft, light, or heavily veined stone, I apply a skim coat and cover the back side of the tile. Not only does this method give the tile better contact, but it fills the pores of the stone with thinset, which helps to solidify a slightly fragile stone.

Clip the corners. Another stone combination begins with 12-in. tumbled marble on the floor and the walls. On the floor, some corners have been clipped to allow the insertion of 2-in. squares of white marble.

Machine-cut bullnose. A specialized profiling machine makes a perfect bullnose edge in less than a minute. It's ideal for jobs where a lot of the material has to be made and consistency is important.

Cutting and Installing Stone Tile

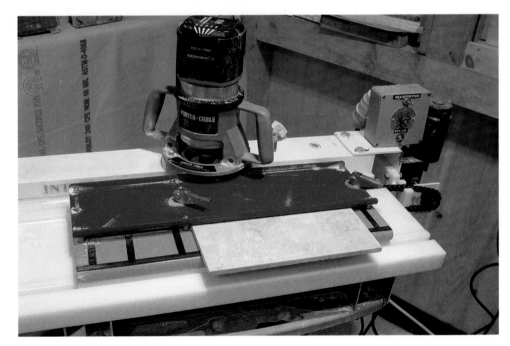

Limestone, marble, and slate should be cut only with a wet saw equipped with a water-cooled diamond-edged blade.

The water cooler is a simple pump in the bottom of the tray on which the saw sits. Water is sprayed continuously on both sides of the blade as the machine runs. Because the blade works by friction rather than a cutting action, it must be cooled or it will wear out in a matter of minutes. When the machine has been properly cared for, it will provide the cleanest and smoothest of cuts.

A snap-cutter is of no use with natural stone because the pieces will hardly ever break in a straight line. A water saw can even be used to cut holes in the middle of a tile (see "Punching a Hole in Stone" on p. 159).

The floor on which stone tile is installed needs twice the resistance to sag as one where ceramic tile is set. For ceramic tile, deflection can be L/360 (that is, the span divided by 360 equals the maximum sag in the floor), but most stone requires a deflection of L/720.

I'm tiling *a large stone floor, and I see that I am going to be short about 20 pieces. Will the shades of the extra tile I buy match what I've already installed?*

You can't predict *whether the shades will match. If you have closets or places on the floor that will be covered by appliances, this would be the place to use that extra tile. If not, do not finish installing all the tile. Leave out about 30 tiles and mix in the two batches to finish up. This will help blend old and new.*

WHAT CAN GO WRONG

I remember seeing a large installation of very light-colored Carrara marble that had been set with grey thinset. The installer told the client the floor would take a couple of weeks to lighten up because the cement had to cure. He got paid that day but the floor never lightened up, and it never will. The grey thinset shows through the somewhat translucent stone. The only way to fix this problem is to take out the tile and start over. When installing any light-colored stone, always use white thinset.

This also means that if you are using a membrane or a cement board as an underlayment over ¾-in. tongue-and-groove plywood, you will have to add another layer of plywood to beef up the floor. (For more on deflection, see "Preventing Cracked Tile and Grout" on p. 196.)

Of course, this means the floor will be higher in doorways. That can be inconvenient, but it can be dealt with and it's better than a job failure. When tiling over wood framing, it is best to use a stress-crack isolation membrane whenever possible.

Pay attention to the joints

It takes more effort to install limestone and marble floor tile than it does ceramic tile. That's because the joints between tiles are smaller and the limestone and marble have a square edge. For appearance's sake, these tiles should be very flat when installed. Most ceramic tile, on the other hand, is installed with a ¼-in. joint, and the outside factory edge has been slightly eased.

With marble, the grout joint should be almost nonexistent. If you're installing polished marble, sanded grout should never be used (the joint should not be wide enough to require it, and sanded grout can scratch the surface of the tile).

If by chance someone has used larger joints and sanded grout on a marble floor and the floor has to be refinished, all the grout has to be removed first so the sand in the grout will not scratch the marble as it is being repolished.

Green marble is even more work than regular polished marble. Because of its chemical makeup, green marble acts negatively on water-based or acrylic thinset cements, causing the tile to warp or break down. It should be set in an epoxy-based material. Epoxy is more difficult to work with than latex-modified thinset. It can sag, it's sticky and messy, and it's quite expensive.

Adding Decorative Details

The options are unlimited for adding a decorative element to stone. You can carve into the stone, add ceramic tiles, or just contrast with another color stone.

Cutting in a decorative tile. To insert a decorative tile into a field of limestone, trace its outline in pencil and then cut away the waste with a water saw.

Install wall tile first. After the prepped field tile has been installed, butter the back of the decorative tile with thinset and set it in place. These are left slightly proud of the wall surface for a three-dimensional effect.

Capping it off. A 2-in. by 12-in. slate border set just below the last course of field tile makes this wall more interesting. These narrow tiles are decorated with a rope design.

Seal backs of green marble

A different solution that has been very successful for me is to seal the backs of green marble tile with epoxy and install the tile with less expensive but very high-quality latex-added or modified thinset.

Seal the back of the tile the day before with epoxy by using the flat side of a spreading trowel or a steel floating trowel. It is important to skim a full thin coat of epoxy over the entire surface.

A wet saw is a must. Stone tile cuts relatively well, but cuts must be made on an electrically driven water saw. A snap-cutter, useful for cutting ceramic tile, doesn't work very well with stone.

GREEN MARBLE TILE CAN LOOK LIKE A SOLID SLAB

Careful choreography of stone. Marble tiles in this shower installation are arranged so that veining and colorations blend smoothly and give the impression that the stone is a solid slab. Diamond shapes are cut from 12-in. pieces of a cream-colored marble.

Seal the back. Green marble reacts badly to water-based cements, so the backs of the tiles are sealed with non-porous epoxy the day before they are installed in the shower.

Keeping it straight. A ledger board keeps the starter course level. Once the thinset bonding this first course has set, the board can be removed and lower tiles installed.

Q & A

I bought *a lot of tile for a large bathroom and some of the corners are broken. Do I send the whole batch back?*

Rather than waste *time and money going back and forth to the store, open all the boxes and see exactly what the damage is. If there are lots of broken corners and only a few broken full tiles, just use the damaged tile for pieces you will have to cut. In most cases, you will have lots of cuts and some waste anyway.*

Then stand the tiles on edge with each one just slightly leaning on the other, like a set of dominos.

The next day, strike all the perimeter edges with a utility knife to get rid of any excess epoxy that would not allow the tile to be installed tightly to the next piece.

Working with slate

Most slate we install today is rustic and uneven in appearance. A lot of the rustic slate is imported from Turkey, India, China, and Brazil. There are slates from the United States, too, but they aren't as rustic in appearance as the imported varieties.

Most imported slate has been coming in 12-in. square pieces, but now there also are a lot of smaller pieces that are mesh-mounted on sheets. This is all quite different from the relatively consistent patterned slate that we installed up through the 1980s.

The colors in today's slate vary greatly from tile to tile and even vary within individual pieces. For this reason, shades really have to be blended in order for the floor to look natural and beautiful. That's why it's a good idea to work out of three or four boxes of tile simultaneously.

Slate tile varies in size and also in thickness by as much as ¼ in. This is why grout joints should be at least ¼-in. wide. If there is a high ridge on a tile, then the grout should be planed with the heel of your hand when you're grouting.

ADDING A CUSTOM MURAL

Laying out a mural. When installing a mural made of hand-molded art tile, the best plan is to lay out the pieces on the floor and take careful measurements before cutting field tile for the wall.

Installing the mural. A narrow band of limestone frames the mural. Plastic wedges are helpful for establishing even grout lines between large limestone tiles on the wall.

Naturally complementary. The completed mural works wonderfully with the natural tones of this French limestone. Light-colored limestone complements almost every color of the rainbow.

Making a Custom Shampoo Shelf

The great thing about working with stone is that you can mold it to a different shape or size. We often make a custom shelf in a shower for shampoo and soap. The stone cuts easily with a water saw. Then we use a grinder and a sander/polisher to shape the stone into a great-looking shelf. The grinder will do the heavy cutting of the stone and the sander/polisher gives it a smooth, finished look. We even cut some holes or slices in the shelf for drainage.

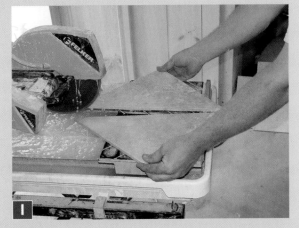

Rough cut. Using a water saw, we cut the tile to a size that will be close to what we want to work with. The tile is a Durango limestone.

Sculpting the edge. A cup grinder with diamond abrasives shapes the shelf.

Smoothing it out. A sander smoothes the curve with 80-grit and then 120-grit paper.

Adding drainage. Slots cut into the stone from the bottom allow soap residue and water to drain away.

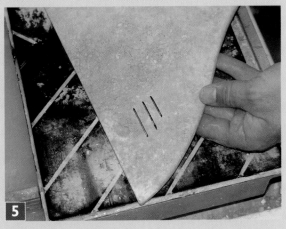

From the top. This piece of stone is now ready to become a finished corner shampoo shelf in a tub or shower.

Our plumber installed *the sinks on our tiled bathroom counters. Now the faucets have dark rings around them, as if the stone is being stained, and the problem seems to be getting worse. What's up?*

The plumber used *pipe dope or some other putty that has oil in it. Remove the faucets right away and clean out any putty. The stone is absorbing the oil, and the stone's porosity is helping it spread. The stains can be taken out with a poultice that will draw out the oils. This will take a professional and it may take a few applications. You will have to be patient.*

TOOLS & MATERIALS

If some tiles are thicker than others, use a trowel with relatively large notches (½ in. by ½ in.). Then take the thin tiles and back-butter them with enough thinset to bring the tiles up to the same plane as the thicker tiles. Keep in mind, however, that thinset should not be more than ½ in. thick. If so, it can shrink, cracking or loosening the tiles.

Protecting stone from grout. All stone tile should be sealed before and after grouting. A coat of sealer prevents the tile from absorbing liquid in the grout and staining.

Stone Should Be Sealed

Slate, like any other stone, should be sealed with a very good sealer. I find that slate, because of its rough surface, should get two coats of sealer before it is grouted. This helps when it's time to clean the surface of the slate after applying grouting.

Grout tends to lodge in the clefts or crevices in the surface of the slate. The sealer works as a grout release. If sealer is not used, it would be extremely difficult to clean the surface of the slate.

After the slate is grouted, cleaned, and has dried out for a few days, a few more coats of sealer should be applied.

If a shine or finish is desired (and that is a good idea), then a top coat or enhancer can be applied.

Seal it a second time. After the grout has cured, applying a second and third coat of sealer blocks stains and protects the stone from water. In some cases, stone should be resealed every two years.

To keep this finish and help build a patina, special stone soap should be used when you're cleaning stone tile.

Limestone also requires a few coats of sealer. The softer and lighter types of limestone require more protection than darker and harder varieties.

Polished marble usually does not require as much sealing, but each kind of stone is a little bit different than the next, so do your research by checking with the manufacturer of the sealer (the line of Miracle Sealants is especially good).

Always test first

"Always test a small area" is a phrase that we hear quite often. I always thought it was just the manufacturer watching his back. I was wrong. This is a very important part of applying any sealer or finish to stone. You never know when a sealer is going to react in a strange way—it doesn't happen every day, but it does happen.

The problem could be that there's too much moisture in the tile, or it may not have been properly cleaned. Take the time to see how the sealer is going to react on an out-of-the way area (if possible, 4 sq. ft. is a good test size) before you seal the whole floor or shower stall.

Testing recently saved me a lot of trouble on a very large job. The homeowners wanted the tile to have a more vibrant color with the addition of a top coat but the sealer blocked the pores of the stone. The finish produced a little shine but it wouldn't darken the stone as we had hoped. Without testing the process in advance, I might have lost a $5,000 job, to say nothing of my credibility.

Punching a Hole in Stone

One way of making a hole in the center of a tile is with a drill. But if you don't have the right bit, a little ingenuity will work just as well. After you make a series of cuts in the tile with a wet saw, the hole can be punched out from the front. Limiting the depth of cut prevents the scoring marks from coming through the front side of the tile.

Back-cut the tile first. To create a hole in the middle of a tile, begin by making a series of scoring cuts on the back side of the tile, centered over the intended location of the hole.

Begin tapping. With the end of a chisel handle (or something like it), begin tapping out the waste from the front side of the tile. Start gently.

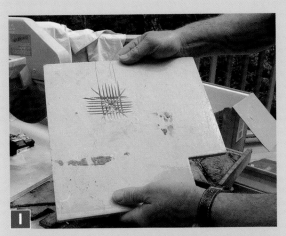

Neat and clean. Keep working the edges of the hole until it's the proper size. Where the tile has been thinned by cuts on the back side, material should break away easily.

DESIGN OPTIONS

Stone is probably the most versatile of all tile products. It can be used anywhere and its natural beauty always shines through.

The warmth of stone. Color tones in the tumbled marble of this backsplash pull together all the colors found in the wood of the counters and hood, plus the stone used on the wall.

The ⅝-in. squares in this shower add texture without a lot of cost.

Repeating patterns. It's easy to clip the corners of this stone floor tile and add an accent color, the same pattern repeated at the top of the wainscot.

Glass

CHAPTER ELEVEN

Tile

1 Glass Tile Installation Is Different, p. 164

2 Glass Tile in a Tub Surround, p. 166

3 Getting the Thinset Right, p. 167

4 Have Patience with Cutting and Grouting, p. 169

Glass tile has become increasingly popular. Many people assume it's contemporary-looking and expensive. In fact, glass tile is something of a chameleon. It can be iridescent, brushed, or tumbled, and there are many ways to use it.

Used alone, it is indeed more expensive than other kinds of tile, but it can be a wonderful and cost-effective accent when incorporated with tumbled marble, limestone, or even ceramic tile.

A square foot of 1-in.-sq. glass tile may cost more than you wanted to spend, but consider how many linear feet of decorative tile you get for that same square-foot price when you cut it into strips. All of a sudden, glass actually begins looking inexpensive.

You can use three or four rows of glass as a decorative band. Or put a cluster of four dots into the floor every 4 ft. Glass is very durable, so you can use it in backsplash applications as well as on floors, and 1-in. or 2-in. squares make good shower floors.

Glass can become the element that ties floors to walls. Ceramic or stone tile on the floor, for example, is accented with glass, while the 6-in. wall tile gets clusters or bands of glass.

163

Q & A

Can I install *glass tiles with mastic?*

Although *there is one glass-tile company that recommends mastic, the answer is generally no. Mastics do not have the bond strength of most recommended thinsets. And mastic can quickly discolor or yellow when used under some translucent glass tile. Always check with the tile manufacturer for the proper adhesive.*

DESIGN MATTERS

Although many people consider glass tile expensive, in reality it's a remarkably affordable way to add a decorative splash of color in an area of ordinary tile at a great price. A square foot of 1-in. by 1-in. glass tile seems costly, but you'll get a lot for your money by cutting it into strips two or three tiles wide and combining them with less expensive field tile.

This glass tile band works well with the white field tile and also picks up the blues and greens in the fish deco tile.

Glass Tile Installation Is Different

Installing glass tile is slightly different than it is for either stone or ceramic tile. It's not that glass tile is an extremely difficult material to work with, but it is less forgiving than other kinds of tile. It calls for precision and strict attention to the instructions provided by manufacturers.

Oceanside Glass Tile, a major manufacturer, offers an excellent instruction manual on installing this material with its product. Keep in mind, though, that different manufacturers might suggest certain modifications for working with their tile. The key is to follow whatever instructions are provided and follow them exactly.

Glass tile is more difficult to cut than ceramic or stone, in part because it is more brittle. In addition, many kinds of glass tile can be scratched, so instructions from manufacturers should be followed before they are installed on a floor.

There are many types and sizes of glass tile and trim pieces, and many have to be installed just a little bit differently than the others. Some are

Sleek, sophisticated, and contemporary, this 1-in. by 1-in. glass tile steals the show and adds to the modern feel of the room.

easier to work with than others (see "Not All Glass Tile Is Fussy," below).

If the tiles are opaque, they must be covered on the back side with thinset cement (this is called "back-buttering"). Tiles that are slightly see-through but have a textured finish should be set on thinset that has been flattened on the wall with the back side of a trowel. Hollow trim pieces should be skim coated with thinset but not filled, or the cement may shrink when it dries and crack the tile.

Take nothing for granted; read the installation specifications and the installation will be successful. The Tile Council of America (see "Resources" on p. 186) can answer questions about this and other types of tile.

Prepare the walls. This glass tile installation starts like that of any tiled tub or shower enclosure, with a layer of cement board seamed with mesh tape and thinset cement. Allow it to dry overnight.

Not All Glass Tile Is Fussy

Many types of glass tile can be finicky and time-consuming to install. But that's not always the case. These Austrian glass tiles, made by Villi, are absolutely beautiful, and they're very easy to install. The tile is perfectly clear, but color has been fired into the back of the tile at 900°F.

They are not antiqued, like those from Oceanside Glass Tile, but the look is still rich and warm. Cutting them is just as easy as cutting ordinary ceramic tile. I use a simple snap cutter and get a perfect cut every time. Some cutting is even possible with tile nippers.

In this project, I've used the glass tiles with a combination of ceramic tiles. The floor is tiled with a stone look-alike that resembles tumbled marble. The threshold is a slab of real marble. The lower two-thirds of the shower stall walls are of Villi-Glass 3-in. by 6-in. blue tile in a brick pattern. Above the decorative checkerboard are 3-in. by 6-in. ceramic tiles, showing that glass and ceramic tiles can be combined to good effect.

I install the tile using the proper thinset and I use rubber spacers to hold the glass tiles in place so they don't slide down before they set up. For this design, I used a 1-in. by 6-in. strip of glass and a checkerboard 1-in. by 1-in. tile as a decorative band. Later, I finished off the wall with a white ceramic 3-in. by 6-in. subway tile.

A snap cutter will do it. Although glass tile can be difficult to cut without a special blade for the saw, this Villi tile cuts cleanly with an ordinary snap cutter.

Q & A

Is plywood *a good substrate for installing glass tile?*

No. *Its high degree of expansion and contraction can cause problems with glass tile. I recommend three methods for glass-tile floors. The first is a wire-reinforced mortar bed (also known as a mud job). It should be allowed to cure for seven days prior to installation. The second is a stress-crack membrane applied over a total of 1⅛ in. of plywood. Last is cement backer board applied over two layers of plywood (total thickness of 1½ in.). Some people recommend cement board over ¾-in. tongue-and-groove plywood, but I think it allows too much deflection.*

Glass Tile in a Tub Surround

For this tub surround, I'm using a little bit of everything. There will be three different types of glass tiles. The lower part of the wall will get 4-in. by 4-in. clear tiles. About two-thirds of the way up, I'll install a 1-in. by 8-in. raised bar liner, a 12-in. band of 1-in. by 1-in. glass mosaics, and then another bar liner. Above this band, the rest of the tub wall will be finished with the same 4-in. by 4-in. tiles with clusters of four 1-in. by 1-in. pieces set on the diagonal. In the middle of the band I will install a preformed shampoo and soap niche that I have tiled with the 1-in. by 1-in. mosaics.

Before I can install any tile, I prep the walls by installing cement backer-board panels with either 1½-in. roofing nails or galvanized screws. I use mesh tape and thinset cement to fill in and bridge all the seams between each sheet of cement board. I try to keep this as flat as possible and then let it dry overnight before starting to tile.

Mosaics above as an accent. Rather than finishing off the upper part of the wall in plain field tile, cut blocks of four 1-in. tiles into tile corners at a diagonal. It's a simple way of tying elements of the wall together visually.

Thinset Techniques for Glass Tiles

Although glass tile, like other kinds of tile, is set with thinset adhesive, its translucent quality calls for a different application technique.

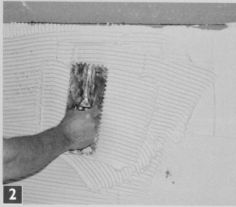

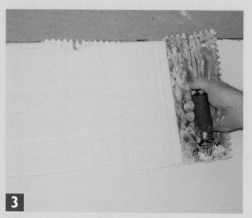

The ABCs of thinset application. For glass tile, applying thinset is a three-step process. Begin by spreading thinset with the flat edge of a trowel (1) before using the notched edge to distribute the cement to a uniform thickness (2), and then returning to the flat edge to remove ridges that might show through the tile (3).

Good layout is balanced

As is the case with any installation, the first task is layout. This installation is not as complicated as it may sound, but it does require some planning. The goal is to make sure that the walls look balanced and to avoid using any very small pieces, which are unsightly.

I can use a measuring tape (and then do the math), but an easier method is to use a story pole on which I've marked exact tile and grout-line spacing. Just remember than once the first tile is set, everything will fall into place.

The back wall of the tub surround is critical because it's what is seen first and most often. To make this wall visually balanced, I decide to cut ½ in. off the tile on each side. The tub is very close to being level (and that's not always the case). The layout shows a full tile along the top of the tub, and a good-sized piece at the ceiling.

Getting the Thinset Right

To start, I draw a level line across the middle of the wall where the border starts. Then I spread the thinset with a ¼-in. notched trowel in three separate steps (see "Thinset Techniques for Glass Tiles" on the facing page).

First, I apply thinset on the wall with the flat side of the trowel. Then I use the ¼-in. notched edge in one direction, a step that spreads the thinset to the desired thickness. Finally, I lightly flat-trowel the thinset again so trowel lines won't show through the tile. I press each tile into the thinset and give it a little slide. This helps to perfect the bond and also rids the thinset of any air bubbles.

When tiling with glass, it is extremely important to use whatever thinset cement the tile manufacturer recommends.

Glass tile expands when the sun beats down on it all day, and that can spell trouble if the wrong

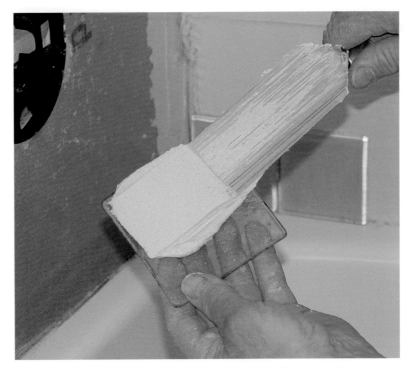

Coat the tiles, too. Each of these clear tiles should be cleaned with a dry cloth to remove dust or dirt and then given a complete, uniform coating of thinset on the back side. Voids will show through.

Don't do this. Although the tile on the left was back-buttered with thinset properly, it was not cleaned well. Dirt will show clearly. On the right, ridges of cement left by the notched edge of a trowel are clearly visible.

Q & A

Should glass *tile installations be sealed?*

Yes. *Glass tile won't absorb sealer, but sealer will protect the grout from staining and from absorbing moisture. Be sure to wipe off any excess sealer with a clean dry towel to avoid leaving a residue of sealer that would leave the tiles appearing streaky*

Can I *drill through glass tile?*

Yes. *MK® Diamond, and I would think other distributors, sell the specialized bits.*

WHAT CAN GO WRONG

I've been setting tile for more than 30 years, and I'd like to think I understand what kind of thinset should be used under different circumstances. But I've had a couple of jobs fail because I trusted my instincts rather than relying on the manufacturer's recommendations. On one floor, I used a full-flex thinset (which is a high quality, latex-modified thinset). More than a dozen pieces of 8-in. by 8-in. tile broke. I replaced the entire 40 sq. ft. floor, which cost me about $1,200.

Cut to fit. Mark tiles for special cuts with a grease pencil or felt-tipped marker.

Special saw for glass tile. This Revolution tile saw will make curved as well as straight cuts with virtually no chatter marks on tile edges. A standard tile saw also would work with a special blade.

kind of thinset is used to set the tile. In addition to choosing the right kind of thinset, you must apply it carefully.

The 4-in. tiles on the lower part of the wall are clear, meaning that every single one of them should have a perfectly uniform coating of thinset on the back side. If I miss a spot, a void will be visible from the front when I'm finished.

Now add the border

Once the 4-in. field tile has been installed on all three walls of the enclosure, I put in the bar liner using the same process. In the corners where the tiles on adjacent walls meet, I miter the cuts at a 45-degree angle.

Before installing tile on the upper portion of the wall, I cut in a shampoo niche and sealed it to the cement board with thinset (for a full discussion of this process, see "Making a Shampoo Niche" on p. 119).

Next are the 1-in. by 1-in. paper-backed mosaics. This time I use a ³⁄₁₆-in. V-notch trowel instead of the ¼-in. notched trowel to apply the thinset (the ¼-in. trowel would apply too much cement) but the same three-step process of spreading it. Mosaics are installed with the paper side up (see "Installing a Mosaic Border" on p. 171).

Push and slide. Giving each tile a push inward and then a slide to the side helps bed it completely, eliminating air pockets that would mar the finished appearance. Very small voids are not a serious problem.

The mosaics are followed by another piece of 1-in. by 8-in. bar liner. All that's left after that is the top quarter of the tub area. Instead of continuing the 4-in. by 4-in. tile straight up to the top, I decided to add some clusters of the 1-in. tiles and cut them in on the diagonal. This breaks up the wall a little and helps the two types of tile to complement each other.

Check top edge before setting border. Horizontal lines at eye level and midwall are particularly noticeable, so checking them with a level is a good idea. These tiles were set to a level line drawn on the wall.

Preformed niche may save time. Using preformed shampoo niches makes installation less complicated, but these sometimes don't conform exactly to tile and grout spacing. Making a custom niche is another solution.

Back-butter the bar liners. These raised bar liners, like the 4-in. field tile, should be coated with thinset on the back side.

Wedges instead of spacers. These pieces can be irregularly shaped, so standard tile spacers may not help keep grout lines uniform. Instead, try tapered plastic wedges to adjust spacing and keep lines straight.

Have Patience with Cutting and Grouting

When cutting glass tile, I use a wet saw with a special blade that's thinner than a standard blade (it also would work on ceramic tile, but it won't last as long as a conventional blade).

Cutting the 4-in. field tile is straightforward, but cutting the 1-in. mosaics gets a little tedious.

Tips for Installing Glass Tile

● When setting glass tiles that are mounted on paper, always keep the paper side up.

● Always take the paper backing off the same day that the tile is installed. Otherwise, you lose the chance to adjust any tiles that may be askew.

● Use white thinset, not gray. Gray cement darkens the tiles and completely changes their appearance.

What options do I have for cutting glass tile?

It is not as easy to cut glass tile as ceramic tile. But it's not that much different. With some glass tile, the hand snap cutter and ordinary carbide-tipped nippers work fine. The electric water saw with a blade that is designed for glass works well. The best tool I've found is the Revolution Saw, from the Gemini Saw Co. It can cut curves as well as straight lines and does not leave a ragged edge, as some of the other methods do.

TOOLS AND MATERIALS
An electric wet saw

A special blade is usually recommended for ¼-in. thick glass tile. The glass-cutting blade is a little thinner than an ordinary blade, and it does not have as much diamond compound in it.

Glass tiles are trickier to cut than other materials. If the tile keeps breaking or has a very ragged edge, the tile saw could be out of balance. Last but not least is blade speed. Some imported tile saws with small, brushless motors run too fast. If the cut is a little rough, it can be sanded with a 3M diamond sanding pad.

When you're cutting mosaic tiles, tile nippers work relatively well. But the nippers should be new or almost new.

Small pieces of tile have a habit of falling into the ½-in. groove in the center of the tile saw's tray and then into the water pan below. To avoid this, I cut mosaics on a piece of 12-in.-sq. limestone in which I've cut a narrow groove. This allows the tiles to sit flat and stable. By cutting another piece of limestone into a 2-in. wide L-shape guide, I can quickly cut a group of mosaics to the same size.

Grouting glass tiles takes some patience, too. It takes more time for the grout to set up, simply because the glass does not absorb any moisture. The less water I use to clean up the grout, the better.

Before I use a sponge and water, I wipe down the surface with a cotton cloth or cheesecloth to remove excess moisture.

After the tiles have been cleaned, I wait at least 15 minutes for a haze to develop. Then I rub off

that film with a clean cloth and bring the tiles to a shine.

It's important to get the tile as clean as possible in order to avoid using heavy-duty cleaners (those containing acid can damage tile or grout). After the grout has dried for a day, I use standard tile-and-grout cleaner available at any tile store or home center.

Sealing the glass tiles and grout should always be done to prevent moisture from penetrating the grout, and also to help provide a clean, crisp grout line.

I like to seal the tiles with a very good impregnator sealer a couple of days after the job has been cleaned. I use either a foam brush or a large spray dispenser (like a garden sprayer). Once I apply the sealer, I always wipe down the walls or floor with clean cotton rags to eliminate streaks.

Wait longer for grout. Grout should be allowed to set up an extra 10-15 minutes before excess is cleaned from the surface. On mosaics, where grout lines are narrow, use cheesecloth instead of water to remove excess.

Buff the surface. Once remaining grout has dried to a dull haze, polish the surface with a soft cotton cloth.

Installing a Mosaic Border

The sheets of 1-in.-square glass mosaics are installed with the paper coating out. After setting them, bed them with a hammer and wood block. After 15 or 20 minutes, wet down the paper with a sponge and let it set for a couple of minutes. When the paper backing is saturated and darkened, slowly pull the paper off with a downward motion (not straight out from the wall). A few pieces may fall off. If so, just dab a little thinset on the back and set them back into place.

1

Setting border mosaics. These sheets of 1-in. by 1-in. glass tile create an eye-level band across the wall. Sheets are applied with paper facing out.

2

Tap, but gently. With sheets of tile in place, use a hammer and a block of wood to bed them firmly and evenly in the thinset cement. Using a rubber mallet is a little less risky.

3

Peel paper gently. Make sure that the paper facing is saturated with water before attempting to peel it away from the tile. Pull downward, not outward. If the paper is hard to remove, try warm (not hot) water and wallpaper remover.

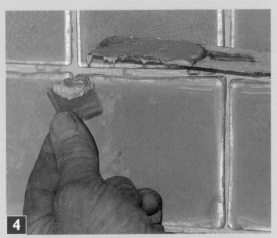

4

Replace any dislodged mosaics. Removing the paper from the front surface of the tile may dislodge some of the glass mosaics. If that's the case, butter the back of the mosaic with thinset and set it back in place.

171

DESIGN OPTIONS

Glass is as durable as it is beautiful. Whether you are tiling a whole wall or using it as an accent, glass can be just the glimmer of surprise that your project needs.

Classic patterns. Glass tile doesn't always have a contemporary look. This border combines glass tile and tumbled marble for a warm yet sophisticated effect

An inexpensive design element. Used alone, glass tile can be more expensive than ceramic tile, but installing just a narrow band of glass is an inexpensive way to add color and texture.

As little as one row of glass top and bottom in the decorative strip increases the whimsical effect for little money.

Mix and match. Combining 1-in. glass tiles in three warm shades of color gives this backsplash the feel of textured wallpaper.

No need for a shower curtain. The glass block wall not only allows light into the shower, it also helps contain the water.

Combining elements. The unexpected combination of slate and glass gives this bathroom a contemporary look but doesn't feel cold, underscoring the versatility of glass as well as stone.

Tile

CHAPTER TWELVE
Repairs

1 Planning a Repair, p. 176

Even the best tile job sometimes needs repair. A leak can cause shower tiles to come loose; a floor that flexes can lead to cracks; changes in plumbing can require the replacement of existing tiles.

Repair work is part of the business, and in this chapter we'll cover the most common repairs— loose tiles, cracked tiles, and tiles that have to come out so that something new can go in. Before you start, there are a few guidelines we always follow when we approach a repair.

First, make sure you solve the problem. If tile fails, it fails for a reason. If it's cracked, it's cracked because the surface behind it has moved. If it's loose, it's because the adhesive or the substrate has failed, usually because of movement in the substrate or water intrusion or both (see "The Trouble with Drywall" on p. 176).

If the grout turns black, it most likely is caused by mildew, but this may also be sign that the wall behind it is constantly wet. Whatever the case, you can't just remount and regrout. You've got to find out what caused the problem and fix it.

2 Replacing Tile around a Shower Valve, p. 177

3 Replacing a Large Area of Tub Surround, p. 182

4 Replacing Floor Tile, p. 184

Q & A

If the grout has separated at the seam between the kitchen counter and backsplash, was the installation done poorly?

No. The wall and the counter are on two separate planes, one horizontal and the other vertical. It is only natural for movement to take place between them as the floor settles. Scrape out the loose grout with a utility knife and regrout the seam.

TOOLS AND MATERIALS

Removing old grout can be a real chore. Over the years I've used utility knives, chisels, carbide tipped cement board cutters, and various other tools for this labor intensive job.

Now, there is a great tool made by Fein Power Tools called the Fein MultiMaster. This tool is the most efficient and effective grout removal system anywhere. It makes very little mess and works by moving a two inch blade back and forth. It does an amazing job with little effort. It even gets into the corners and does not damage the tile. The Fein MultiMaster can run from $250 to $300 and is worth every penny.

Planning a Repair

It's tricky to match new to old. Don't expect to buy a tile today and have it match the one you bought yesterday, much less 10 years ago when the shower was new. Tile color changes from batch to batch, not to mention from year to year and manufacturer to manufacturer.

If you're repairing natural stone tile, it will be virtually impossible to match the shades of new and old. The only sure match for a tile is a tile from the original batch.

When you put in tiles, buy a few extra. Put them in a safe place, and save them in case you need them.

A repair doesn't have to be just a patch. Repairs are seldom invisible. Use this to your advantage, and make the repair look as though it was part of your design rather than an afterthought. Instead of trying to match an old tile color, for example, put in new colors that accent the old ones.

If you can't match the size, frame the new tiles with a border to make the change in size look like something you planned. Or install the new tile on the diagonal, creating a pattern that camouflages the size difference.

If you have a problem with tiles in the upper row of a shower stall, take out the top three rows and replace them with a checkerboard pattern. If

The Trouble with Drywall

The invention of gypsum drywall promised to simplify the lives of tile installers. Instead of elaborately coating all surfaces to be tiled with a thick layer of mortar and mesh, we could now install tile directly over water-resistant drywall, which is much faster and easier. Unfortunately, the promise was short-lived. Drywall installations broke down after a number of years, and once water penetrated the paper backing, the walls harbored mildew. Grout turned black with mold, not from a lack of cleaning, but because bacteria worked its way back out through the grout.

Tile showers got a deservedly bad name in those years. In fact, the unreliability of drywall for this specific application virtually launched the fiberglass tub-surround industry. In the mid-1970s, the ceramic tile industry took a turn that would alter the way tile was installed for generations to come.

Cement backer board—a sheet of concrete sandwiched between two layers of fiberglass mesh—slowly replaced gypsum drywall as a substrate in showers. (Drywall, by the way, is still a perfectly good tile substrate in parts of the bathroom that aren't wet. It's just not suitable for showers and tub surrounds.)

The change was met with great skepticism, but backer board finally triumphed, and because it is so durable, repairs are limited to problems caused by settling, movement, deflection, broken pipes, or poor workmanship. Done well, a new shower installation should outlast the installer.

These days, the only time you'll encounter drywall in a shower is on one of the countless installations done before backer board became the industry standard. There are fewer and fewer every day, but be prepared—if you encounter a drywall shower substrate, water will have damaged much of it, and mold may require removing even more.

Before starting the demolition of tile around the mixing valve, I first remove the finish plate over the valve. This is also a good time to locate the water main, just in case I nick a pipe with a chisel and cause a water leak. When I start breaking out the tile, I start close to the hole to relieve pressure on the other tiles. The hole around the valve is the weakest point so it is easy to chisel from this point and then work my way out further into the wall. If I had started in the middle of the wall, more tiles would crack and tiles that were not meant to come out might be damaged.

the bottom half of your tub surround needs repair, install a decorative band at wainscot height to form a border between the old and new tile.

Be inventive. A repair should never be "just a repair"; it should be an improvement.

Replacing Tile around a Shower Valve

Every now and then the water-control valve or mixing valve has to be replaced in a tub enclosure or a shower stall. It's only a matter of a dozen tiles or so, but we're going to start with it because it shows you most of the techniques you'll use in any repair.

We did have a bit of good luck on this job, however. On many repairs the tile has been discontinued, and you can't find a good match. In this case, however, we had installed three baths in this house two years ago, and the homeowners had saved a box of tile and left it in the cellar.

Remove the old tile

Removing tile is usually a messy job. Keep the windows open when possible and keep the doors to the rest of the house closed. Cover up the tub to protect it—we use scrap pieces of

Remove the old tile by chipping away at it with a hammer and cold chisel. Try not to damage the outer edge (2 in.) of the cement board too badly so later you can tape the joint to make the new wall a seamless part of the existing wall. By doing this, the repair will have less chance of leaking.

Easy does it. Cut through the grout line first with a right-angle grinder and abrasive wheel to separate tile that must be removed from tile that can stay. Then remove tile inside the cut with a cold chisel and a hammer.

A two-person job. One person handles the grinder with both hands while another holds a vacuum nozzle nearby to catch dust as the blade cuts through the cement board substrate.

Q & A

Is it normal for the grout in between tiles on the wall and floor to fall out?

If the grout falls out between two planes—a wall and a floor for example—it's usually because of settling. Remove the loose grout and apply new grout. If the grout falls out between tiles in the same plane, they are probably loose and will need to be replaced.

WHAT CAN GO WRONG

Chipped or cracked tiles should be replaced, and that means digging out what's there without damaging the tile that's still good. You can't just attack the problem with a hammer and chisel. When you use indiscriminate force on tiles that have been set with thinset cement over cement board, there is a very good chance that the next tile over may crack, chip, or shale. Begin by breaking out a tile in the center of the repair, then work carefully from the outside edge inward. The trick is not to exert pressure on tiles you don't want damaged.

Supporting the patch. When there's nothing to support the edges of a backer board patch, you have to make your own supports. Cut a piece of wood that you can slip into the opening, and coat it and the inside of the wall with construction adhesive.

shower-pan liner, but you can use a tarp or even a piece of plywood cut to cover the entire tub.

Removing the tile starts when you break loose a few tiles with a hammer. Remove only those that the plumber needs to do the job. Chip away at them carefully with a hammer and cold chisel. It doesn't matter if you take out a little bit of backer board in the process—you'll need to remove and replace any backer board you've exposed anyway.

As you plan the repair, make sure that new tiles won't meet over a joint between the old and new backer board—that's the weakest point in the wall. Try to lay out the tile so that half falls on the new surface and half on the old. Bridging the seam with tile will prevent both leaking and separation between the walls.

As you get closer to the end of the opening, be careful as you chip. You need to leave an inch or so of backer board exposed. You'll want a straight, clean edge along the exposed backer board in order to simplify fitting in the patch. The best way to get a good edge is with a grinder and a vacuum

Attaching the support. Screw through the existing backer board to attach the support firmly to the wall.

Applying mud. Put a bed of thinset on the supports to fill any gaps that might occur between the patch and the supports.

Cutting backer board. Lay out your cut on backer board with a marker, and then guide a knife along the line to start the cut. Flex the board along the line until it snaps, and then cut any remaining fibers to free the piece.

Before cutting out the hole for the mixing valve, I measured off the wall and mark where the hole is to be on the cement board to be installed on the wall. I used a utility knife to cut into the marked circles. Once scored, the hammer will do the rest.

(see "What Can Go Wrong" on the facing page). It's precise and does the least amount of damage to the surrounding tile.

Cut and support the patch

When you're replacing backer board, the horizontal seam between the new and old board needs to fall over the middle of a stud. If not, the backer board will flex, and the tile above it will either crack or pop off. Unfortunately, a repair that is only a few tiles wide isn't enough to span two studs, and cutting away enough backer board to reach the studs means removing good tile. Installers solve this problem by cutting the smallest hole necessary and then adding extra support.

Start by cutting a piece of plywood or 2x4 that is 3 in. to 4 in. wide and a foot or so longer than the opening. Cut the longest piece that you can slide inside the opening. Apply construction adhesive to the inside surface of the walls and to the edge of the wood. Put the wood in the opening, leaving half the width exposed. Screw the existing backer board into the wood to lock it into place while the adhesive is setting.

Making the cutout. Cut along the layout line for the mixing valve with a knife, and then break away the backer board with a hammer. Cut away any remaining fibers before attaching the patch.

Use the exposed surface of the wood as a base for the new piece of backer board you're adding. Trowel on some thinset and screw the patch to the nailers as well as to any other support. Apply thinset across the seam and reinforce it with fiberglass tape. Let the thinset dry, then tile as you normally would.

When you're replacing backer board over a shower mixing valve, the process is a bit more complicated. Start by tracing around the mounting plate to lay out the hole. Score around the outside of the line with a utility knife to lay out a hole slightly larger than the valve. Break away the

When doing *a tile repair, can I use mastic over the cement wallboard?*

You can, *but it's not a good idea. The bacteria that causes damage to walls thrives in mastic if it gets wet, and will cause the mastic to break down. Thinset is portland-based cement and holds up well when wet.*

Repairing a Shower Pan

The most difficult repair, and certainly the most expensive, is replacing a leaky shower pan. The old pans, made of copper or lead, had a life expectancy of 18 to 30 years before they deteriorated from chemicals in the water, soaps, and shampoos. Replacing the pans requires removing and replacing the threshold, the shower floor, the bottom 2 ft. of the walls, and of course the shower door. At this point we're talking thousands of dollars and one big mess. And then the big question, "Could the tile be matched?"

If you decide to repair instead of replace, take the tile out the way you would on any other patch—grind along the edges, and chip away elsewhere. Remove tile along the bottom of the shower and at least partway up the wall. Then pull the pan away from the framing—it usually falls apart in the process. Remove any nails holding it in and run a utility knife around the drain to disconnect it from the pan. The plumber will take care of the rest.

When the demolition and plumbing are done, replace the pan with a modern liner like the one discussed in Chapter Nine. Modern shower pans, which are flexible membranes instead of metal liners, should last almost forever. Be careful during installation, however. If by chance someone punctures the pan while the tile is being installed, the pan will leak, and the repair will be as extensive and expensive as replacing a metal pan.

Attaching the patch. Screw the backer-board patch to the supports to hold them in place.

Taping the gaps. The gaps between two pieces of backer board need to be reinforced to prevent cracking. Apply thinset and mesh tape to fill the gap and strengthen the bond.

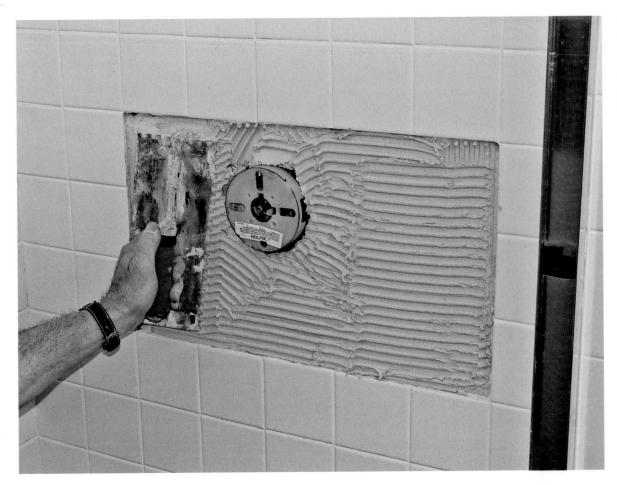

Spread the thinset in one direction for better contact. It can be awkward to spread cement in a small area, so a smaller trowel or back buttering may be necessary.

Replacing tile. Once you've replaced the backer board, replacing the tile is like any other tile job—apply thinset and set the tile.

backer board inside the knife lines with a hammer and cut away the mesh with a knife before putting the patch on the wall.

Now apply the tile

With the supports in place, cut a backer-board patch to fit and then fasten it with either 1½-in. galvanized roofing nails or special backer-board screws, spaced every 6 in. to 8 in. Fill the gaps between old and new backer board with thinset and cover the seam with mesh tape while the thinset is still wet. Let it dry and you are ready to install the tile.

Installation is an easier task than the prep work. Use a latex-modified thinset cement, and apply it as you would on any other tub enclosure.

Cut the curves around the mixing valve with tile nippers after marking the tile with a pencil or marker. Apply standard wall grout the next day.

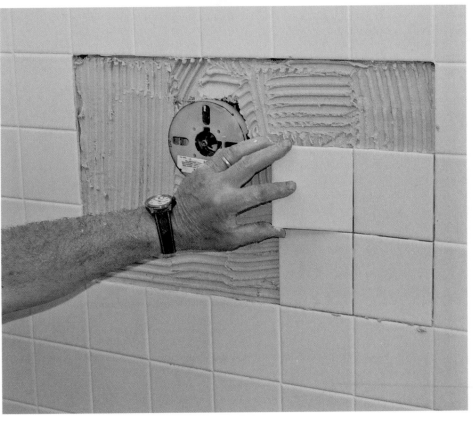

Q & A

When I walk *on my tiled kitchen floor, it sounds like I'm wearing tap shoes. Why?*

More than likely, *the tiles have separated from the substrate and are being held in place by the grout alone. Remove and replace the tiles that make the tapping sound. If this sound is everywhere, you are better off leaving the tile alone until you are ready to replace it. You may still get a few years out of it.*

Replacing a Large Area of Tub Surround

The tub area shown here is typical of many problem tubs: A leak started around a loose soap dish that had a grab handle across the top. After years of use, the soap dish worked loose. Water seeped down a hairline crack where the fixture met the tile. Once the deterioration started there was no stopping it.

With time, the damage went more than halfway up the wall. In addition to removing the tile, we had to rip out the damaged area and root out rotten material in the walls.

There are two key elements in repairing a damaged wall. The first is to make sure that the entire damaged area is taken out so that only a dry, stable surface remains. The second is to remove enough wall, if possible, to reach a stud that will provide a stable base for the replacement backer board.

It was fairly straightforward on this tub: The framing in the corners would support the edge of the new backer board, and studs provided additional support. There would be no need for nailers on this job.

We removed the tile, cut the backer board to fit, applied mud, and taped the seam, the same way we had when replacing the mixing valve.

The problem of matching

But installing the tile—usually the easiest part of the job—was going to be difficult. The company that made the tile for this shower went out of business many years ago. This left two problems: Matching the color and matching the size. Even the smallest difference creates a problem: A tile that is off by $\frac{1}{16}$ in. throws the pattern off by a full inch after only 16 tiles.

If the new tile is too small, you can often solve the problem by increasing the width of the grout

Removing damaged tile. Drywall is a poor substrate for tile in a shower stall or as a tub surround. What started out as a hairline crack around the soap dish eventually damaged the entire lower portion of this wall, which had to be removed.

Killing the mold. If there's enough water to cause a tile job to fail, there's enough water to encourage mold. Spray the walls with a good disinfectant before you close them back up. Then let them air out for a few days.

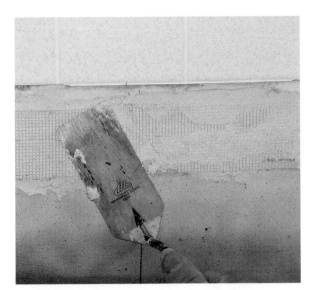

Reinforcing the seam. Apply thinset and tape across the seam between the new and old substrates to prevent movement that could cause the tile to crack.

Setting the tile. The repair starts at the top with a pencil trim piece that makes the change from old to new tile look intentional. Work your way across and down the wall, one row at a time.

joints a little as you go along. On this job, however, the new tile was larger than the old.

The only remedy was camouflage—using an entirely different tile in such a way that the change looks intentional. We installed a pencil trim piece as a border between the old and new tile. Below the pencil, on the bottom half of the tub, we replaced the 4-in. tile with 6-in. tile. Instead of looking like a patch, the pencil served as a decorative transition.

Planning the new layout

Ordinarily, you would start a repair like this by putting in the pencil trim that separates the new tile from the old.

Once it's in place, you work your way across the repair, one or two rows at a time. When you get to the bottom, you cut the row immediately above the tub to fit. We probably should have seen this coming, but on this tub this last row was very narrow—too narrow.

Visually, it's always better to have a big piece instead of a small one. Structurally, the larger tile

Be inventive. An awkward gap appeared inevitable at the top of the tub, but adding a pencil below the first row of tiles and sliding the others down solved the problem.

is stronger, which is especially important at the bottom of the tub. To fix what was obviously a problem, we slid everything down and added another pencil, as shown. The result—a full tile in the top course and a full tile in the bottom course.

Q & A

I'm putting in *a shower with six showerheads. Should I put plastic sheeting between the backer board and wall?*

Plastic sheeting *behind the backer board only encourages mold, and we don't use it. With this much water involved, however, you should put a waterproof membrane over the backer board.*

TOOLS AND MATERIALS

A grinder and vacuum used together can be a big help in removing old tile. It's a two-person job. One holds the vacuum in the line of fire to suck up dust as the grinder plows through the tile. The other mans the grinder, and the hands have to be very steady. This takes practice. Another important tool is a cold chisel because after the grinder has made a cut, the tile still has to be taken out with a hammer and a chisel. Cold chisels come in all different sizes, but I find a ¼-in. chisel good for intricate work when I can't afford to chip the next tile.

Replacing Floor Tile

One of the most common tile failures is a long crack in the floor that runs through several tiles. Nine out of ten times the crack follows a seam of the plywood that has moved or settled as the result of deflection in the floor.

Proper construction can usually prevent this problem, but once a crack develops, you have three choices: Live with it, repair it, or replace the whole floor.

The floor shown here had a crack that ran through three tiles, and as expected, the crack was right along the seam between two pieces of plywood.

Begin with removing the old

To remove the tiles we once again used the two-person grinder and vacuum system, cutting along the perimeter of the damaged area to

Removing the grout. Cut through the grout with a grinder so that removing the damaged tiles won't damage neighboring tiles.

I pulverize the center of the tile and then chisel the tile from the outside toward the middle to relieve pressure against other tiles.

Repairing a floor. Movement in the subfloor has caused these three tiles to crack. To repair them, you'll have to repair the subfloor and then replace the tiles.

isolate the damaged tiles so they could be removed without damaging any other tiles.

Once you've ground out the grout, break out the damaged tiles with a hammer and chisel, starting in the middle of the tile. Take the tile out—it will be in about a million pieces—and chisel out the old thinset.

Fix the flex first

Now it's time to try and fix the problem. Deflection is usually only a problem on large floors, and large floors tend to be on the first floor. If the joists are exposed in the basement below, you can often reinforce them.

First find the problem: Walk along the floor until you can feel it flexing. Measure so that you can find the same spot from the basement. Cut a board the same size as the floor joists to a length that fits tightly between the two joists that flex. Coat the ends with construction adhesive and nail the board between the joists. Repeat as needed until the floor is rigid.

Sometimes, however, the joists are covered, either because of a finished basement or because the problem is on the second floor. If so, drive screws every few inches through the plywood on both sides of the seam to lock it into place and limit the movement.

There's about a 50/50 chance of long-term success. No matter how successful we think we have been at reinforcing the floor, we always improve the odds with a piece of stress-crack membrane.

Making the repair

Start by putting down a coat of latex-modified thinset. Then, while the thinset is still wet, put the membrane over the entire damaged area, bridging the seams and, hopefully, absorbing any future movement. Immediately apply more thinset and set the tile in it.

Repairing the subfloor. Start the repair by screwing the subfloor securely to the framing every few inches. Isolate any future movement from the tile by spreading latex-modified thinset on the subfloor and putting in a stress-crack membrane.

Applying thinset. Spread more thinset once the membrane is in place.

Tiling. Set tile in the thinset and grout as you normally would.

Resources

Tile Companies

Elon
358 Saw Mill River Rd.
Millwood, NY 10546
(914) 941-7800
(stone and specialty tile)

Artistic Tile
520 Secaucus Rd.
Secaucus, NJ 07094
(201) 864-7000
www.artistictile.com
(stone & specialty tile)

Fire & Ice Casting, Inc.
P.O. Box 985
Spearfish, SD 57783
(605) 642-1015
(specialty tile)

Island Stone
P.O. Box 400
Capitola, CA 95010
(800) 371-0001
www.Islandstoneusa.com
(stone-pebbles)

Suzanne Crane Fine Stoneware
4225 Earlysville Rd.
Earlysville, VA 22936
(434) 973-8379
www.suzannecrane.com
(specialty tile)

Akdo International
675 E. Washington Ave.
Bridgeport, CT 06608
(800) 811-2536
www.akdointertrade.com
(stone)

Arizona Hot Dots
P.O. Box 14735
Scottsdale, AZ 85267
(480) 451-3687
www.azhotdots.com
(metal tile)

Artistone Tile Import
1400 Hempstead Tpk.
Suite 100
Elmont, NY 11003
(516) 775-7757
www.artistonetile.com
(specialty tile)

Cancos Tile
1085 Portion Rd.
Farmingville, NY 11738
(631) 736-0777
www.cancos.com
(tile)

Lutz Tile
445 East Main St.
E. Puyallup, WA 98372
(253) 840-5011
www.lutztiles.com
(specialty tile)

Marzi Sinks
1220 Broadway
Seaside, CA 93955
(831) 394-9382
www.marzisinks.com
(custom sinks)

Bass River Designs
Kathleen O'Neil
128 Pleasant St.
South Yarmouth, MA 02664
(508) 398-0233
(specialty tile)

Euro Tile
6100 Mid Metro Dr., Suite 6
Fort Myers, FL 33912
(941) 275-8033
www.euro-tile.com
(villi glass tile)

Meredith Art Tile by Meredith
    Collection
1201 Millerton St. SE
Canton, OH 44707
(330) 484-1656
www.meredithtile.com
(specialty tile)

Onyx France
10 South Bradley Rd.
Woodbridge, CT 06525
(203) 389-8833
www.onyxfrance.com
(stone)

Pittsburgh Corning
800 Presque Isle Dr.
Pittsburgh, PA 15239-2799
(800) 624-2120
www.pittsburghcorning.com
(glass block)

American Olean
    Daltile Corp.
7834 C. F. Hawn Frwy.
Dallas, TX 75217
(214) 398-1411
www.americanolean.com

Sonoma Tile
7750 Bell Rd.
Windsor, CA 95492
(707) 837-8177
www.sonomatilemakers.com
(specialty tile)

Stone Art
P.O. Box 434
330 N. Lampasas St.
Bertram, TX 78605
(512) 355-2722
www.antiquestone.com
(etched stone by water jet)

Wizard Tile
1522 West 135th St.
Gardena, CA 90249
(310) 323-4975
(specialty tile)

Phoenician Stone
430 E. Princeton St.
Ontario, CA 91764
(909) 391-6944
(stone)

Timeless Tile
5445 Hwy 9
Felton, CA 95018
(831) 335-0771
www.timeless-tile.com
(specialty tile)

Oceanside Glass
2293 Cosmos Ct.
Carlsbad, CA 92009
(760) 929-4000
www.glasstile.com
(glass tile)

Marin Designworks
    Glass Tile
21-H Pamaron Way
Novato, CA 94949
(415) 884-2605
www.marindesignworks.com
(glass tile)

Antiquity Tile
12 Shaw Hill Rd.
Hampden, ME 04444
(207) 862-3513
www.antiquitytile.com
(specialty tile)

Surving Studio
Natalie Surving
17 Millsburg Rd.
Middletown, NY 10940
(800) 768-4954
www.surving.com
(specialty tile)

Walker Zanger
13190 Telfair Ave.
Sylmar, CA 91342
(800) 634-0866
www.walkerzanger.com
(specialty tile)

Original Style
Falcon Rd.
Sowton Industrial Estate,
Exeter, Devon England
    EX2 7LF
www.originalstyle.com
(866) 881-6609
(specialty tile)

Tools and Materials

Cement board
Denshield
Georgia-Pacific
133 Peachtree St. NE
Atlanta, GA 30303
(404) 652-4000
www.gp.com

Durock
United States Gypsum Co.
125 S. Franklin St.
Chicago, IL 60606-4678
312-606-4495

Hardibacker
James Hardie Building Products
26300 La Alameda, Suite 250
Mission Viejo, CA 92691
(888) 542-7343
www.jameshardie.com

Wonderboard
Custom Building Products
13001 Seal Beach Blvd.
Seal Beach, CA 90740
(800) 272-8786
www.custombuildingproducts.com

Tile cutting and installation tools
Superior Tile Cutter, Inc.
1566 W. 134th St.
Gardina, CA 90249
(800) 787-2152

Superior Custom
    Building Products
13001 Seal Beach Blvd.
Seal Beach, CA 90740
(800) 272-8786
www.custombuildingproducts.com

Felker Wet Saw
17400 West 119th St.
Olathe, KS 66061
(800) 365-4003
www.felkersaws.com

Gemini Saw Co.
3300 Kashiwa St.
Torrance, CA 90505
(310) 891-0288
www.geminisaw.com
(revolution and ring cutting saw)

Rubi Tools USA
9900 NW 21 St.
Miami, FL 33172
(305) 715-9892
www.rubi.com
(trowels and cutting tools)

North American
    Tile Tool Co.
7960 Kentucky Dr.
Florence, KY 41042
(800) 406-tile
www.nattco.com

Marshalltown Company
104 South 8th Ave.
Marshalltown, IA 50158
(641) 753-0127
www.marshalltown.com

Target
Electrolux Construction Products
    North America
17400 West 119th St.
Olathe, KS 66061
(800) 365-5040
(tile saws and diamond products)

Saw Master
Diamond Tools Inc.
1595 E. 6th St., Suite 102
Corona, CA 92879
(888) 688-6899
www.sawmaster.com
(tile saws)

MK Diamond Product, Inc.
1315 Storm Pkwy.
Torrance, CA 90501
(800) 845-3729
www.mkdiamond.com
(tile saws and other cutting devices)

DeWalt Industrial Tool Co.
701 E. Joppa Rd., TW425
Baltimore, MD 21286
(800) 4-DeWalt
www.dewalt.com

Sealants and Maintenance Products

Miracle Sealants Co.
12318 Lower Azusa Rd.
Arcadia, CA 91006
(800) 350-1901
www.miraclesealants.com

HMK Stone Care System
1555 Burke Ave., Suite C
San Francisco, CA 94124
(415) 643-5603
www.hmkstonecare.com

Aqua Mix
P.O. Box 4127
Santa Fe Springs, CA 90670
(800) 366-6877
www.aquamix.com

Stonecare International
P.O. Box 703
Owings Mill, MD 21117-0703
(800) 839-1654
www.stonecare.com

Membranes

Schluter Systems L. P.
194 Pleasant Ridge Rd.
Plattsburgh, NY 12901-5841
(800) 472-4588
www.schluter.com
(waterproofing and
    crack membrane systems)

Noble Seal
P.O. Box 350
Grand Haven, MI 49417-0350
(800) 878-5788
www.noblecompany.com

Mer-krete
501 South Van Ness Ave.
Torrance, CA 90501
(800) 851-6303
www.merkote.com

Laticrete International
1 Laticrete Park North
North Bethany, CT 06524
(800) 243-4788
www.laticrete.com

Thinset and Grout

C-Cure
13001 Seal Beach Blvd.
Seal Beach, CA 90740
(800) 895-2874
www.c-cure.com
(full installation product line)

Hydroment
211 Boston St.
Middletown, MA 01949-2128
(888) 603-8558
www.bostikfindley
(full installation product line)

Laticrete International Inc.
1 Laticrete Park North
Bethany, CT 06524
(800) 243-4788
www.laticrete.com
(full installation product line)

TEC Grout
601 W. Campus Dr., Suite C7
Arlington Heights, IL 60004
(800) tec-9002
www.tecspecialty.com

Mapei
1144 E. Newport Center Dr.
Deerfield Beach, FL 33442
(800) 426-2734
www.mapei.com

Tools

Fein
1030 Alcon St.
Pittsburgh, PA 15220
(800) 441-9878
www.feinus.com

Beno J. Gundlach Co.
211 North 21st St.
P. O. Box 544
Belleville, IL 62222
(618) 233-1781
www.benojgundlachco.com

Racatac Products Inc.
3229 West Gloria Switch Rd.
Church Point, LA 70525
(877) 722-2822
www.racatac.com
(kneeling and rolling trays)

Alpha Professional Tools
250 Braen Ave.
Wyckoff, NJ 07481
(800) 648-7229
www.alpha-tools.com
(fabrication tools)

Intertool
1607 Abram Ct.
San Leandro, CA 94577
(800) 926-9244
www.inter-tool.com;
www.leitchco.com
(tile bullnose machine
    and fabrication tools)

Levels

Stabila
332 Industrial Drive
South Elgin, IL 60177
(800) 869-7460
www.stabila.com
(levels and lasers)

Trowels

Marshalltown Co.
104 South 8th Ave.
Marshalltown, IA 50158
(641) 753-0127
www.marshalltown.com
(trowels and full tool line)

Lasers

Stabila
332 Industrial Dr.
South Elgin, IL 60177
(800) 869-7460
www.stabila.com

Laser Products
1335 Lakeside Dr.
Romeoville, IL 60446
(877) 679-1300
www.lasersquare.com

Slip-Resistant Coatings

Slip Tech
1111 La Mesa Ave.
Spring Valley, CA 91977
(800) 667-5470
www.sliptech.com

Trusty-Step International
271 Western Ave.
Lynn, MA 01904
(800) 323-0047
www.trusty-step.com

Preformed Shower Pans, Niches, and Benches

Better Bench
Innovis Corp.
1008 Clegg Ct.
Petaluma, CA 94952
(800) 382-9653
www.innoviscorp.com
(prefabricated seats and shelves that can be tiled)

Bonsal
P.O. Box 241148
Charlotte, NC 28224-1148
(800) 334-0784
www.bonsal.com
(prefabricated pans and niches, full setting material)

Heated Floors

Nuheat
1689 Cliveden Ave.
Delta, BC Canada V3M 6V5
(800) 778-9276
www.nuheat.com
(electric comfort heated floors)

SunTouch
Watts Radiant, Inc.
3131 W. Chestnut Expressway
Springfield MO 65802
(888) 432-8932
www.suntouch.net

Easy Heat
2 Connecticut South Dr.
East Granby, CT 06026
(860) 653-1600
www.easyheat.com

Warmly Yours
1400 E. Lake Cook Rd.
Suite 140
Buffalo Grove, IL 60089
(800) 875-5285
www.warmlyyours.com

Educational

Ceramic Tile
Education Foundation
5326 Highway 76
Pendleton, SC 29670
(864) 222-2131
www.tileschool.org

National Tile Contractors
Association
626 Lakeland East Dr.
P. O. Box 13629
Jackson, MS 39232
(601) 939-2071
www.tile-assn.com

Tile Council of America
100 Clemson Research Blvd.
Anderson, SC 29625
(864) 646-8453
www.tileusa.com

Marble Institute of America
28901 Clemens Rd., Suite 100
Cleveland, OH 44145
(440) 250-9222
www.marble-institute.com

Tile Heritage Foundation
P.O. Box 1850
Healdsburg, CA 95448
(707) 431-8453
www.tileheritage.org

The National Training Center for
Stone and Masonry Trades
(NIC)
International Stone Institute
70 Westside Drive
Ashville, NC 28806
828-255-4510
www.internationalstone-institute.com

A World of Tile

Many factors go into choosing tile—cost, ease of upkeep, and, of course, the look. Ceramic tile is a very durable, man-made product that is generally homogeneous and roughly half the cost of natural stone. Stone is unpredictable in the way it looks and how well it wears and resists stains. Yet there is no way to completely replicate the natural beauty of stone in a man-made product. There are many potential choices, no matter which type of tile you ultimately select.

Ceramic tile

Ceramic tile is often relatively inexpensive and is available in many different shapes, sizes, and colors. Common ceramic floor tiles have either a glazed or unglazed surface. Glazed tiles have a special ceramic coating that is applied to the body of the tile and fired under tremendous heat. The glazing becomes hard and nonporous, resulting in a floor that resists stains, scratches, and fading from sunlight. It's also easy to keep clean and provides good footing.

Ceramic tile is also rated for durability and hardness. The Porcelain Enamel Institute's scale, which runs from 0 to 5, is not a measurement of quality but an indication of where manufacturers recommend their tile be installed. Tile intended for use on walls (where foot traffic is not an issue) are rated at 1 or 2. Industrial tile designed to withstand very high traffic in commercial areas is rated at 5. Ceramic tile of any rating can be used on a wall, but make sure you choose a good-quality tile for floors. As a rule of thumb, choose tile with a rating of between 3 and 4 for a floor in a residential area with moderate traffic, including kitchens. If you live in an area with a lot of sand, keep in mind that you need a tile that can withstand a lot of abrasion. A good

ceramic tile that has been installed properly should outlast all of us. It is stain resistant but grout should be sealed with a good sealer, such as an impregnating sealer from Miracle Sealants or Stone Care International.

Porcelain tiles also are ceramic tiles. Typically made with porcelain clay, they are dense and have low water-absorption rates. They are usually, although not always, frost resistant. Some people refer to unglazed porcelain tile as "through body" because the color goes all the way through. With true porcelain tile the clay body goes through and if the tile is chipped the color will remain the same, provided the tile is not glazed on top. Porcelain is quite durable (harder than granite). Many glazed porcelains also have extremely good durability. Although the color in the glaze layer may be different from the body, the surface is usually sufficiently resistant to abrasion to resist wear in typical applications.

Nonporcelain tiles typically are glazed (although unglazed quarry tile is the exception) and the glazed layer can be extremely durable. However, because there are differences from one glaze to another, it is important to check that the tile has been tested and will be durable enough for its intended use. Nonporcelain tiles have water absorption rates greater than 0.5 percent. There are many nonporcelain tiles that can be used in freeze–thaw environments and are manufactured with properties similar to porcelain tiles.

Handmade ceramic tile

This tile is typically used on walls, but there also are some very beautiful handmade floor tiles that have been fired at a higher temperature to increase their durability and finished with special glazes. Handmade tile will usually have a beautiful irregularity to it. Remember, you are paying extra for slight imperfections and slight variations in the glaze colors. If you want them to all be the same then stay with machine-made ceramic or porcelain tile. Due to their irregularities, handcrafted tile will need a slightly larger grout joint. When grout joints are too tight, the installation doesn't look straight. Handmade field tile can cost four times as much as machine-made ceramic tile. Hand-sculpted specialty tiles will be even more.

Slate

Like other kinds of stone tile, slate is mined all over the world and its point of origin affects its color and in some cases its porosity and hardness as well. Many of the types of slates from Vermont, for instance, are harder and denser than slate from India, but Indian slate has more variation in color and often is considered more desirable. This is where a good sealer steps in and protects a softer stone.

Slate tile is versatile. It can be used in floors, fireplace surrounds, counters, and even showers. Its natural beauty, varying color and relative affordability help to make it popular. Slate is a wonderful choice to use around a fireplace because it can easily be rounded and finished off at the fireplace opening with an orbital sander, giving it a finished look without a bullnose or cap. Slate is not as uniform as other types of stone tile—limestone or granite, for example—and varies greatly in thickness. The irregular surface will add to its slip resistance, though, when used in a wet area like a shower.

Limestone

Limestone is a sedimentary rock with colors ranging from very neutral shades of beige from

Mexico to taupe from France and golden tones from Israel. Like a simple black dress, limestone can be dressed up or kept more casual. It has more of a cloudlike appearance than the veining of marble, and if you're lucky some incredible fossils, too. Unlike polished marble or granite, limestone can be sanded with fine sandpaper to remove a scratch.

Like slate, limestone can be used in many areas of the house and is offered in many different sizes, shapes, and finishes. The most common is a 12-in. by 12-in. tile with a honed surface, which is smooth with any holes filled and a low-luster finish. Many other sizes are available, as well as chair rails, pencils, and mosaics. Limestone has a simple elegance that doesn't need much embellishment. To change the look or give the stone your personal touch, you can add touches of glass, metal, ceramic, or even contrasting stone, polished, honed, or tumbled.

Limestone is more porous than either marble or granite, but don't forget that it's been used to

create building facades that survive a host of environmental challenges, including acid rain. Limestone is roughly twice the cost of ceramic tile.

Marble

Polished marble has a beautifully classic, even formal, look and is used frequently for fireplaces, bathrooms, or foyers. But it also is available in other finishes, such as tumbled or honed. Polished marble is available in a greater range of colors, from dark greens (which pose certain installation challenges), to blues, jades, whites, gold, and browns with dramatic veining through them. In a polished state, marble is no more or less porous than tumbled marble. Remember that the stone was not polished when it was mined, but became polished by the use of diamond pads and chemicals.

Polished marble is used more in certain regions than others, for either aesthetic or practical reasons. In sandy beach areas, polished marble doesn't have a chance in high-traffic areas. On Cape Cod, for example, we may use its reflective property as an accent, mixing it with ceramic tile or as a contrast to a matte-finished limestone. With its mirrorlike finish, polished marble can sometimes show water spots or etch marks when used for a shower wall or on countertops. If it is scratched, you will need a professional to grind it and bring the polish back.

Tumbled marble gives the same full array of color without the glossy finish, and it's available in a complete spectrum of sizes. Tumbled marble is just that—marble that is blasted or tumbled with water. Large sizes are usually sanded on the edges and then blasted with water jets.

Marble's colors and veining can be emphasized with an impregnating enhancer without giving the stone a high gloss. Edges can be eased with an orbital sander or variable-speed marble polisher. As with any tumbled stone or hand-crafted tile, grout lines for tumbled marble should be kept slightly larger than normal to accommodate the irregularities of each stone. Tumbled marble costs slightly more than polished marble because of the added processing needed to create this wonderful texture. It's less formal than polished marble, with a softer, river-rock look about it.

Granite

Like marble, granite is often polished, but it also can have a honed surface that is less formal but still very durable. Granite is often used for counters and fireplace surrounds. It is available in a magnificent array of colors and patterns.

Granite used on kitchen counters are usually, but not always, in slab form. Either way, it's a very practical surface, highly heat resistant and able to make a dramatic design statement with a wave of color. There are, however, a few types of granite that are affected by high heat, such as absolute black granite. Even though granite is very hard, it is still porous. Hot grease and red wine, left over night, have the ability to do considerable damage to some stones.

Saltillo

These tile are sometimes called terra-cotta, meaning burnt from the earth. They are made of unprocessed clays and fired in Saltillo, Mexico. Saltillo tile is reasonably priced, and it can be purchased sealed, unsealed, or glazed. Unsealed tile is the least expensive, but it will have to be sealed by the installer. This type of tile wears more easily than others, but that's part of its rustic look.

Glass tile

Glass tile has become increasing popular and is found in every area of the home, from bathrooms and back splashes to certain floors, pools, and spas. It adds a wonderful flair to any installation and can be incorporated into any style home. The finishes are almost as varied as the colors. The addition of an iridescent finish, for example, can add just the right amount of glimmer, while a brushed or texture finish may provide a softer look. Glass is available in many different sizes—from 1-in. to 12-in. squares—as well as mosaics and basket-weave patterns, to name a few.

Installing glass tile is not like installing stone or ceramic tile. Because you can see through some types of glass tile, the color of the thinset used to set it is very important and can actually change the entire look of the tile.

Although glass tile is relatively expensive, it can make a very effective accent. For example, buying 1 sq. ft. of 1-in. by 1-in. tile and cutting it into rows of three for use in a shower adds zest to an installation of 6-in. white tile without costing a lot.

Metal

More types of metal tile—bronze and nickel, to name just two—and more applications are showing up every year. But metal is still primarily used as a decorative accent, whether it is a button or bug in a grout joint or a full 4-in. by 4-in. oak leaf inserted into a slate or ceramic floor. Square-foot sheets are also available in many different patterns, which make spectacular back splashes that accent stainless steel appliances. Always check with your manufacturer with regard to acid washing just in case the metal will oxidize. There are many different types of metal tiles, so always check with the distributor before installation. As a general rule, metal tiles are installed just like ceramic tile.

Sealing stone tile

People are rightfully concerned that stone is porous. All stone, no matter what kind, should be sealed. But as long as the tile is maintained and sealed properly it should develop a beautiful patina over the years. Europe is known for the beauty of antique stones that have been used for hundreds of years. Determine which stone is best suited for your application, then make sure you maintain it properly. First and foremost, make sure the surface is clean before applying a sealer. Stone should be resealed roughly every two years.

Tools and Materials

Manufacturers offer a variety of products that make setting tile easier and more predictable than it's ever been.

Backer board

There are three types of backer board: the original cement and fiberglass panel (Wonderboard®, from Custom Building Products, was the first of them), a fiber-cement board (Hardibacker made by James Hardie Building Products), and a waterproof gypsum board with a vinyl-like coating (DensShield from Georgia Pacific).

There are a few companies making the cement and fiberglass panels. Most of these products come in different sizes, such as 3 ft. by 5 ft., 4 ft. by 8 ft., and 4 ft. by 4 ft. There are two thicknesses, ½ in. and ¼ in. All of these panels can used on walls and floors.

Thinset cements

There are many manufacturers that offer a variety of thinset cements for different applications. Three types are commonly used: dry-set mortar, which is mixed with water and has no latex added to it; latex-modified, which has latex or polymers added to the dry powder and is mixed with water; and dry-set with latex or polymer that is added in a liquid form (no water at all is used).

Most of the latex-modified and latex-added thinsets have the ability to bond to plywood substrates and other products, such as stress-crack membranes and vinyl flooring. Dry-set thinset bonds to concrete, cement board, Ditra-Mat membrane, and unpainted drywall.

Always read the label on the packaging. It will list contents, limitations, and abilities. If you have doubts, call the toll-free number and ask.

Don't use the product until you get the information that you need

Grout

The two basic grouts are wall and floor grout. The terminology actually springs from the width of the grout joint, not where it's used. On walls, where the grout line is typically ⅛ in. or less, use an unsanded grout. On floors, where grout lines are usually wider than ⅛ in., use a sanded grout. The added sand helps reduce shrinkage, and therefore cracking, in wider grout lines.

Epoxy grouts are great in both commercial and residential jobs where there may be chemicals present or on a kitchen counter that's used as a work area for foods and liquids that stain. Epoxy grout is more expensive and it's labor intensive to use, although it has improved over the years. A new epoxylike grout by Laticrete, called SpectraLOCK, seams to be much easier to use. It's a good idea to check with the manufacturer for limitations and recommendations when using epoxy grout.

Membranes

The three most common types are stress-crack isolation membrane, waterproofing membrane, and uncoupling membrane.

A sheet membrane made by the Noble Company can be used for waterproofing and for blocking stress cracks. NobelSeal CIS can be bonded directly to a ¾-in. tongue-and-groove plywood subfloor (use two layers of plywood for stone, one for ceramic tile).

Liquid waterproofing membranes and some stress-crack membranes are applied with a brush, trowel, or roller. Some are two-part systems consisting of a fabric and a liquid that are used together, while others are simply a liquid.

The other type of membrane is an uncoupling membrane, which allows independent movement between the tile covering and the substrate. It neutralizes differential movement in the substrate and prevents the transfer of stresses to the tile. This type of membrane is ⅛ in. thick and has wafflelike chambers that allow vapor pressure equalization. It also serves as the substrate directly over a ¾-in. tongue-and-groove plywood subfloor. Because of its wafflelike squares, dry-set mortar is recommended for bonding tile to the surface, which saves time and money. When the mat is installed over a wood subfloor, it must be bonded with latex-modified thinset. Ditra-Mat, made by the Schluter Co., is by far the most common uncoupling membrane.

Trowels for Tiling

Steel and wood floating trowels are used to spread and smooth a cement bed that will be tiled. Either a 4¼ in. by 11½ in. or 4¼ in. by 16-in. steel floating trowel is useful.

Notched trowels for spreading thinset or mastic come in many different sizes and have many different uses. There are about five common sizes that cover the majority of tile installations. The ¼-in. by ³⁄₁₆-in. notched trowel can be used for standard 4¼-in. bathroom tile and for spreading thinnest under stress-crack membranes.

A ¼-in. by ¼-in. notched trowel is used for a little larger tile (like 6 in. by 6 in.) or tiles that are irregular. The slightly larger notch size removes less thinset, so it helps to fill in any voids in the back of the tile.

A ¼-in. by ⅜-in. or ¼-in. by ½-in. square-notched trowel is used for larger floor tiles. As tiles become larger in size or are manufactured with wafflelike indentations on the back, they call for larger notched teeth.

A ½-in. by ½-in. notched trowel is used for very large and uneven tiles. I use this trowel for large and uneven terra-cotta tile from Mexico.

There is another kind of tooth trowel, called a U-notched trowel. This is a newer style and its configuration is designed to provide a better bond for large tile. It is highly recommended by tile-industry leaders. Its ¼-in. by ⅜-in. or ½-in. notch is rounded at the top.

Grouting trowels are rubber floats that are used for spreading the grout over the tile and then scraping off the excess off with a squeegee effect. The trowels vary a little for different textures of grout, which include unsanded wall grout (a softer trowel), and a harder trowel for sanded floor grout or epoxy grout.

Mixing and buttering trowels are used for just that. The trowel that I use the most is the 2-in. by 5-in. margin trowel (which I have always called a square-nosed trowel). It is great for mixing and cutting in the corners when I grout, among many other things. There are a few other hand-mixing trowels, such as the V-shaped buttering trowel and the long, thin, duck-nosed trowel.

Preventing Cracked Tile and Grout

By Frank Woeste and Peter A. Nielsen

The 2003–2004 Tile Council of America's *Handbook for Ceramic Tile Installation* contains numerous details for a double-layer wood floor system supporting ceramic tile. The thicknesses of the subfloor and underlayment are given in each case.

Specific guidance on where to butt the underlayment end joints is not given for any detail. The purpose of this article is to propose specific guidelines for the orientation and placement of underlayment, including end and edge joints, beyond the rules given in the TCA *Handbook*, to improve the performance of double-layer wood systems. These guidelines are based on engineering science and field observations.

The Tile Council of America's standard formula for measuring maximum deflection under a tile floor is called L-360. Divide the total span of the floor joists by 360 for the maximum amount the floor can give in the middle. For example, if the floor joists span 15 ft.: 15x12 (in.) = 180 in. divided by 360 = 0.5. The maximum allowable deflection for a joist span of 15 ft. is ½ in. The l-360 standard applies to most ceramic, porcelain, and hard stone. But for certain soft stone tile such as limestone or light marble, the L-720 formula applies, cutting the maximum allowable deflection in half. Ways of reducing deflection include adding extra layers of plywood underlayment or installing additional support under the floor framing.

Background

While many factors can contribute to an installation failure, we believe that the localized bending or curvature of the subfloor–underlayment assembly produced by vertical loads can lead to tile and grout cracks. When cracked tiles are observed, it is common for them to be above a joist and run (generally) parallel to the joist. This crack pattern is physical evidence that the subfloor and underlayment on top of the joists experienced enough curvature to break the brittle materials above.

The term "curvature" in this discussion relates to how much an originally flat surface is "bent." For example, the surface of the earth has only a slight curvature, whereas a basketball has extreme curvature relative to the earth. Excessive curvature under a tile is shown in the drawing below. When installing tile over double wood floor systems, we believe the two-layer wood substrate under service loads should have minimum curvature in order to prevent tile and grout cracking. How, then, can we position the underlayment relative to the

subfloor to yield an area having the least curvature when loaded in service?

Intuition can be misleading

Aside from the instructions in the TCA *Handbook*, many contractors butt the underlayment end joints directly over the joists because their intuition leads them to believe it's the best way. The logic might be, after all, that since you always butt the subfloor end joints on a joist for the obvious support, why not butt the underlayment end joints on a joist as well? We believe that this logic is flawed for a brittle surface covering because the curvature of the subfloor is the greatest directly over the joist where there is no help from the butted underlayment. This non-intuitive fact stems from the bending stress diagram of continuous beams.

If you apply bridge design principles to underlayment placement, the goal is to place the underlayment end joint splice at a point where the bending stresses in the subfloor are relatively low. The idea presented here is to have two layers of sheathing at those points where the

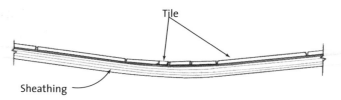

Excessive curvature under a tile duct, due to the bending of the
floor sheathing from service loads, can produce cracked tile and grout.

bending stresses are greatest—over the joists. We thus propose the "¼-point rule" for the placement of underlayment end joint butts. For example, abut underlayment panels on either side of the joist centerline at 4 in. for 16-in. on-center joists, 5 in. for 19.2-in. o.c. joists, or 6 in. for 24-in. o.c. joists. Underlayment end joints should be placed as far away from subfloor end joints as possible. The end joint butt positioning is depicted in the drawing at right.

Edge joint offset

While the TCA *Handbook* and American Plywood Association (APA) literature permit the edge joints of the subfloor and underlayment panels to be as close as 2 in., we believe the underlayment should overlap the edge joints of the subfloor by one-half the width of the subfloor panel (that is, 24 in.) to prevent potential damaging curvature from occurring between the sides of adjoining panels. This practice simply requires that the first set of underlayment panels be ripped lengthwise (no extra materials should be required).

General recommendations for underlayment

To assist contractors and installers, we've summarized our ideas for underlayment placement and orientation; panel end, edge, and perimeter gaps; and nailing. The recommendations given for nailing

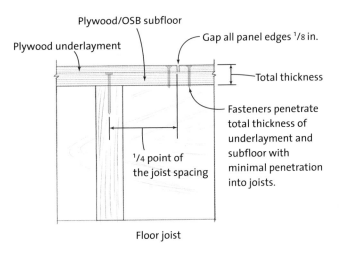

Overlap ½ width of subfloor panel 24 in. (610 mm)

Abut underlayment at ¼ point of joist spacing (typical).

Subfloor

Underlayment

Subfloor

Typical wood-floor joist spacing

Plywood/OSB subfloor

Plywood underlayment

Gap all panel edges ⅛ in.

Total thickness

Fasteners penetrate total thickness of underlayment and subfloor with minimal penetration into joists.

¼ point of the joist spacing

Floor joist

are more conservative than specified in ANSI A108-1999, Section AN-3.4.1.3, which states, "locate nails at 6-inch centers along panel edges and 8-inch centers each way throughout the panel." Closer nail spacing as given in Table 1 on p. 198 will better guard against voids between the subfloor and underlayment sheathing panels, improve the composite action of the two layers of sheathing, thus reducing sheathing curvature under service loads, and increase the buckling resistance of the underlayment, thereby minimizing the potential for buckling of the underlayment due to seasonal moisture-content changes. This closer fastener spacing also eliminates the need for panel adhesive between the underlayment panels and the subfloor. The potential value of this practice is important to note, as the use of panel adhesive can be problematic if not applied properly. Many panel adhesives are applied with a caulking gun and can skin over quickly. In this type of adhesive application, the underlayment panels may rest on top of skinned-over "beads" of adhesive, creating voids between the underlayment panels and the subfloor. Any gap between the two sheathing layers will reduce the shear stiffness of the nail or screw connections, and thus to some extent reduce the composite action of the sheathing layers. In this case, the adhesive can create more problems than it solves.

Place underlayment panels (Exposure 1, plugged-face plywood of minimum ⅜-in. thickness) such that the following conditions are met:

Butt all underlayment end joints at the ¼-point between joists. Underlayment end joints should be placed as far away from subfloor end joints as possible.

Underlayment should overlap edge joints of subfloor by one-half the width of the subfloor panel. At restraining surfaces, overlap may be less than 24 in. when the subfloor panel is less than 48 in. wide.

Gap underlayment panels ⅛ in. on all ends and edges and ¼ in. at perimeter walls, cabinetry, or other restraining surfaces.

TABLE 1. Maximum on-center fastener spacings for installing underlayment panels. Minimum thickness of underlayment should be obtained from the latest edition of the TCA *Handbook*.

Plywood Grades	Plywood Thickness (in.)	Maximum On-Center Fastener Spacing (in.)	
		PANEL EDGES	**FIELD**
Exposure 1, plugged-face plywood	⅜	4	6
	½	4	6
	Greater than ½	6	6

Credits

All photos appearing in *Working with Tile* are © Tom Meehan and Lane Meehan, except:

p. ii: Photo © Rob Karosis.

p. 9: Photos courtesy Cape Cod Tileworks.

p. 12: (left) Photo © Rob Karosis.

p. 24: Photo © Rob Karosis.

p. 25: (right) Photo by Roe A. Osborn, courtesy *Fine Homebuilding*, © The Taunton Press, Inc.

p. 26 (center & right) Photos by Roe A. Osborn, courtesy *Fine Homebuilding*, © The Taunton Press, Inc.

p. 30: Photos by Roe A. Osborn, courtesy *Fine Homebuilding*, © The Taunton Press, Inc.

pp. 32–33: Photos by Roe A. Osborn, courtesy *Fine Homebuilding*, © The Taunton Press, Inc.

pp. 34–35: Photos by Roe A. Osborn, courtesy *Fine Homebuilding*, © The Taunton Press, Inc.

pp. 36–37: Photos by Roe A. Osborn, courtesy *Fine Homebuilding*, © The Taunton Press, Inc., except photo on p. 37 (top right) © Rob Karosis.

p. 38: Photo © Rob Karosis.

p. 39: (top right) Photo courtesy Walker Zanger; (bottom, left & right) Photos courtesy Meredith Collection.

p. 42: (left) Photo courtesy Meredith Collection; (right) Photo courtesy Cancos Tile Showroom.

pp. 54: Photo courtesy Sonoma Tilemakers.

p. 55: (top right & bottom) Photos courtesy Sonoma Tilemakers.

p. 55: (top left) Photo courtesy Original Style.

p. 58: Photo courtesy Maline Tile Co. Inc.

p. 59: (left) Photo courtesy Antiquestone, Inc.; (right) Photo courtesy Celine Newell.

p. 63: Photo courtesy Surving Studio.

p. 70: (left) Photo courtesy Oceanside Glass; (right, top & bottom) Photos courtesy Meredith Collection.

p. 71: (left) Photo courtesy Sonoma Tilemakers.

p. 99: Photo courtesy Lutz Tile.

p. 108: (left) Photo courtesy Oceanside Glasstile™; (top right) Photo courtesy Island Stone; (bottom right) Photo courtesy Cancos Tile Showroom.

p. 109: (top left) Photo courtesy Cancos Tile Showroom; (top right) Photo courtesy Meredith Collection; (bottom) Photo courtesy Lutz Tile.

p. 126: Photo courtesy Original Style.

p. 127: (top left) Photo courtesy Oceanside Tile; (bottom left) Photo courtesy Cancos Tile Showroom; (right) Photo courtesy Oceanside Tile.

p. 130: Photo courtesy Island Tile.

p. 146: (top right) Photo courtesy Oceanside Glass.

p. 147: (left) Photo courtesy Island Store.

p. 155: (bottom, left to right) Photos by Jefferson Kolle, courtesy *Fine Homebuilding*, © The Taunton Press, Inc.

p. 156: (center & right) Photos by Roe A. Osborn, courtesy *Fine Homebuilding*, © The Taunton Press, Inc.

p. 158: (top) Photo by Roe A. Osborn, courtesy *Fine Homebuilding*, © The Taunton Press, Inc.

p. 160: (top) Photo courtesy Artist Stone.

Index

A

Accent tiles. *See* Decorative (accent) tiles

B

Backer board. *See* Cement backer boards
Backsplash, 72–85
    accents in, 74–75, 76
    choosing tile, 74
    color/texture of, 74
    design ideas, 73, 74–75, 76, 78, 84–85
    dry run, 77
    grouting, 81–82
    irregular tile lines, 79–81
    laying up tile, 79–81
    layout, 77–79
    leveling, 80
    partial tiles, 79
    protecting work area, 76
    reducing glare of, 74
    sealing, 80, 81, 82–83
    tiling around outlets, 76, 78, 79
    tumbled marble, installing, 76–81
    wainscot and, 50
    where to start, 74
Baseboards, 32
Bathroom tile size, 24
Beveling tile, 68
Book, using, 4–5
Borders
    around mirrors, 9
    glass tile, 168–69, 171
    mosaic, 171
    stone tiling, 154
    three-piece, 43
    wainscot, 43, 45, 52–53
Broken tiles. *See* Repairing tile
Budgeting, 7
Bullnose tiles, making, 18, 66, 150, 152, 153

C

Cement backer boards, 12–13
    cutting, 18, 117, 178–79
    drywall vs., 176
    keeping out of water, 117, 140, 142,
        144
    leveling areas with, 62
    for repairing tile, 178–79
    for shower pans, 138, 140–42, 144
    for showers, 116–17
    taping joints, 102, 116, 117, 180
    for tub surrounds, 98, 100, 101–102
Colors
    of backsplashes, 74
    classic black and white, 21
    of floors/walls, 10
    stone tile, 151–52, 154
    timeless white, 42
    transitions of, 10
Countertops, 86–95
    cleanliness concerns, 88
    cutting tiles, 91, 92–93
    design ideas, 87, 88, 89, 94–95
    edgings, 89, 90, 93
    grouting, 88–89, 93
    membranes for, 90–91
    overhangs over 10 inches, 89
    over laminate, 88
    practicality of tile, 88, 92
    rounded ends, 91–93
    wet saw for, 88
Cutting tile
    bevels, 68
    for ceilings/showers, 121
    glass tile, 165, 168, 169–70
    miter cuts, 51, 65
    radius corners, 90, 91, 92
    safety, 50
    selecting tool for, 50
    stone tiling, 153, 155, 159
Cutting tools, 16–17, 18

D

Decorative (accent) tiles, 8, 10, 34
    in backsplashes, 74–75, 76
    picture framing, 67
    stone tiling, 154
Deflection tolerance, 25, 30, 153
Design ideas
    backsplashes, 73, 74–75, 76, 78, 84–85
    choosing tile, 12, 20, 34, 112–13
    countertops, 87, 88, 89, 94–95
    decorative (accent) tiles, 8, 10, 34, 67,
        154
    fireplace tile, 57, 58–61, 64, 70–71
    floor tiling, 10, 23, 24, 38–39
    flow/continuity, 8, 10, 75
    glass tile, 172–73
    grout selection, 12
    intricate designs, 16
    mixing different tile types, 11, 52, 104,
        172
    options, 20–21, 38–39
    picture framing, 67
    planning for future, 8–10
    shower pans, 130, 146–47
    showers, 111, 112–13, 126–27
    small vs. large tile, 10–11
    stone tiling, 150–52, 160–61
    style considerations, 8
    tile orientation, 10
    translating ideas into tile, 10–12
    tub surrounds, 97, 98, 102, 104,
        108–109
    wainscot, 41, 42–43, 46, 50, 54–55,
        126, 161
Diagonal tile floors, 10, 11
Drywall
    problems, 176, 182
    tiling on, 42, 118

E

Edge-forming tools, 17, 18, 90
Epoxy grout, 88
Epoxy thinset, 154, 155
Expansion joints, 33, 34–35

F

Fireplace tile, 56–71
    around stoves, 63
    avoiding cracks, 58, 60
    choosing tile, 64
    design ideas, 57, 58–61, 64, 70–71
    grouting/joints, 68
    hearths, 59–61, 68
    holistic approach, 58
    mantels, 59–60, 64–66
    mastic, 66
    membranes, 61, 62–63, 68
    over firebox, 61–63
    over masonry, 60
    planning, 58–61
    prep work, 65
    sealing, 68
    structure supporting, 65, 69
    thinset, 60, 61–62, 65–66
    tiling walls, 66, 67–68
Floor tiling, 22–39
    advantages of, 12
    baseboards and, 32
    choosing tile, 10, 12
    color considerations, 10
    compensating for irregularities,
        30–31, 32–33
    cracks in, 184–85
    deflection tolerance, 25, 30, 153–54
    design ideas, 10, 23, 24, 38–39
    eliminating bounce, 25, 30, 185
    expansion joints, 33, 34–35
    glass tile, 28–29
    grout coming out, 30
    grouting, 29, 36–37
    heat mats under, 14, 27
    installing, 32–35
    layout, 30–31
    loose tiles, 182
    maintaining style flow, 10, 24
    membranes, 25–26, 28–29
    on oak floors, 28
    on particleboard, 28
    replacing, 184–85
    sealing, 34, 35, 36
    showers, 121
    small vs. large tile, 10–11
    substrates, 24–26, 28
    thinset, 26, 32, 33
    tile orientation, 10, 11
    uncoupling layer, 26
    on vinyl, 34
    where to start, 8, 26

G

Glass-block wall, 122–25
Glass tile, 162–73
    affordability, 163, 164
    borders, 168–69, 171
    cutting, 165, 168, 169–70
    design ideas, 172–73
    drilling through, 168

easy-to-install, 165
floors, 28–29
general characteristics, 163
grouting, 29, 170
installing, 164–69, 171
layout, 167
mastic for, 164
mixing other tile types with, 52, 172
mosaic border, 171
sealing, 168, 170
substrates, 165, 166
thinset, 165, 166, 167–68
in tub surround, 166–67
Grout(ing)
backsplashes, 81–82
choosing, 12
colored, with stone tile, 150
coming out, 30, 178
countertops, 88–89, 93
cracking, 80
epoxy, 88
fireplace tile, 68
floor tile, 29, 36–37
floor tiling, 29, 36–37
glass tile, 29, 170
joints/spacers for, 68, 78, 81, 154
mixing, 13
redoing, in tub surrounds, 106
sealing, 88, 107, 170
separating at seams, 176, 178
stain-reducing agents in, 13, 88
stone tiling, 150, 151, 158
tumbled marble, 93
types of, 13
when to start, 82
Gypsum drywall. See Drywall

H
Heating systems (under tile)
effectiveness of, 14
heat mats, 14, 27
installing, 27
membranes, 14
Hole cutters, 17
Holes, in backer board, 117, 179

I
Irregular tile lines, 79–81

L
Laminate, tile on, 88
Lasers, 15
Layout tools, 17
Levels, 15, 98, 140
Lifestyle, 8
Limestone. See Stone tiling

M
Marble backsplash. See Backsplash
Masonry, tile over, 60
Mastics, 13
for fireplace tile, 66
for glass tile, 164

spreading, 49–50
for wainscoting, 48, 49–50
Measuring tapes, 17
Membrane heat systems, 14
Membranes
for countertops, 90–91
for fireplace tile, 62–63
as shower-pan liner, 131, 133–38, 142, 143, 145
for tile floors, 25–26, 28–29
for tub surrounds, 101
Mildew/mold, 176, 182
Mirrors, tiled, 9
Miter cuts, 51, 65
Miter wet saws, 19, 51
Mortar
beds, 88, 139–40, 142, 143–44
for glass block, 123–25
mixing, 132
for shower pans, 132–33, 139–40, 142, 143–44
Mural, stone tile, 156

N
Nippers, 17, 18, 107

O
Oak floor substrates, 28
Oceanside Glass Tile, 164, 165
Ogee tile, 45, 53
Outlets, tiling around, 76, 78, 79

P
Particleboard substrates, 28
Picture framing, 67
Planning. See also specific projects
budgeting and, 7
finding information for, 4–5
for future, 8–10
importance of, 4
prioritizing projects, 7
style considerations, 8
Polished marble. See Stone tiling
Prioritizing projects, 7

R
Radius edges, 90, 91, 92
Repairing tile, 174–85
applying tile, 181
around shower valves, 177–81
backer board for, 178–79
cutting/supporting patch, 178, 179–81
drywall problems and, 176, 182
floor tiling, 184–85
mastic for, 180
planning for, 176–77
removing old tile, 177–79, 184–85
thinset for, 180, 183, 185
tub surrounds, 182–83
Revolution saw, 16, 88
Right-angle grinders, 18
Router, for edging tile, 17

S
Safety tools, 18–19
Sealers
grout, 88
tile, 14–15, 37, 151
Sealing
backsplashes, 80, 81, 82–83
fireplace tile, 68
floors, 34, 36–37
glass-block mortar, 125
glass tile, 168, 170
grout, 88, 107, 170
natural stone tile, 34, 35, 36–37, 68, 80, 81, 82–83, 155–56, 158–59
pre-sealing tile backs, 155–56
testing before, 159
Shampoo niches
custom, 157, 169
preformed, 119, 169
Shower pan, 115, 116, 128–47
backer board, 138, 140–42, 144
coordinating colors of, 130
curb (threshold), 131–32, 138, 139, 141–42
curbless, 143–45
design ideas, 130, 146–47
drain/liner junction, 136, 137–38
drain positioning, 140
felt paper liner, 133
installing backer board/tile, 140–42
layers, illustrated, 136
leak precautions, 138
leveling/screeding, 140, 143
minimizing grout joints, 142
mortar for, 132–33, 139–40, 142, 143–44
patching membrane, 138
preformed thresholds, 132
repairing, 180
subfloors, 131–33
testing, 138–39
tiling threshold, 141–42
tools/materials for, 136, 140
waterproof liner (membrane), 131, 133–38, 142, 143, 145
wire mesh on curbs, 139
Shower(s), 110–27. See also Shower pan
backer board, 116–17
choosing tile, 112–13
cutting tiles, 121
design ideas, 111, 112–13, 126–27
drain removal, 114
floor tiling, 121
glass-block wall for, 122–25
glass tile, 165, 173
handicapped stall, 142, 143
handling water leaks, 112
installing pan, 115, 116
installing tile, 120–21
layout for, 118–20
leak precautions, 116, 118
mixing ceramic/stone tile, 11

planning around showerhead/valve, 112

plastic sheeting behind backer board, 184

plumber jobs, 114, 115

removing old units, 112, 113–15, 116

replacing tile in, 177–81

shampoo niches, 119

soap shelves, 119

story sticks, 118–20

turning off main water supply, 113

wainscoting and, 43, 126

Size of tile

design ideas, 10–11

perceived room size and, 10, 24

for small bathrooms, 24

small vs. large, 10–11

Skim coating, 65

Slate. *See* Stone tiling

Snap cutters, 16–17, 100, 106

Squares, 17

Stone tiling, 148–61

absorbing putty oils, 158

advantages of, 37

choosing tile/style, 150–52

color/texture of, 151–52, 154

commonly used, 151

countertops. *See* Countertops

custom shampoo shelf, 157

cutting, 153, 155, 159

decorative details in, 154

deflection tolerance, 153–54

design ideas, 150–52, 160–61

floors. *See* Floor tiling

general characteristics, 149

grout/grouting, 150, 151, 158

grout joints, 154

installing, 153–57

irregular tile lines, 79–81

limestone, 150, 151, 154, 159

marble (polished), 150, 151, 154, 155–56, 159

marble (tumbled). *See* Backsplash

matching color, 154

mixing ceramic tiles with, 11, 52, 104

mural, 156

pre-sealing back of, 155–56

protecting from grout, 158

punching hole in, 159

reclaimed, 150, 151

repairing scratches, 152

sealers, 14–15, 37, 151

sealing, 34, 35, 36–37, 68, 80, 81, 82–83, 155–56, 158–59

slate, 151, 156, 158–59

solid-slab look with, 155

thinset, 152, 154

tools/materials, 152, 158

using broken tiles, 156

Story poles

making, 44

for showers, 118–20

for tub surrounds, 99–101

for wainscoting, 44, 46–47

Stoves, tiling around, 63

Style, 8

Substrates. *See also* Cement backer boards

bridging two different, 58, 60

drywall, 42, 118

for floor tiling, 24–26, 28

glass tile, 165, 166

masonry, 60

oak floor, 28

particleboard, 28

plywood, 166

vinyl, 34

for wainscot, 42, 48

T

Thinset cement, 13

for fireplace tile, 60, 61–62, 65–66

for glass tile, 165, 166, 167–68

mixing, 13

for repairing tile, 180, 181, 183, 185

skim coating with, 65

stone tiling, 152, 154

Three-piece borders, 43

TileLetter, 16

Tools, 15–19

for cutting cement board, 18

edge-forming, 17, 18, 90

hole cutters, 17

lasers, 15

layout, 17

levels, 15, 98, 140

miter wet saws, 19

nippers, 17, 18, 107

precision cuts with, 16

right-angle grinders, 18

safety, 18–19

snap cutters, 16–17, 100, 106

story pole. *See* Story poles

suppliers for, 16

trowels, 15–16, 152

undercut jam saws, 18

water (wet) saws, 16, 19, 30, 88, 153

Trim pieces. *See also* Borders

corners, 52

cutting. *See* Cutting tile

pencil moldings, 58, 121

Troubleshooting. *See also* Repairing tile

bridging two substrates, 58, 60

floor tile noise/movement, 25, 30, 182

grout coming out, 30

grout cracking, 80

limestone scratches, 152

membrane holes, 138

out-of-level tubs, 98

out-of-square rooms, 26

pipe leaks, 112

rings around faucet tiles, 158

shower leaks, 130

stone tile shortage, 154

Trowels, 15–16, 152

Tub surrounds, 96–109

adjusting for irregularity, 103

cement backer board, 98, 100, 101–102

checking for plumb/level, 99, 102, 103

cutting corner/edge tiles, 105–107

design ideas, 97, 98, 102, 104, 108–109

glass tile, 166–67

grouting, 107

important considerations, 98–99

installing tile, 104–107

layout, 99–101

membranes, 101

minimizing small pieces, 101

mixing different tile types, 104

out-of-level tubs and, 98

planning installation, 102–103

protecting tubs, 98

re-grouting, 106

repairing, 182–83

sealing grout, 107

soaking tubs, 98, 99

story pole for, 99–101

tapering backer board/tub lip seam, 100

tools/materials for, 98, 100, 106

wainscot in, 46

waterproofing tub seat, 101

where to start, 104–105

U

Undercut jam saws, 18

V

Villi-Glass tile, 165

Vinyl, tiling over, 34

W

Wainscot, 40–55

borders/trim, 43, 45, 52–53

checking horizontal spacing, 47–48

corners, 52

design ideas, 41, 42–43, 46, 50, 54–55, 126, 161

features/advantages of, 41, 42

height, 42, 44

installing tile, 49–53

layout, 45–48

level lines, 46–47

mastic for, 48, 49–50

obstructions, 44, 46–47

story pole, 44, 46–47

substrates, 42, 48

tools/materials for, 48

in tub area, 45, 46

where to start, 48

Water (wet) saws, 16, 19, 30, 88, 153